Geoffrey. L. Green.
6 May 1989.

# The Royal Navy and Anglo-Jewry 1740-1820

# THE ROYAL NAVY AND ANGLO-JEWRY 1740-1820

Traders and those who served

*

Geoffrey L. Green

First published in 1989 by
GEOFFREY GREEN,
Naval and Maritime Bookshop,
104 Pitshanger Lane, Ealing,
London W5 lQX
in association with
The Self Publishing Association Ltd


ISBN 1 85421 025 4



Typeset by Printit-Now, Upton-upon-Severn
Printed and bound in Great Britain by
Billing & Sons Ltd, Worcester

Dedicated to the Hebrew Congregations
in the naval towns of Portsmouth,
Plymouth and Chatham

# CONTENTS

# LIST OF ILLUSTRATIONS



The author has made every effort to find the source of any copyright material, and can therefore only apologise for any possible oversight, which is unintentional.

# FOREWORD AND ACKNOWLEDGEMENTS

The oldest Ashkenazic Synagogue in the whole of the English speaking world is found in the naval town of Plymouth. Built in 1762 and miraculously surviving the devastation of March 1941, when the centre of Plymouth was completely destroyed, there this synagogue stands surrounded by the new Plymouth, symbolically reminding us of the long history of the Jews in England. Arguably the oldest Jewish Community outside London is in the premier naval town of Portsmouth, and it was founded before 1750. Chatham and Sheerness were shortly to follow, resulting in a continuous Jewish association with the Royal Navy.

Two basic factors were to bring about these early Jewish Settlements and expansion in the naval towns. Firstly, the Jewish immigrants of the mid-eighteenth century being restricted in the occupation they could take-up resorted to peddling and the selling of secondhand clothes, whilst others became jewellers and silversmiths. These petty traders discovered that seamen delighted in the goods they had to offer. Why necessarily peddle your wares about the country when more or less captive customers were to be found in the men-of-war lying at Portsmouth, Plymouth, Chatham and Sheeness? At that time only the most trusted seamen were allowed ashore for fear of desertion and so, to ease this restriction on the crews, traders were from long usage allowed to go aboard the warships to trade. Secondly, 1740 saw the outbreak of the War of the Austrian Succession with the expansion of the Royal Navy, to be followed by the three great continental conflicts culminating in the Napoleonic Wars.

It is partially through the trading activities of the Jews that naval historians can find fruitful research into the experiences of the seamen when they came into port. We know, for instance, of Prize Money being the greatest incentive mainly distributed to the Officers, but what of the Seamen? Who were the Navy Agents, what function did they perform? The Jews were not ships chandlers; the early settlers knew nothing of the sea, but it was their instinctive trading ability and acumen which forged a link between often credulous seamen and those in authority ashore. Both the Jews and the seamen knew hardship, with little consideration from the public at large. Economic necessity brought them together.

There were of course Jewish Seamen in the Royal Navy. Their number has always been small. Until the time of Roman Catholic emancipation in 1829 only Protestants could officially join the Royal Navy and until fairly recent times candidates had to be of British nationality and sons of British-born parents. So we find of the 60,000 British Jews who joined the colours in the First World War, only about 1,000 or so found their way into the Royal Navy.

Without admitting to it, those of the Jewish faith who served in the Royal Navy, Royal Marines and WRNS have an intense pride in their time under the white ensign. Because of the small numbers they are looked upon as an oddity by their co-religionists and with surprise and curiosity by their shipmates. The eventual traditional tolerance of the Royal Navy towards all religious denominations overcame the isolated manifestations of anti-semitism. To be the only Jewish seaman aboard a warship meant he felt isolated on occasions and obviously unable to follow the tenets of his religion.

The regulations were often disregarded by the Admiralty to suit their manning requirements and about 15% of the Royal Navy's strength during the Napoleonic Wars consisted of foreigners. The discovery of Jewish ratings among the muster books in the Public Record Office has set me an incomplete task. A seaman's religion was never stated in the muster books or service records until late into the nineteenth century. Many changed their names and it has been physically impossible to examine over 10,000 musters in the Public Record Office. I therefore went through the Naval General Service Medal Rolls, Trafalgar Roll and Greenwich Hospital Registers extracting distinctive Jewish names, then finding their place of birth from the muster books. Where considerable doubt exists they have been excluded. Other indications from general research were followed up so that a broad representation evolved, enabling a select but incomplete muster-roll of Jewish ratings. I crave forgiveness for any errors of omission and commission, but trust the roll will be of particular interest to genealogists and at least can be built upon by future researchers.

Originally it was my intention to set down a history of Anglo-Jewry's involvement with the Royal Navy up to the present time. However, so much material about the early period revealed itself eventually that it merited a volume to itself. I trust, therefore, that all those who have assisted me with their own personal experiences during both World Wars will continue to bear with me. Many of them were unknowingly following a long tradition. In the meantime I present this volume.

I have of course, received considerable interest and encouragement from many directions which have been important to me in helping to achieve a cherished ambition. My acknowledgements therefore are not to be construed in any order of importance. Unfortunately, some who assisted have gone to their eternal rest.

It is only correct to start by expressing my thanks to the Hebrew Congregations in the Naval Towns – Portsmouth, Reverend A. Dee and Secretary Joseph Daufman; Plymouth, Rabbi Doctor Bernard Susser, Bertram Emdon; Chatham, G. Lancaster, Secretary. Cyril Drukker Secretary of the Jewish Historical Society of England. Captain M. Beeching RN and David Brown successive Heads of the Naval Historical Library; Ministry of Defence, Members of staff and in particular A.J. Francis and A. Wilkins. The attentive staff at the National Maritime Museum Library particularly A.W.H. Pearsal and D. Bradley. The archivists at the Head Offices of Barclays, Lloyds, National Westminster, and Williams & Glyn's Banks. Yvonne Moss of the Rothschild archive. The staff at the British Library Reference and Newspaper Library, Colindale. Bridget Spiers at the Royal Marines' Library and Museum. V. Mawhinney, Sheerness Library. Mrs M. Guy, District Librarian, Central Library, Guildhall, Portsmouth, with additional thanks for particular kindness shown to me by the staff in the naval and local history reference section. John Smith and members of staff in the naval and local history section of Plymouth Reference Library. G. Fordham, Chatham Reference Library. A. Corney, City of Portsmouth Museum and Art Gallery. The staff at Portsmouth Polytechnic Library. The librarian and staff at the *Jewish Chronicle.* J Munk, Anglo-Jewish Archives, Mocatta Library, University College London. The Staff at Guildhall Library City of London. The invaluable assistance shown to me at the Portsmouth, Plymouth and Liverpool Records Offices. Dr N.A.M. Rodger, Assistant Keeper of the Public Records and Honorary Secretary of the Navy Records Society, together with all the staff at the Public Record Office, Kew and at Chancery Lane. Phineas May of the Jewish Museum. I. Maundy, genealogist of Anglo-Jewry. All my collegues in the book trade and the notable kindness of B. Hirschler. Friendly assistance from David Spector and Lynne Edwards of the younger generation, and visitors to my bookshop who gave assistance in many ways, including Lord Ambrose Greenway, Grahame Hunt, Gordon Connell, Alan Norris and Mark Loost. My loyal book shop staff, over the years, June Petty, Margaret Teuton, Betty Breton and Pauline Fox who between them corrected the manuscript and typed it. Gwyn Petty for the sketch map of Portsmouth. I owe a special debt of gratitude to my mentors, Doctor Vivien and Sonia Lipman. To all the staff at the Self Publishing Association.

Crown – Copyright material in the Public Record Office in reproduced by permission of the Controller of Her Majesty's Stationery Office.

To my wife Valerie for her support and understanding over the years and for the quiet encouragement of my son Keith. Last, but not least, my appreciation to Laura my daughter for looking after our bookshop while father was absent without leave.

Ealing,
West London.
1989

# CHAPTER 1

## Historical Introduction – Prior to 1740

*'The nations which have received and in any way dealt fairly and mercifully with the Jew have prospered; and that the nations that have tortured and oppressed him have written out their own curse.'*

Olive Schreiner 1906

A commemorative tablet on the Cunard Building in Bury Street on the corner of Leadenhall Street in the City of London calls our attention to the site of the first London Synagogue of the re-settlement established by the associates of Menasseh ben Israel in 1657.

To this synagogue, converted from two dwelling houses, came Samuel Pepys on Sabbath day 3 December 1659, then a clerk at the Exchequer. As it transpired the service being held in the first floor had a special importance being the end of the Sheloshim, the thirty days of mourning for Antonio Ferdinando Carvajal, founder and owner of the synagogue – "The first English Jew".

In fact Jews were known to have escaped from the massacre in Rouen in 1096 finding refuge across the channel in England under William II and his successor Henry I. Here they stayed under Royal Charter until 18 July 1290 when Edward II decreed the Jews were to leave by 1 November. Their usefulness as mechants had run out; the Exchequer could not tax them any more, and the country could do without their economic function. Some returned to France and others to Spain and Germany.

Another expulsion of the Jews occurred in 1492 from Spain, some however keeping their Judaism secret under the cloak of Catholicism – thus grew the community of Marranos. But under the Spanish Inquisition the position of these Marranos became untenable, some finding refuge in England without disclosing their true religious beliefs; here they stayed unmolested until Queen Mary came to the English throne in 1553. Opportunities returned for the Marranos with the accession of Queen Elizabeth I and the wars with Spain.

At the head of the 100 or so community was Hector Nunez whose connections abroad were particularly useful to the Government with whom he had access, bringing news of the Spanish Armada's arrival at Lisbon. One of his sons, Francis, was employed for intelligence work in the Azores by Sir Francis Drake. Another Marrano, Dr Rodrigo Lopez, was the Queen's physician. By the end of the 16th century this community declined, and all Portuguese merchants suspected of Judaizing were forced to leave the country in 1609.

In the place of Nunez came Antonio Ferdinando Carvajal, from the Canary Islands. He settled in England some time between 1630 and 1635 and subsequently built up a considerable overseas trade using his own ships. Still as a Crypto-Jew with wide contacts all over the world, he organised practically the whole of Cromwell's secret service. Important information on Spanish naval armaments against England was given by David Nasy and Manoel Grasian. Spanish shipping movements were watched and reported by Carvajal's agents and passed on, enabling many a Spanish galleon to be captured. Then again in 1657 Carvajel's agents led to the capture of Royalist shipping at Ostend.[1]

Meanwhile an army chaplain, William Erbury, observed no purpose would be effected in allowing the Jews to return to England if not giving them the right to exercise their religion. In fact the Council of Officers were in favour of re-admission. The Navy was in like mind when, for example, a contemporary newspaper reported that after visiting the Leghorn Synagogue the crew of the thirty eight gun *Phoenix* felt the Jews should be allowed to return in peace.[2]

Under the Puritans the political and religious atmosphere had completely changed. Business, enterprise and profits could and should harmonise with the most deeply held religious beliefs. Cromwell expounded "liberty of conscience is a natural right; he that would have it, ought to give it". In the rest of Europe the opposite had occurred – the Spanish Inquisition, the most vehement attacks on the Jews in Poland, and the Chmielnicki massacres in the Ukraine were examples.

The Jews had turned to Amsterdam, which became the most prosperous of the European trade centres, mainly through their business acumen and, most important, the world wide connections of the Jewish merchants.

Among the Marranos community in Amsterdam was a mystic, Menasseh ben Israel, who not only acted as a rabbi but was considered a courtier of considerable learning. He felt that the political and religious views of the Puritans in England with their more favourable attitude towards the people of the Old Testament would be a haven for the Jews from the atrocities in the rest of Europe. Cromwell, on the other hand was more hard headed, recognising that the admission of the Jews with their far flung financial and commercial connections would make an invaluable contribution to England's overseas trade and economic wealth.

The two men came together at the outbreak of war between Spain and England. The London Marranos found themselves in a difficult position – being Spanish, their property would be forfeited. There was no alternative but to disclose their Jewish indentity. After long deliberations and disappointments for Menasseh ben Israel, the Council of State exempted the Marranos community. At the famous Whitehall Conference in December 1656 Cromwell realised he could not resolve all the matters in dispute, so he broke up the Conference, but did not use his prerogative to grant the Jews lawful establishment. Most important was the fact that there was no law forbidding the Jews to return – so in a country where compromise did more than legislation, after 365 years the Jews returned.

The small community of 100 or so were treated with a certain amount of curiosity, with the Synogogue in Creechurch Lane becoming a place to visit. So we learn from Samuel Pepys' Diary, now Clerk of the Acts to the Navy Board, dated 14 October 1663:

> "I saw the men and boys in their vayles and the women behind a lattice out of sight; and some things stand up which I believe is their law, in a press, to which all coming in do bow; and at the putting on their vayles do say something, to which others that hear the priest do cry amen, and the party to kiss his vayle. Their service all in a singing way, and in Hebrew. And in the end they had a prayer for the King, which they pronounced his name in Portugall, but the prayer, like the rest in Hebrew. But Lord, to see the disorder, laughing, sporting, and no attention but confusion in all their service, more like Brutes than people knowing the true God, would make a man forswear ever seeing them more, and indeed, I never did see so much, or could have imagined there had been any religion in the whole world so absurdly performed as this."

Jews will immediately recognise this visit as Simchath Torah, 'Rejoicing of the Law', when for one day of the religious year the synagogue has a carnival atmosphere. This gave Pepys the wrong impression – on every other occasion decorum and devotion ensues. Reference to Vayles was the prayer shawls worn by the men, and the press is the Ark.

This synagogue proved too small as the original community expanded to more than 100 families. A contract was signed in 1699 with Joseph Avis, already responsible for St Bride's Church, Fleet Street, for the erection of a synagogue in Bevis Marks, costing £2,650. Eventually the amount turned out to be less as Avis, a Quaker, refused to accept the agreed sum, not wishing to profit from a House of God. According to a report, Queen Anne presented one of the beams taken from a man-of-war. Bevis Marks, the Spanish and Portugese community synagogue opened in 1701 and is now listed as a Historic Monument as the oldest synagogue in Britain.[3]

Soon after the re-admission of the Jews to England, in 1660, Charles II came to the throne conferring on the Commonwealth Fleet the title 'Royal Navy'. Thus two totally unconnected events came about. The Royal Navy was to become the heritage of the nation with a tradition the envy of the world, whilst those Jews who served at sea and in their various trading activities with the Royal Navy were particularly proud to be part of that heritage.

Seaman 1663.

# CHAPTER 2

## "A Sea Officer"

*"Persevere"*. The motto of the Schomberg family.

The National Maritime Museum at Greenwich holds a special place for all those interested in naval and maritime history with its collection of about 1,000 ships models, 3,400 paintings, innumerable maps, books, drawings and figureheads. It is one of the finest museums in the world, fitting for a maritime nation.

*Sir Alexander Schomberg 1720-1804, by William Hogarth. National Maritime Museum.*

In the first floor gallery the visitor cannot help but be struck by a painting in oils, 24" x 19", – "A Sea Officer" by William Hogarth, depicting a captain of over three years standing – this portrait dated about 1760 is of Captain Sir Alexander Schomberg 1720-1804, the son of a German-Jewish doctor.

Meyer Loew Schomberg settled in England about 1720 obtaining his doctorate of medicine in Germany, where he was born in 1690. The Royal College of Physicians, knowing his financial position to be so poor, thoughtfully allowed him to pay the fees for licentiateship by bond for payment twelve months later. The name of his wife is unknown but in all probability she was a Jewess, if only because of the vehement way Meyer Schomberg was later to attack those Jews who married out of the faith.

He set up practice in Fenchurch Street, within a relatively short time becoming one of the wealthiest and best known doctors in the City, mainly through his early acquaintance with the leading merchants of Bevis Marks Synagogue. In fact Meyer was for a short time physician to the Great Synagogue in Dukes Place, City, at a salary of £30 per annum, a communal dignitary of some importance. This synagogue had been established in 1690 by the Ashkenazim (the Jews of German and Slavonic speaking countries, as distinguished from the Sephardim of Spanish and Portuguese origin) who were now arriving in England in increasing numbers from persecution in Central and Eastern Europe and who were soon to outnumber the Sephardim.

Meyer Schomberg became at odds with both Jewish communities. He accused them of breaking the Ten Commandments, affecting business on the Sabath, eating forbidden food, and not marrying Jewish girls of poorer position than themselves. The community in reply accused him of carrying a sword on the Sabbath and of riding in a coach on the Sabath day to visit his patients. He also wrote a pamphlet denouncing much of Judaism.[1] It is therefore no real surprise that his gifted family of six sons (a daughter died young) virtually abandoned the Jewish faith, thus being able to achieve very successful careers, free from all disabilities, with the wealth of their father to smooth the way. We are concerned with the fifth son, Alexander Schomberg, the first successful Royal Navy officer of Jewish birth – precursor of a distinguished and notable naval family.[2]

Born 1720, presumably in London, Alexander was educated at St Paul's School, brought up as a Jew but probably in a far from orthodox fashion. It must be remembered that under the Test Act of 1673 all persons holding any office or place of trust under the crown, whether civil or military, were compelled to publicly receive the sacrament according to the rites of the Church of England. So we find Alexander giving up the Jewish religion in order to be an officer in the Royal Navy, joining at the comparatively late age of twenty three because of the Test Act as by this time virtually all his family had abandoned Judaism.

Meyer Schomberg, with his contacts throughout the City, was introduced to Captain Pratten and probably with his influence Alexander joined his ship, the seventy gun *Suffolk*, on the 14 November 1743, where he was to serve for four years except for a short period of about four months aboard the fifty gun *Deptford* early in his career.

The War of Austrian Succession had broken out, England finding herself once again at war with France and, as was to recur time and again, the Royal Navy at the start of the country's wars, found itself ill-equipped with ships and stores. With the run down of the fleet, few officers had gained experience at sea and were in the main elderly. In February 1744 Admiral of the Fleet Sir John Norris, then a tough old man of eighty-four, took command of the fleet assembled in the Downs and proceeded to Dungeness, where the French fleet had anchored. The French left on seeing the British were superior in numbers, thus a fleet action was avoided and any invasion attempt frustrated.

In Sir John Norris's fleet was the *Suffolk* with the young Schomberg not yet a lieutenant, and the *Shrewsbury*, an eighty gun ship with 600 men commanded by Captain Solomon Gideon, also of Jewish birth. It is possible he was a relation of Samson Gideon, one of the twelve Jewish brokers admitted to the Royal Exchange, who had risen to be one of the most important City financiers, 'the pillar of state credit'. In fact with the French fleet in the Channel and the risk of invasion, government funds were falling and a crisis developed. Gideon granted the Prime Minister, Pelham, an immediate loan of £1,700,000 for the government. Other Jewish brokers and merchants rallied round assisting Gideon, who with ready cash had pledged his name and reputation, thus supporting the credit of the state. Jews enlisted in the Militia and with the backing of the synagogue authorities were encouraged to pay money into the Bank of England. Those who owned sea vessels put them at the government's disposal without reservation. The Anglo-Jewish tradition of unbounded loyalty to the country in time of crisis under war time conditions had been founded.

Solomon Gideon had joined the Navy at the turn of the eighteenth century with periods ashore, being a magistrate at Penryn, Cornwall, in 1719, serving as Master (Navigator) and Lieutenant, then as Captain of the *Blaze*, a fire ship of eight guns with a crew of forty five. Then early in 1741 Gideon was employed in home waters before moving on to be Captain of the *Panther*, a fourth rate of fifty guns, which joined the British fleet under the command of Vice-Admiral Haddock in the Mediterranean. Once, on returning from a cruise to Gibraltar, the *Panther* nearly drifted under the Spanish batteries at Algeciras. Vice-Admiral Haddock, lying with his fleet at Gibraltar, dispatched boats to Captain Gideon's assistance in order to tow him to safety. On arrival Solomon Gideon enquired, with some little emotion, what they wanted. On being told, to get him out of reach of the enemy's batteries on to which he was drifting, he replied perfectly unconcerned, 'Well then, I will cast loose my lower-deck guns and fire at them'. It was said he was a man of good humour and eccentric at times. The *Panther* was afterwards part of the squadron under Commodore Martin sent to Naples in August 1742 which successfully put pressure on the King to withdraw his troops under threat of bombardment.

In 1755 Solomon Gideon was put on the superannuated list with the rank and half pay of Rear-Admiral, dying soon after in England on 3 September 1756.[3]

Alexander Schomberg was to see further service in the *Suffolk,* the largest ship in Commodore Peter Warren's squadron to the Leeward Islands, capturing twenty four large vessels and valuable prizes in a relatively short time. The *Suffolk* returned with a convoy in company with the *Lyme,* a twenty gun ship which foundered on the way home, all the crew being lost. In October 1744, the *Suffolk* was nearly lost in a violent storm when returning with the British and Dutch fleets, under Sir John Balchen after seeing store ships safely into Gibraltar and trying to catch the French off the Tagus.

It was now time for Schomberg to obtain his Lieutenant's Certificate from the Navy Board:-[4]

> Alexander Schomberg . In pursuance of the 7th November 1747. We have examined Mr Alexander Schomberg who appears to be 21 years of age and find he has gone to sea more than 3 years in the ships and quality undermentioned viz:-

| | | | Years | Months | Weeks | Days |
|---|---|---|---|---|---|---|
| *Suffolk* | Ordinary | | | 1 | | 6 |
| *Deptford* | Ordinary | | | 4 | 1 | 6 |
| *Suffolk* | Ordinary | | | 10 | 2 | 1 |
| *Suffolk* | Midshipman | | 2 | 7 | | 1 |
| *Suffolk* | Acting Lieutenant | | | 2 | 1 | 5 |
| | | i.e. | 4 years | 1 month | 2weeks | 5 days |

He produced Journals kept by him in the *Suffolk* and Certificates from Captain Pratten of his diligence, etc. He can splice knot, reef sail etc. and is qualified to do the duty of an able Seaman and Midshipman.

| | |
|---|---|
| Dated | 3rd December 1747 |
| Signed | R. Haddock (Controller) |
| | E. Falkingham and |
| | A. Geddes (Extra Commissioner) |

Schomberg was of course really six years older than quoted and on 11th December 1747, now a Lieutenant, was appointed to the *Hornet,* a fourteen gun sloop of 272 tons and 125 men, employed in convoy and packet service. In the spring of 1750 Schomberg took passage home in the *Speedwell* also a fourteen gun sloop, until she was paid off in the following July, remaining on half pay until February 1755 when appointed to the *Medway,* a fourth rate of sixty guns, 1204 tons and a crew of 420 under Captain Peter Denis. The *Medway* with eighteen other ships of the line sailed from Spithead under Vice-Admiral Sir Edward Hawke on 21 July to cruise off Cape Finisterre in the hope of intercepting a French convoy, but to no avail.

After a short period on half pay in 1756 he again served under Captain Pratten, this time on the *Intrepid,* a third rate of sixty four guns, until on 5 April 1757, he was promoted Post Captain. His first command was the *Richmond,* a fifth rate of thirty two guns, but not for long, being appointed to the *Diana* in August 1757, then fitting out at Deptford.[5] She was a brand new frigate, the second ship to bear the name after the daughter of Jupiter in Roman Mythology, built at Limehouse of 668 tons, length 124 feet, beam 35 feet and a draught of 12 feet. By comparing the size of say, a garden, one can begin to appreciate what it must have been like aboard these small vessels with a crew of 220 men, armed with thirty two twelve-pounders and smaller guns. It was as Captain of this ship that Alexander Schomberg was to establish his career and become known for his part in the capture of French Canada.

His Majesty's Ship *Diana* joined the fleet at the Nore by the end of September, her first duty in December to be part of the escort accompanying a large convoy of fifty-two merchant vessels from the Downs to Plymouth, where she was to stay provisioning ship for foreign service.

The Seven Year War with France had commenced the year before and Britain found herself in a position to concentrate her attention on the French hold in North America, the Gulf of St Lawrence being the key.

Flying the broad pennant of Commodore Philip Durrell, the *Diana* left Plymouth in February 1758 to blockade Louisberg in Cape Breton Island and to await the arrival of the main fleet under Admiral The Hon. Edward Boscawen. Gabarus Bay was appointed the point of rendezvous. 167 sail of various kinds arrived there on 2 June. After Commodore Durrell was ordered to explore the coast in the *Diana,* he reported troops could be landed at Flat Point Cove abut four miles from Louisberg, without danger from the surf which made many parts of the coast inaccessible. Accordingly, Admiral Boscawen gave orders for seven frigates, including the *Diana,* to place themselves opposite the enemy's batteries and cover the disembarkation of the troops under Brigadier General Wolfe. On the 8th, *Diana,* with the *Shannon* in company, covered a feint attack in the centre, her barge and cutter being used to land troops, whilst keeping up a fire on the enemy's entrenchments for five hours. Meanwhile, Wolfe's main attack through the surf had succeeded with all the troops safely landed. Siege operations against Louisberg now began.

On the 26th, whilst off Louisberg, the *Diana* went close in between a small island and lighthouse at the mouth of the harbour to engage a French sloop and to protect the British store ships unloading cannon. The sloop soon retired after being damaged by the *Diana's* broadsides. But this success had not been without damage to herself. She had four men killed and seven wounded. The next day, other French ships loosed their topsails in readiness to engage the *Diana,* who made the signal 'Enemy was superior'. HM Ships *York* and *Bedford* came up in support and on the 29th *Diana* received orders to proceed to Gabarus Bay and erect tents on shore for the sick, her carpenters assisting.

The main attack on the remaining French ships in Louisberg Harbour was made on 25 July when 600 seaman boarded and carried the *Prudent* 74 and *Bienfaisent* 64, *Diana* providing a boat's crew. All resistance ended and the Govenor surrendered the next day. Cape Breton and Prince Edward Islands were in British hands. *Diana* left North American waters on 1 October, arriving at Spithead on 19 November. To commemorate the action at Louisberg, a medal was struck and awarded to officers who had distinguished themselves, including Captain Alexander Schomberg.

The war with France was at last turning England's way and 1759 was to be the "Glorious Year of Hearts of Oak". The *Diana* was not to remain in England for long, Schomberg being under some pressure from the Admiralty to get the *Diana* ready for sea again. Two of his letters give us an insight into his problems in turning the ship round:[6]

7th January 1759 *Diana*, Portsmouth Harbour

I have received their Lordships Directions for fitting and storing His Majesty's Ship under my command for Foreign Service and I shall use the utmost dispatch in getting her ready accordingly.

As the new guns were not likely to come round, nor the new sails in a way to be finished soon, it was judged most prudent to waive docking the *Diana* till the next Spring Tide, but now the sail-makers have orders to dispatch the sails I believe in preference to any other ships and we shall I hope be got into the Dock tomorrow. By a letter I have received of my secretary of Ordnance I am informed that there are not sufficient numbers of short guns ready for the Diana. I shall therefore take in the old ones as soon as I am out of Dock.

J. Cleveland. Secretary Board of Admiralty.

Then again a week later:

12th January 1759 *Diana*, Portsmouth Harbour

As you have directed me to give you an account of the manner I became so short of my complement I beg leave to acquaint you that during the siege of Louisberg seven of my people were killed, a malignant fever carried off twenty-nine and eight of the oldest sailors have deserted me since I have been in this Harbour, these added together will show what appears in my weekly account namely that I am 44 short of complement as I am ordered on Foreign Service I have no doubt you will soon complete me.

J. Cleveland. Secretary Board of Admiralty.

Just over another month was to pass before *Diana* left Spithead on 17 February 1759 in a fleet of forty nine ships plus transports, under the command of Vice-Admiral Charles Saunders. After calling in at New York, *Diana* arrived in Louisberg Harbour on 24 May which was not free of ice until 2 June. Embarking a large body of troops under the command of Major General Wolfe, the armada of ships and transports made their difficult journey of a thousand miles up the St Lawrence Seaway. What was to follow was brilliant co-operation between the Navy and Army, primarily brought about by the harmony of Wolfe and Saunders. It was a classic of combined operations. By constantly anchoring and weighing to take advantage of wind and tide, and by superb navigation, the army was brought with its stores to the Isle D'Orleans, anchoring on 26 June a few miles below Quebec. The fleet repulsed the French fire ships and it was decided to work *HMS Sutherland* (fifty guns) and some smaller ships beyond Quebec to gain the upper river. The *Diana* was in company, hugging the southern shore under cover of the army's guns on Point Louis, when her luck ran out. On 19 July, when almost abreast of the town, a small sloop nearly collided with her. *Diana* swung away, but in so doing was trapped in an eddy. The wind suddenly died away and she went aground. The ship had to be lightened as fast as possible. Down came the top gallant yards and topmast. The lashing were quickly cut off the booms and used to shore the damage. Gunpowder, shot and iron ballast was sent ashore in the ship's boats, with assistance from other men of war in the near vicinity. Thirteen of her guns were hove overboard. Meanwhile, the French guns opened up from the town. Their floating batteries hit *Diana,* whose remaining guns were not able to reply. Help was however at hand when the army's field pieces opened fire forcing the floating batteries to retire, saving *Diana* from an awkward position. The next day, HM ships *Pembroke* and *Richmond* came to the frigate's assistance. On board the former was James Cook, who had so brilliantly navigated and surveyed the St Lawrence. Cables and hawsers were passed across, and *Diana* was pulled off the rocks into seven fathoms of water. After a further twelve guns were hove overboard repairs were carried out, sufficient to get her down to Boston where she headed whilst the operation continued. Schomberg was not to see the surrender of Quebec on 17 September.

The *Diana* left Boston on 1 November in charge of a convoy of nine ships, arriving at Spithead on 27 December. Schomberg reported to the Admiralty about his concern over the condition of *Diana's* stern and requested that her bottom be further strengthened. The ship was still on his mind whilst he was on leave. He wrote to the Admiralty from his Norfolk Street, London, address on 7 January 1760.[7]

> When I fitted out last year the time would not admit of my waiting for the short twelve pounders which their Lordships were pleased to order for *HMS Diana.* There may now be time to have them round if their Lordships will be pleased to give their directions to the Office of Ordnance.

and again on 16th January.

> I have received your letter and am obliged to their Lordships for their futher leave of 10 days absence from *HMS Diana.*
>
> Although I found on my arrival in England that Vice-Admiral Holburn had directions from their Lordships to give me 10 days leave, I nevertheless would not quit Portsmouth till my ship was in the Harbour.
>
> I now wish I had staid while she had been cleared for the Dock as I find her progress is not pleasing to their Lordships.

Captain Schomberg, with his experience of the St Lawrence, was needed again as further expeditions in Canada were planned. Early in February, he was ordered to get the *Diana* provisioned and stored with the utmost despatch for foreign service and so on 11 March *Diana* left Spithead in company with HM ships *Penzance* and *Lowestoft* under Commodore Swanton in the*Vanguard* for the St Lawrence as a reinforcement to Commodore Lord Colville. *Diana* made a good start, finding the French store ship *Deux Freres* in Gaspy Bay, at the mouth of the St Lawrence. Although the Frenchman was frozen fast, *Diana* successfully executed a cutting out operation and took her prize.

Meanwhile, the French, knowing something further was afoot, attempted to recapture Quebec before the river was clear of ice. They met with success, defeating General Murray on 28 April at Ste. Foy, about five miles from the town. The British withdrew within the city gates, which Murray had previously fortified, both sides now waiting expectantly for reinforcements. Who would get to Quebec first? Round the point of the island came a small frigate, the troops peered, then gave a resounding cheer. She flew English colours! It was the *Lowestoft* (twenty eight guns, Captain Deane) the advance ship of Swanton's squadron. Commodore Swanton did not arrive in the *Vanguard* until six days later on 15 May. He did not wait – the desperate situation merited immediate action.

The very next day, as soon as the tide turned, the *Diana* and *Lowestoft* slipped their cables to work up towards the French naval force of two frigates, two armed ships and many smaller vessels. The enemy fled up river, the *Pomona* (thirty six guns) was forced aground and burnt near Cape Diamond. The *Vanguard* joined and enfiladed the French entrenchments at Sibery whilst the *Diana* led the *Lowestoft* further up river in chase, four more of the Frenchmen going aground. The last, the *Atlante* (thirty two guns), was eventually over-hauled about thirty miles above Quebec and, in making for the shore, also went aground. The *Diana* anchored in five fathoms abreast of *Atlante* and engaged her for two and a half hours. When the tide went down the Frenchman struck her colours and was burnt. The *Diana* was badly damaged in masts, rigging and sails, losing one man killed and five wounded. Quebec had been relieved.

Over the next few days repairs to *Diana* were carried out and a jury bowsprit rigged for the return down river on 18 May. The *Lowestoft* in company struck a sunken rock and was a total loss. None of her crew were lost being all taken off by the *Diana* who, with the assistance of the sloop *Hunter*, recovered much of the *Lowestoft's* stores. The *Diana* now continued her passage downstream, firing several shots at enemy troops ashore and rejoining the fleet abreast the town of Quebec on 21 May.

It was time for Captain Alexander Schomberg to make his last entry in *Diana's* log[8] on 23 May:-

> Off Quebec. Point Levy E.N.E. Wind E.N.E. to S.S.W. Moderate and clear. Came on board Captain Deane late of His Majesty's ship *Lowestoft* to take the Command here, and I was this day discharged by order of Lord Colville.

So ended two and a half years as Captain of the *Diana*, which was to add Louisberg and Quebec to her battle honours. During this time, those serving under Schomberg included the two Midshipmen Isaac Lewis and Samuel Morris whilst Able Seaman John Morris and Francis Silver were in his boat's crew.[9] Could there have been Jewish blood here as well?

In fact, Schomberg had asked Lord Colville to be relieved because of failing health, which was readily granted. He was sent home in the *Hunter*, with the honour of delivering Lord Colville's despatches.[10]

After recovering his health, Schomberg's next appointment was to the *Essex*, a brand new third rate of sixty four guns. It was the sixth ship to bear that name, built on the Thames, of 1,379 tons, 158 feet in length, beam 45 feet and a 16 feet draught, manned by a crew of 500. He remained her Captain until the end of the Seven Years War in 1763.

On 29 March 1761, the *Essex* was part of the squadron of thirty one vessels under Commodore, the Hon. Augustus Keppel, which sailed from St Helens with 100 transports, carrying 10,000 men for the attack on Belle Isle. This fortified islet lay off the south-east coast of Brittany and was of strategic importance being midway between Brest and Bordeaux. After initial setbacks the enemy was overcome. The Marines excelled and it is traditionally believed that the laurel wreath in the Corps badge was awarded for their contribution in capturing the island.

The following year, the *Essex* was employed in home waters, taking part in testing a new chronometer for the Board of Longitude in the Bay of Biscay, meeting the inventor, a Mr Harrison, off the Scillies in May, 1762. She returned home the following month after having escorted a convoy of troops to Belle Isle and to Lisbon.

Captain Schomberg, now aged forty-three, came ashore after the Peace of Amiens and in August 1763 married Arabella, the only child of the Reverend James Chalmers. They were to have five children, all baptized. He was re-called for a short time in command of the *Prudent,* a third rate of sixty four guns, having been joined by his nephew, Isaac Schomberg. At the end of 1771 Alexander was appointed to the yacht *Dorset* (with a complement of fifty) attached to the Lord-Lieutenant of Ireland, much against the liking of Lord Sandwich, First Lord of the Admiralty. He told Schomberg that such an appointment must be considered as retirement from the line of active service and when Schomberg quoted precedents to the contrary, replied, 'I was not then at the Admiralty.' Schomberg persisted in his right to accept the appointment. Sandwich could only write: 'He is either extremely indigent, infatuated or may think my situation at the Admiralty not permanent.' So Schomberg did not see any more active service, nor obtain his flag during the American War, continuing command of the *Dorset.* Knighted by the Lord-Lieutenant in 1777 for his outstanding merits on active service, he was the author in 1789 of "A Sea Manual recommended to the Young Officers of the Royal Navy as a Companion to the Signal Book", now a very rare book indeed.

Having for many years headed the list of Captains, Sir Alexander Schomberg died in March 1804. He was buried in the churchyard of St Peter's, Dublin (just four months after his wife).

His long life of 84 years had seen the expansion of England overseas as a maritime nation and he will be particularly remembered for his services in Canada. He had the satisfaction of seeing two of his sons into the Royal Navy. The eldest, Admiral Alexander Wilmot Schomberg (1774-1850), had a distinguished and varied career, whilst the other, Sir Charles March Schomberg (1779-1835) was a Lieutenant in the *Minotaur* at the Battle of the Nile, and afterwards Flag-Captain to Sir Sidney Smith in 1807. He is best known for his action as Captain of the frigate *Astrea* when, as senior officer at Mauritius in May, 1811, in company with two other frigates and a sloop, the British Squadron fell in with three large French frigates. After a brisk action, the *Renommée* of forty guns, was forced to strike her colours to the *Astrea*. Commander-in- Chief at the Cape of Good Hope from 1828-1832, Sir Charles finished his career as Lieutenant Governor of Dominica.

The other naval grandson of Doctor Meyer Schomberg was Captain Isaac Schomberg (1753-1813). He was in command of the *Culloden* at the Glorious Battle of the First of June in 1794. In 1802 he wrote one of the first major works on the Royal Navy entitled "Naval Chronology, or an Historical summary of Naval and Military events from the time of the Romans to the Treaty of Peace 1802". It went to five volumes, published in 1802. He dedicated this most valuable and still used work of reference to Lord Samuel Hood for his steady patronage over many years, reflecting the support Lord Hood gave to Isaac Schomberg when, as a Lieutenant in the frigate *Pegasus*, he had a disagreement over discipline with his younger Captain Prince William in 1787, involving Lord Nelson whilst in the West Indies.

As Sir Alexander Schomberg's sons and nephews were gaining prominence, he was still at sea in command of the *Dorset*, acting as a form of dispatch vessel between Dublin, Holyhead, Park Gate and Milford Haven, right up until he died. The passing of the Navy's veteran is simply recorded in the *Dorset's* log.[11]

> Wednesday 21st March 1804. Moored in Dublin Harbour. Wind E.S.E. Fresh Gales. A.M. The Captain Sir Alexander Schomberg departed this life.

A near contemporary of Alexander Schomberg was Captain Maximillian Jacobs of foreign extraction and probably of Jewish birth. He joined the Royal Navy as a Captain's Servant in the *Hampton Court* (sixty four) about 1745, being present at the dispersal and capture of part of a French convoy from the West Indies in June 1747, and afterwards in the *Centurion* (fifty) where he obtained his Lieutenant's Certificate in November 1752. Commander in June 1757, he was promoted quickly afterwards to Post Captain on 4 January 1758 in command of the *Kennington* (twenty), but only for a short period. Captain of the *Deal Castle* (twenty guns) on the North American Station until 1772, he was not given another appointment until February 1776 when given command of the relatively new thirty two gun frigate *Amazon*. Jacobs took a convoy of nineteen sail to Quebec in the September where he remained as Senior Officer in the River St Lawrence until the end of 1776. After returning to England in 1779 he was appointed to the *Defiance*, a third rate mounting sixty four guns under orders from North America. Jacobs arrived in New York during

September with a convoy of twenty five merchants vessels. It was during this time that he succeeded in putting down a serious mutiny among the 500 complement of the *Defiance*. Afterwards he sailed from New York on 26 December 1779 in a fleet of sixteen warships and transports with 7550 troops under Vice-Admiral Arbuthnot, flying his flag in the *Europe* for an attack on Charleston in South Carolina. Whilst on passage the fleet put into Savannah and captured Port Royal but unfortunately the *Defiance* was a total wreck on the bar to the entrance of the River Savannah. Captain Jacobs never held any subsequent appointments, being placed on the superannuated captains' list at an annual pension of £182.10s.0d until he died in 1800.[12]

It will be seen how, owing to the Test Acts, there were but few officers of Jewish birth prepared to give up their religion. But one who did was Donald Fernandez. Of a Sephardic family, he joined as a Midshipman at the age of nineteen in 1790. He was to see service in the *Assistance* (fifty guns) followed by two seventy four's, the *Edgar* and *Thunderer.* As Master's Mate in the latter ship, he was present at the Battle of the Glorious First of June under Lord Howe in 1794, then with Lord Bridport a year later at the inconclusive action off Groix. Towards the close of 1795, Fernandez accompanied Sir John Jervis to the Mediterranean as Acting-Lieutenant of the thirty-two gun frigate *Lively,* then was promoted Lieutenant in February 1797 a few days before the Battle of St Vincent. He then saw service off Cadiz, engaging Spanish gun-boats and batteries. Until the short-lived peace of 1802, Fernandez was aboard the flagships *Victory, London* and *Princess Royal.* His only command was the fourteen gun brig *Speedwell,* employed for a few months in 1803 on the Home Station. He did not see any further active service, being on half-pay when made Commander in 1838. Fernandez died at Southampton aged 80.[13]

Seaman 1744.

# CHAPTER 3

## "Rings, Trinkets and Gold Seals!"

*How strange it seems! These Hebrews in their graves,*
*Close by the street of this fair seaport town,*
*Silent beside the never-silent waves,*
*At rest in all this moving up and down.*
*How came they here? What burst of Christian hate,*
*What persecution, merciless and blind,*
*Drove o'er the sea – that desert desolate –*
*These Ishmaels and Hagars of mankind?*

*H.W. Longfellow 1858*

*HMS Lancaster* of sixty six guns was lying at Spithead, her log for Friday 10th February 1758 simply reading,

> Wind W to W.N.W. Paid the ships company (520 men) 6 months pay. Loosed sails to dry, set up the lower shrouds, at 5 sent the longboat on shore for Boatswains Stores.[1]

What it did not record was a major loss to the small Jewish community of Portsmouth.

For many years a custom had grown up of allowing tradesmen to board men-of-war mainly because of leave not being allowed to the crew for fear of desertion. On this particular day a number of Jews were aboard trying to sell their wares, time was getting on, the sun was going down, the Jewish Sabbath would be due, being quite early at this time of year. A number got into a hired sailing boat, the wind suddenly got up, the sail jibbed and the boat overturned. The *Lancaster's* boat immediately put off, but help was virtually too late, five bodies were never recovered, seven were brought aboard but all dead or dying. Their graves can be seen in the small Jewish burial ground in Fawcett Road, Southsea. The only survivor was Samuel Emanuel an ancestor of a future Jewish Mayor of Portsmouth.[2]

How was it Jews came to settle in the premier naval port of Portsmouth, being in all probability the oldest community in England outside of London?

By 1743 the Jewish population in England had grown to about 7,000, virtually all being in London. A small number of the more wealthy lived and traded in the City. This was forbidden to the very poor immigrants emanating from Poland and Germany who were crowded into a tiny area mainly on the eastern side, to be followed by a further influx caused by persecution in Bohemia. In spite of the parent Ashkenazic and Sephardic sense of community towards their poorer brethren, synagogue funds were insufficient to support them – the east side of London became crowded, a self-imposed ghetto in an alien world. Yet in England the Jews were under the protection of the law and able to settle where they pleased, unlike the persecution in the majority of European countries. Rising crime, overcrowding and unrest were overcome because the ghetto system found abroad within a walled city did not apply to England – a "Jewish Problem" was avoided. However, the established Jews became concerned. They looked unfavourably upon this continuous influx of a poor class of immigrant. They could not be sent back, so the answer was to encourage them to leave London for the countryside. A small loan was given, or a stock of commodities to pedal their wares. Not all the German and Polish immigrants were destitute, some arrived with a little capital and had a trade such as jeweller, silversmith or engraver. Others, particularly from Alsace and the German Rhineland had been small shopkeepers. They saw that their position in London was untenable, compounded by the difficulties of obtaining employment caused by Sabbath observance and restrictions on retail trade, so they left.

The Naval Ports of Portsmouth, Plymouth, Chatham and Sheerness were about to receive their first Jewish immigrants, trading connections with the Royal Navy were to follow and continue to the present day.

Not that the founders of these communities deliberately set out primarily to trade with the navy. The economic necessity of moving from London coincided with the expansion of the Royal Navy about to embark on the breaking of French sea power. It is not therefore surprising that the Jews, an essentially trading and commercial people, gradually established themselves at the ports, selling among other items to the seamen, old clothes, slops, trinkets, watches and cheap jewellery. These shopkeepers would send destitute pedlars inland with boxes of trinkets, laces, cigars and other portable goods to sell to farmers and their wives. Accounts were settled at the ports once a week on Friday afternoons after which the shopkeeepers and their dependent hawkers would assemble for the inauguration of the Sabbath either in the shop or hired room. On the Sunday, the pack would be replenished and the following day the pedlars trudge off again on their rounds. As soon as a pedlar had saved a little money he would marry his patron's daughter, or the daughter of an itinerant colleague, or would send for his wife from abroad. Then he would set up shop on his own, preferentially in the centre of the district which he had worked as a pedlar, blossoming out into a jeweller and silversmith, buying his goods from the great London gem and bullion merchants like Franks, Simons and Keysers.[3]

So we find a Benjamin Levy, originally from Wiesbaden, an artist and engraver of some repute, trading at the corner of Union and Queen Street, Portsmouth Common, who was to become the founder of the Portsmouth Jewish community in about 1742. Other leading members were Mordecai Samuel, originally from Rondelheim, a jeweller; Lazarus Moses from Furth and Mordecai Moses from Konigsberg, both pedlars.[4] Prayers were originally held in a private house, possibly that of a Nathan Jacobs in Oyster Street, Portsmouth Common. A burial ground was consecrated in 1747 in what is now Fawcett Road, Southsea, and is still in partial use. The first synagogue was built in White's Row, off Queen Street in 1749, whilst the Official Seal of the Portsmouth community dates from about 1746.[5]

Situated to the north of the original town of Portsmouth with its small natural harbour entrance and peninsula known as The Point, was Portsmouth Common. This was rapidly developing owing to the expansion of the dockyard. Queen Street bisects the area with Lion Gate at the east end and The Hard on the west. The streets were extremely narrow, badly paved, unlighted and uncleansed with no proper sanitation, the only water supply coming from wells and pumps, which did not improve until the 1760's. Public houses, brandy shops and coffee houses abounded especially on The Point and Hard, with scenes of debauchery and violence.

Into this environment came the Jewish immigrant, easily recognisable by his peculiar foreign dress. Giving an unkempt appearance of an untrimmed beard and side-locks; of boots to the knees; of a longcoat down to the heels; and wide-brimmed hat that was never removed. Generally Yiddish speaking, he had only a small English vocabulary and pronounced "W" as "V", "B" as "P" and "Th" as "D". Poverty and long years of persecution had sharpened his mind. First he must survive, then, with determination, succeed.

His first opportunity came by trading aboard the numerous warships coming and going from Portsmouth during the long French Wars, either to refit, store or bringing in prizes. There were also convoys and the large fleet assemblies at the anchorage of Spithead. Mingled with the bumboat woman was the Jewish pedlar. The scene is best pictured in *"Jack Nastyface", the Memoirs of an English Seaman,* and although William Robinson is writing at the time of the Napoleonic Wars his description of life on the lower deck had little changed since the time of the first Jewish pedlars.[6]

> Our ship having been in dock, she was prepared and got ready for sea again. A day or two previous to our sailing, the ship's crew was paid agreeably to an Admiralty order, and, to picture the scenes which at this time occurred is a task almost impossible. In the early part of the day the commissioners came on board, bringing the money which is paid the ship's crew, with the exception of six months pay, which it is the rule of the government to hold back from each man. The mode of paying is, as the names are, by rotation on the books: every man when called, is asked for his hat, which is returned to him with his wages in it, and the amount chalked on the rim. There is not perhaps one in twenty who actually knows what he is going to receive, nor does the particular amount seem to be a matter of much concern; for, when paid, they hurry down to their respective berths, redeem their honour with their several ladies and bumboat men, and then they turn their thoughts to the Jew pedlars, who are ranged round the decks and in the hatch-way gratings, in fact, the ship is crowded with them.

*Scene in port on the main deck of a Man-of-War. A Trader can be discerned – left hand background (from a colour aquatint by T Sutherland 1820). National Maritime Museum*

They are furnished with every article that will rig out a sailor, never omitting, in their parkains, a fine large watch and appendages, all warranted, and with which many an honest tar has been taken in; they can supply them likewise with fashionable rings and trinkets for their ladies, of pure gold, oh! nothing can be purer! Yet with all Mordecai's asservations, it's purity may be doubted . . .

. . . By the evening, when the Jews were all ordered out of the ship; he then made it known to the captain, who caused an enquiry to be made: the boatswain's mates were called aft, but none of them knew of a man having been started at the time the Jew mentioned; the captain then told Moses that he could do no more for him unless the men who had played off the trick were brought to him, and then he would take care they should be punished. On this promise the Jew went below; he looked with piercing eyes between the guns fore and aft, where the men mess, but could not find the skulker who had so ingeniously taken his revenge and possessed himself of a suit of clothes. Mortified to think he should be done, he swore by Moses and the Prophets, he would find the villain; became exasperated, and left the ship, amidst the grins and jeers of the whole crew, who were much diverted and pleased to think that any of their shipmates had tact enough to retaliate so nicely on a Jew.'

*Pay day in port aboard a Man-of-War. Seamen and others skylarking with a Jewish pedlar. circa 1820 from an etching by G. Cruikshank*

The seamen delighted in sky-larking with the Jewish pedlars. An etching of the time shows a grating being pulled from under the feet of a pedlar, his goods spilling everywhere causing much merriment between decks. Fiction and non-fiction alike of the period make reference to Moses the pedlar, sometimes in a degrading manner, but most usually as a figure of fun. The novelist can often set the scene – Captain Marryat in *"Peter Simple"*:-[7]

> At last the frigate was full manned; and, as we had received drafts of men from other ships, we were ordered to be paid previously to our going to sea. The people on shore always find out when a ship is to be paid, and very early in the morning we were surrounded with wherries, laden with Jews and other people, some requesting admittance to sell their goods, others to get paid for what they had allowed the sailors to take up upon credit. But the first lieutenant would not allow any of them to come on board until after the ship was paid; although they were so urgent, that he was forced to place sentries in the chains with cold shot, to stave the boats if they came alongside . . .
>
> About eleven o'clock the dock-yard boat, with all the pay clerks, and the cashier, with his chest of money, came on board, and was shown into the fore-cabin, where the captain attended the pay-table. The ship was now in a state of confusion and uproar; there were Jews trying to sell clothes, or to obtain money for clothes which they had sold; bumboat men and bumboat women showing their long bills, and demanding or coaxing for payment; other people from the shore, with hundreds of small debts; and the sailor's wives, sticking close to them, and disputing every bill presented, as an extortion or a robbery. There were such bawling and threatening, laughing and crying – for the women were all to quit the ship before sunset – at one moment a Jew was upset, and all his hamper of clothes tossed into the hold; at another, a sailor was seen hunting everywhere for a Jew who had cheated him, – all squabbling or skylarking, and many of them very drunk . . .

"A Leg for a Boot, or the Jew outwitted"[8] is another example:-

> This circumstance we are about to relate might, or might not, have occurred on board the *Royal William* (which ship it is well known nearly suffered shipwreck, by grounding on her own beef bones at Spithead), but if it did not take place on board that ship, it must, nevertheless, be treated with respect.
>
> An individual of the Jewish persuasion, by name Isaac Isaacs, the lower extremities of whose face were distinguished by a beard of no

> mean pretensions, had established, by the good-will of the first–lieutenant, tolerably extensive premises on the middle deck of the ship above referred to, where he carried on a very considerable trade. Dead-eye buttons, scissors, and thread, – jackets, thick and thin, – shirts of all sizes, hats, caps, and looking glasses, for either sex, – watches, gold chains, stockings, shoes, and a mass of indescribables were there heaped together; in fact it was "a Jew's shop". Among other valuables exhibited in this Jewish collection Mr Isaacs had not forgotten to provide some fine large strong fishermen's boots, at that time in great request for washing decks . . .
>
> . . . But it occasionally happened that articles, notwithstanding the lynx-eye and ubiquitous nature of the owner, walked off without his being able to bring the proceeds to account. Such was the case with his wash-deck boots: one of a pair was missed from its accustomed place; but by whom removed no one was bold enough to say . . .
>
> . . . Mr Isaacs leaving his shop in care of his faithful servant, ascended to the quarter-deck, with the seaman to make his complaint; and the first-lieutenant undertook to be the arbitrator. The Jew's case was, that there was proof presumptive that the sailor either had the missing boot himself, or else knew the thief . . .
>
> The first-lieutenant having heard Isaacs to an end, then turned to the man, and asked what he had to say in reply, when Jack, with very little hesitation, said, "You see, your honour, old Tom, the cook, since I've been aboard the Royal Billy, has acted the part of a father to me, in taking care of me like, and I wished to make him some return; so, seein' the odd boot hanging up in Isaac's shop, and knowing that old Tom had a wooden leg, and did'nt want a pair of boots, I thought as how this would be a good chance, so I axed the price of it, and the Jew swore directly I'd a stole the other; and brought me afore your honour.
>
> Isaac's beard dropped below his girdle, and the lieutenant's countenance evinced a strong disposition towards a broad grin. The former made the best of his way back to his shop, and the sailor remained in full possession of the victory. Overtures were shortly after made by Isaacs, and the sailor became possessed of a pair of boots for the price of one.

So we learn what it was like for the original Jewish traders going aboard the men-of-war in harbour, the scenes of drunkenness, the bumboat women taken below decks by the young seamen after not seeing a woman for many months – not a place for the prudish. The Jew was blamed for excessive prices on faulty goods, and outlandish interest on money lent, a butt for the authorities keeping the seamen in low pay and not allowing them ashore for fear of desertion. The practice of trading could have been easily stopped, but it gave the seamen some laxity in the harsh discipline whilst keeping them in the confines of the ship. The navy had enough manning problems and the wars had to be won.

As for the seamen themselves and the pedlars one senses a certain affinity behind all the skylarking. Both knew hardship – the immigrant from a persecuted homeland into an alien society: the seaman risking shipwreck, disease, flogging and the chance of being killed or wounded in action or simply falling from the rigging.

*Interior of Portsmouth Synagogue, White's Row, Portsea.*

Not that all was accord in the Portsmouth Jewish community itself, with some of the scenes of violence spilling into the Synagogue where one Jew physically attacked another whilst the congregation was at prayer.[9] In 1766 after a long and sometimes bitter argument over which London Synagogue the community should be affiliated to for spiritual guidance, a split occurred with another synagogue being formed virtually opposite in Daniel's Row. They came together again in 1789 after the original community in White's Row had re-built the synagogue nine years previously. It was destined to stand for another 156 years. The interior was adorned with gilding, six elegant chandeliers and brazen candlesticks, the ark of solid mahogany, holding the Scrolls of the Law, in the centre the reading desk and elders' seats, with ladies' gallery above. Seating 200 with a vestry room built on the side, the whole was unobtrusively sited in White's Row (now Curzon Howe Road) out of sight from the main Queen Street. Later the Royal Arms was affixed to the gallery on the west side in honour presumably of some member of George III's family who was associated with Portsmouth and quite possibly visited the synagogue.[10]

To the south side of Royal Parade, Plymouth, close to St Andrew's Church and the Law Courts, is a small turning called Catherine Street. A little way down on the right is an old building. Walk slowly up the side "ope". You are approaching an ancient synagogue – the oldest in continuous use for the Ashkenazi service in the whole of the English speaking world. The entrance is apparently at the back because in all synagogues the Ark holding the sacred scrolls faces towards the Holy Land. Look up and see the Foundation Stone, "Built in the year 1762".

On your approach you will be struck by this old building surrounded by the re-built Plymouth. Miraculously the synagogue survived the blitz of March 1941. Let us enter with due reverence.

In the oak panelled vestibule can be seen a small silver shield-like plaque on which are engraved the names of the nine founders. Here also is the Prayer for the Royal Family, painted on canvas. The inside of the synagogue is small, but beautifully proportioned. The slender pillars supporting the gallery add to its delicacy, while the stained glass windows fill the interior with colour. In the centre is the Bimah, a raised reading desk, around which are the eight great brass candlesticks which the founders had to pawn to pay for the completion of the building. The Holy Ark, covered with gold and silver leaf is a masterpiece of exquisite carving by skilled craftsmen producing an elaborate baroque effect. Local custom relates how it may have been transhipped from Italy on board one of His Majesty's ships through the possible connivance in one way or another by the community's trading connection with officers of the Royal Navy. Bearing in mind the transport of the time, it was unlikely it could have been brought overland. In the Ark are the Sacred Scrolls of the Law, some of which were used by the original members in 1742. Over all, are the Tablets of the Ten Commandments.

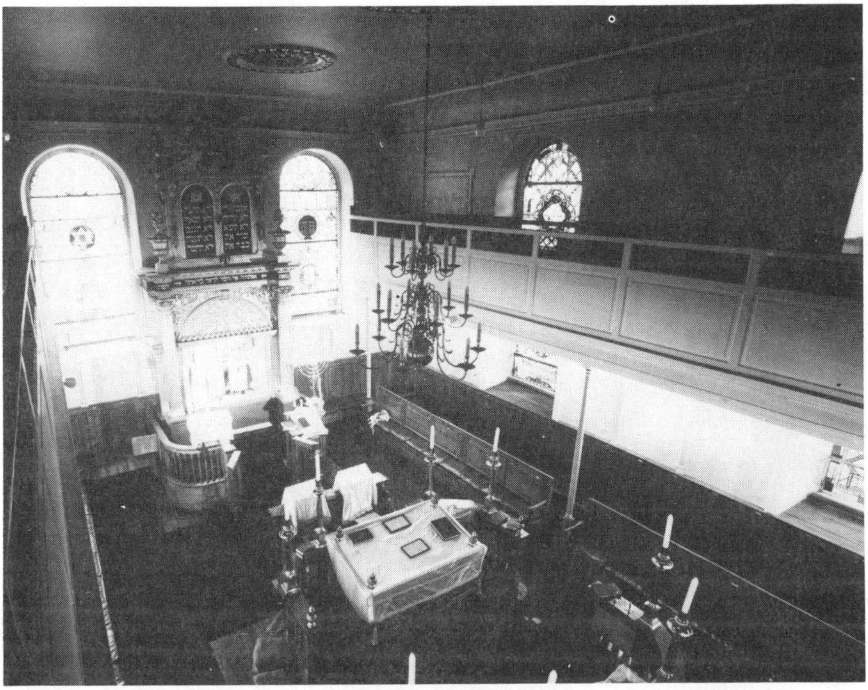

*Interior of Plymouth Synagogue. The oldest Ashkanazic Synagogue in the English speaking world built 1763. Miraculously saved from destruction in March 1941 when the centre of Plymouth was virtually destroyed by German aircraft. (Authors collection)*

The great central chandelier, the side lights, the Everlasting Light and the silver Menorah are all modern, but the little brass offertory box facing the door dates back to 1762 and is still in use.[11] The wooden benches seating ninety-nine gentlemen and eighty ladies ranged round the walls, were discovered on renovation early in the 1970s to be of rather cheap pine, reflecting the community's poor financial state. It was found, on stripping down, that none of the main woodwork is nailed or screwed, but plugged with pieces of dowel the way shipwrights used to work. Therefore it could be that shipwrights from the dockyard carried out the original work at a small charge or for some returned favour.

The warmth of this little gem of a synagogue, steeped in history, grips into your very being, an enduring monument of Israel's faith and to the Glory of God.

*Plymouth Jewish Cemetery, consecrated in 1752. Situated at The Hoe on the west side of New Street. (Author's collection).*

We have seen how the Jews first came to Portsmouth and it was the same conditions and process which brought them to Plymouth about 1740, settling around Notte and Southside Streets, probably holding services in private houses, it is said in Woolster and Holgate Streets. A cemetery was acquired in 1752 on the north side of the Hoe, now disused. A lease of land was granted by the Mayor and Commonalty of Plymouth to Samuel Chapman as Jews could not at that time own land. He in turn granted a Trust Deed to the elders of the synagogue "That Jews should enjoy the use of the Land and Premises". So the synagogue was built, with the help of a £300 mortgage raised to complete the building in 1762.[12] By 1797, Jews were allowed to own property, a lease was granted for ninety-nine years, converted to a Freehold in 1834. The vestry alongside the synagogue was built in 1874.

The synagogue elders had laid down rules of strict behaviour with an eye to the future, particularly in the Hebrew education of the children, who had special seats with their teacher on the western side. No Jew dared summons a fellow Jew before secular courts and the poor were particularly taken care of. In August 1779, with the threat of French invasion from the combined fleets of France and Spain, the Jewish community donated £50 to the government.[13]

From the Plymouth Aliens List of 1798,[14] the early settlers in the 1760s and 1770s were roughly between the ages of thirty and thirty-five, mainly from Germany, with a high proportion of silversmiths. They had arrived in England through Harwich and come thence to Plymouth, often via London. A Barnett Levy first went to Portsmouth and then on to Plymouth in 1775, possibly the presage of the Jewish inter-movement between the two naval ports.

At that time Plymouth consisted of only about 1,500 houses clustered round Sutton Harbour, with the present Royal Parade the northern extremity of the town. Part of Catherine Street was open towards the west, whilst southward a succession of fields spread towards the Hoe. Millbay had not been developed and Devonport Dockyard was in its infancy.[15] As with Portsmouth, the naval military base was to expand, increased trading opportunities the result. The pedlars and others amassed a little capital, opening slop shops ashore, performing a useful but dubious function with the seamens' wage tickets.

The seamens' pay was very poor, not having risen between 1653 and 1797. Paid on a monthly basis, from which sixpence was deducted as a contribution to the Royal Hospital, Greenwich, a Landsman received eighteen shillings, an Ordinary Seaman nineteen shillings, and an Able Seaman twenty four shillings. They were all paid at least six months in arrears. On leaving his ship each seaman was given a wage ticket, not the money. It was encashable only by personal visit to the Navy Pay Office at Tower Hill in London. Those few who did make the journey found they had to give some consideration to the Pay Clerks. Many subterfuges were piled on the seamen, with any excuse not to pay them, as for instance, the immediate transfer from one ship to another. The authorities set up the situation for a large traffic in these "wage tickets". The seamen, needing the money as soon as they came ashore, had no other recourse but to the "ticket buyers", often at scandalous rates of discount. The unscrupulous publicans, prostitutes and other parasites swindled the susceptible seamen. Before the age of paper money, ships could not carry large amounts of coin, due to the prospect of capture, so the seamen and their families suffered. But so did the slopsellers who took them. At least from them, the seamen received some clothing in exchange for the "wage tickets". But the traders in turn had difficulty cashing them in.

Popular writers and some historians blame the Jews, among others, for taking advantage of the seamen's circumstances. No doubt some did. In a dishonest age nobody was immune from such actions. Moreover the impression given of large numbers of grasping Jews in the naval ports is exaggerated as all traders dealing in "wage tickets", whether Jew or Gentile, were given the name of "Jew" by the seamen.[16] By 1800, we know from census returns the population of Plymouth, including Plymouth Dock (later Devonport), was about 40,000 and Portsmouth in the region of 32,000. To gauge the number of Jews is difficult, but as some guide Patrick Colquhon, the police magistrate, estimated 5,000 outside of London. This is thought to be a little exaggerated. The German pastor Frederick Wenderborn, on a visit to England recorded 1,000 in 1791, possibly an under-estimation. The seating accommodation of the synagogue gives some guide, so it would appear something under one per cent of the population were Jews in the naval ports. They tended to congregate in certain parts, were noticeable in speech, looks and attire, and so gave the impression of large numbers. By no means all the slopsellers were Jews. Here reads the colourful language of one:-[17]

> MORGAN. MERCER AND SEA DRAPER
> NUMBER 85 OPPOSITE THE FOUNTAIN INN
> HIGH STREET, PORTSMOUTH
>
> Sailors rigged complete from stem to stern, viz. chapeau, napeau, flying jib and flesh bag, inner pea, outer pea and cold defender; rudder case and service to the same; up haulers and down traders, fore shoes, lacing gaskets, etc.
>
> With canvas bags,
> To hold your cags,
> And chests to sit upon;
> Clasp knives your meat
> To cut and eat
> When ship does lay along.

In fact the clothing sold to the seamen in the second half of the eighteenth century did not conform with any laid down regulations but was usually much more colourful and distinctive than that issued by the purser aboard ship. For example, trim straw hats with ribbons and the ship's name painted on, glazed tarpaulin hats, gaudy waistcoats and neckerchiefs, baggy blue and white striped trousers and seamen's gear such as knives and hammock stretchers. The seamen purchased second hand clothing of variety including double fronted jackets of blue baize with eight buttons, red petticoat breeches, white waistcoats and black shoes having square metal buckles.[18]

*Trade Card of Abraham Joseph 1731 - 1794. (from an engraving)*

Bailey's Directory for Plymouth of 1783 lists Abraham Joseph as a Mercer and Draper of Barbican Quay, a man of some substance probably setting up in business during the 1760's. He was appointed by Royal Warrant to be slopman and agent to Prince William Henry, third son of King George III in 1780, then a Midshipman, together with his elder brother the Prince of Wales. Stothard painted a picture in 1779 showing the Prince in Midshipman's uniform of blue coat, white waistcoat and knee-breeches. No doubt Abraham Joseph supplied Admirals with frocks having narrow lapels down to the waist, small coat-cuffs, and single lace of mousequetaire pattern down the side skirts. The lapels on the captain's and commander's frocks went down to the waist and lieutenant's the same but with slash white cuffs and lapels like the commander's without lace. Flat buttons with an engraved anchor and cable, plain waistcoats and white breeches were worn. It was not until 1795 that epaulettes were introduced.

During the time of Prince William Henry's disfavour with the King in 1786 he often sought the help of Abraham Joseph. The royal friendship was to continue with Abraham's son Joseph. *The Gentleman's Magazine* of 1794:

> There died in Plymouth aged 63 years, Abraham Joseph. Popularly known in the South West of England as "The King of the Jews", a wholesale dealer in slops for the Navy. He was one of the people called Jews but the actions of his whole life would have done honour to any persuasion. He amassed a considerable fortune by very fair and honest means. As an agent for seamen, his practice was well worth the imitation of every person in that business as several orphans and indigent widows can testify.

War had broken out the year before with Revolutionary France, the classic age of Britain's naval achievement was about to begin. Portsmouth Common became Portsea in 1792 where the majority of Jews lived, worked and prayed. Instead of trading aboard the warships some of the pedlars established their own shops, the next stage in the Jewish trading activities had been reached.

Seaman 1777.

# CHAPTER 4

## "His Brothers are at Sea in the King's Ships"

*The security of the kingdom is increased by every man being more or less a sailor.*

Captain Marryat

The frigate *HMS Magicienne* lay at her moorings in Sheerness Harbour. It was a clear cold winter's day, 3 February 1802. At eight o'clock in the morning a gun was fired breaking the silence over the harbour and the Union Flag hoisted at the *Magicienne's* peak[1] – the signal for a Court Martial.

On the quarterdeck were twelve Captains of some of the ships moored at Sheerness, with the President of the Court Martial, Rear-Admiral Bartholomew Rowley, assembled behind a table covered with green baize. From below was brought the prisoner, John Cook, late belonging to His Majesty's cutter *Dolphin,* charged with desertion and robbing Mr Robert Jackson, Midshipman, of the same vessel. The trial opened. Cook faced the Court standing beside the Master-at-Arms who had his sword drawn[2].

It transpired that on 8 September 1801, the prisoner was given permission by Midshipman Jackson to go ashore at Sheerness from the *Dolphin* to conduct some private business, and to be back aboard the same evening. It was alleged Cook took with him some of Midshipman Jackson's dirty linen for washing, which had not been seen again. Under examination the owner could not recollect what had been lost and admitted the clothes were of little value. The Boatswain and Carpenter's Mate both remembered the prisoner going ashore about the beginning of September, but not of taking any linen with him. The minutes of the Court Martial continued:-

> The Prisoner (John Cook) was now put upon his Defence and the Court cleared – Upon the Court being re-opened, the Charge against the Prisoner was read to Mr Isaac Joseph, Slopseller, in Blue Town,

Sheerness, who was Sworn, as a Jew, upon the Old Testament.

Court. Do you know the Prisoner?

Answer. Yes – John Levy – I have known him from his infancy ("Cook" was obviously an alias. G.G.)

Prisoner. Did I, in the month of September last, leave some clothes with you, at your house?

Answer. No.

Prisoner. What is my general character.

Answer. A very honest Lad, but very wild – you are of a very good family, and if you had stayed with them, you would probably have had Five Thousand Pounds – I believe there is about a Thousand Pounds left to you now, by your Uncle.

The Prisoner addressed the Court and most solemnly averred that he left Mr Jackson's Linen with Mr Isaac Joseph, and that from motives of fear he did not return to the *Dolphin,* having exceeded his leave. He then called upon Lieutenant Shirley, who said the prisoner behaved himself very well and like an honest man, whilst acting as his Servant in the *Dolphin.*

The Prisoner having no further evidence to call, threw Himself upon the mercy of the Court.

The Court was then cleared and the Judge Advocate having read the Minutes, the Court very seriously and maturely considered the same and agreed in opinion, that the charge of desertion was proved and that the charge of having robbed Mr Jackson, Midshipman, was not proved, and therefore adjudged the Prisoner, John Cook, to receive One Hundred and Fifty Lashes on his bare back, with a Cat-of-Nine Tails, alongside such of his Majesty's Ships and Vessels, and at such time, as the Commander in Chief of His Majesty's Ships and Vessels in the River Medway and at the Buoy of the Nore shall direct.

On dispersal the prisoner was removed to the guardship *Zealand* to await his punishment.[3] Five days later, on Monday 8 February, the signal was made with many of the warships lying at the Nore sending a boat manned with a marine guard to attend the punishment. At 8 o'clock in the morning the *Zealand's* launch was lowered into the water.[4] Levy then appeared under guard, stripped to the waist. He came down the ladder and was lashed by the wrists to a capstan bar running the length of the launch. In attendance was the Surgeon and Master-at-Arms. Captain William Mitchell read the sentence from the gangway, a Boatswain's Mate followed, being ordered to do his duty. The cat-of-nine-tails was produced from its bag. The Boatswain's Mate took a full swing of the arm and crashed it down on Levy's back. After six lashes another mate took over. And so it went on. In all, twenty-five lashes were inflicted. The prisoner was cast loose and collapsed. When a blanket was wrapped around him, he revived. Meanwhile, the launch was rowed away from the *Zealand's* side to the sound of the half-minute bell, the oars keeping time to the drummer who beat the Rogue's March beside the victim. The attendant boats followed slowly in procession to the same melancholy beat. The launch approached the fifty gun *Isis* and was tied up.[5] From the top of the gangway her Captain, Thomas Masterman Hardy, read the charge, and so the torture was repeated, this time with twenty-six lashes. On he was taken to the next ships, until, after seventy-five lashes, it was stopped. Levy was then returned to the *Zealand* and taken below to the sick quarters. There, he was told he would receive the remaining seventy-five lashes after recovering.

However, the Surgeon of the *Zealand,* Alexander Duncan, wrote to his Captain, William Mitchell, on 14 February,[6] six days after the flogging:

> I beg leave to represent to you, that John Cook (a Jew) who was some time ago sentenced by a Court Martial to receive 150 lashes for desertion from the *Dolphin* Cutter, had 75 of them inflicted on Monday last, at which time he fainted, was brought on Board here, where he had for the space of an hour such a succession of severe convulsion fits, that I thought at one time his recovery extremely doubtful. It is necessary to remark, that previous to his trial, he was a poor emaciated hectic creature and I am well informed, from the day of sentence being passed to that of its execution he neither ate or slept (except in a very limited degree) and since I can from my own observations aver the same thing – this I conceive to be partly owing to his deteriorated state both of body and mind, aggravated by the remaining part of his punishment hanging over his head – which in my opinion, he cannot possibly bear without the immediate risk of his life, or at least rendering an already broken constitution to the lowest ebb – I have therefore to request you will be pleased to represent the same to the Commander in Chief or otherwise as you may think proper.
>
> I am, Sir,
>
> Your most obedient Servant,
>
> Alexander Duncan.

The letter was immediately passed to the Admiralty through the Commander-in-Chief Nore, Vice-Admiral Graeme, with a reply on 17 February to remit the remainder of the punishment.

Levy recovered enough to be moved to the Hospital Ship *Spanker,* moored in the Swale at Queensboro not far from Sheerness, on 2 March, suffering from rheumatism.[7]

The *Spanker* was nearing the end of her usefulness. She was being converted into a hospital ship and all her guns were being removed. With timbers rotting, low deck space, poor food, and dirty wards, Levy must have been relieved to learn that, after seventeen days, he was to be discharged on 19 March 1802, as unserviceable. In fact, the Admiralty had already directed Admiral Graeme on 3 February[8] that, after Cook had received his punishment, he was to be considered a disposable man.

So ended almost six years' service in the Royal Navy. Levy first entered as a volunteer with a bounty of £1.10s.0d. on 13 May 1796, into the receiving ship *Enterprise,* having been born twenty years previously in London.[9] He was then sent to the new sixteengun sloop *HMS Merlin* as a landsman on 16 May 1796, where he was to remain for about five years,[10] seeing action in the West Indies. In September 1798 the *Merlin,* under Commander John Moss, found herself the only ship of the Royal Navy at Belize facing Spanish attacks in the Gulf of Honduras. Commander Moss organised and armed a small force of schooners and launches from the colony, leading them against a superior Spanish flotilla including transports carrying 2,000 troops. After a series of spirited actions the Spaniards were forced to retire.[11]

On paying off the *Merlin,* Levy's next ship was the cutter *Dolphin* which he joined on 31 July 1801 only soon to desert with fateful consequences.[12] What subsequently happened to John Levy and how long he lived is unknown. Perhaps he sought out the Jewish community and Isaac Joseph the slopseller in Sheerness. Jews had first settled there in 1790, having moved on from Chatham where the original synagogue had been constructed thirty years previously. Perhaps his legacy, if it really existed, helped. But, as with many others, the flogging he had endured left him a broken man.

So we learn without doubt of a Jew serving in the Royal Navy during the Napoleonic Wars. Little could he have realised he was to go down in the annals of Anglo-Jewry as a symbol to those Jews who were to follow him into the Royal Navy right down to the present day. 'Remember John Levy, flogged round the fleet in 1802!'

Life in the Royal Navy was harsh. In addition to the floggings for the smaller offences, between thirty-four seamen and marines were tried by Courts Martial (between 5 February and 16 May 1800). Two were aquitted, two had sentences of 500 lashes, seven of 300, six of 200, two of 150, seven of 100, one of 60 and seven of 50 lashes. Not that it was any better ashore, it was being normal practice to flog even the youngest for petty larceny. It was a brutal age.

*"A Flogging at the Gangway" circa 1820 from an etching by G. Cruikshank. National Maritime Museum.*

Although the Muster Books of the period did not give an individual's religion, it is possible to detect other Jews from the distinctive names, reinforced by birth places where it is known Jewish communities existed.

There was the enterprising Ordinary Seaman John Jacobs of Portsmouth who tried to beat the system in December 1796, having joined the frigate *Eurus* after receiving a bounty of £5.19s.0d, from the parish of Portsea. Within a few days, whilst on duty in Portsmouth dockyard to collect stores for the *Eurus,* he deserted, volunteered again and received another bounty of £2.10s.Od., this time as John Francis aboard the *Royal William* Guardship at Portsmouth. Meanwhile, the Master of the *Eurus,* who was looking for six men to complete his crew, came aboard the *Royal William.* It was the practice to man ships under sailing orders from the Guardships. Unfortunately for John Jacobs he was recognised, put aboard the *Eurus* and sent off to the West Indies. At his subsequent Courts Martial, aboard HMS *Bellona* at Martinique in March 1797, after not offering any defence, he was sentenced to reimburse the bounty and to receive 300 lashes.[13]

When the war had broken out in February 1793, against revolutionary France, for once the Royal Navy had been reasonably prepared. The reverses of the War of American Independence had not gone unheeded by the Admiralty. Howe, Hood, Jervis, Duncan, Collingwood, Saumarez and Nelson were unsurpassed in their professional excellence and knowledge.

The reaction of the Jews to the emergency was much the same as other Englishmen. Although treated as virtual social outcasts, but able to follow their religion under the protection of the law, they came forward. The leaders of the Jewish community encouraged devotion to King and Country through the Rabbis of the Portugese and Great Synagogues preaching sermons and prayers for the success of the British Arms.[14] This was also to help ward off the anti-foreign agitation against the Jews, accused, among other things, of Jacobin sympathies. Under the Aliens Act of 1793, which gave the government strict control over foreigners' movements, some Jewish pedlars and small traders were deported. On the other hand, all further immigration of penniless Jews from Europe was stopped, thus relieving further embarrassment to the acclimatized. The war now brought about a chance for the younger Jews to break out of their poor, inhibiting surroundings. The Jewish population had grown to about 25,000 (approximately 0.25% of the whole country) with roughly 20,000 in London. They were mainly very poor, with a great gulf between a few wealthy families and those who were petty shopkeepers, dealers in old clothes, pedlars and costermongers. Young Jewish boys lived by their wits. They became street hawkers and turned to disreputable callings, including crime, with no hope of improving themselves. The war was to bring social and economic change. As far as the lower deck was concerned, the rule that only Protestants could serve was quietly overlooked. The Royal Navy, albeit unwittingly, gave English Jews an opportunity to make an impression in their long search for acclimatisation and acceptance.

The nucleus of the fleet was formed round the regular volunteers who were serving in small numbers at the war's commencement. They were mainly from the Marine Society which had been founded in 1756. It is still in existence today.

The Society, supported by public subscription, performed the function of sending young boys from poor families, orphans and others, to sea in the Royal and Merchant Navies. After being cleansed and fully kitted out they were given a rudimentary education and some maritime instruction. Other young men, not seamen, but willing to volunteer, (often because they were in some trouble), were also helped along in the same way. These men and boys were ideal. They could stand the rigours of life at sea and, above all, did not desert, if only because they had nowhere to go. On the outbreak of hostilities, with the rapid expansion of the Royal Navy, the best of the Marine Society men and boys eventually found themselves in the better lower deck posts, such as Captain of Guns and Petty Officers.

An examination of the Marine Society Records[15] of the boys as young as twelve and the older "landsmen" reveals a roll of probable Jewish volunteers (See Appendix Six & Seven – Muster Rolls of Jews who served in the Royal Navy from the Maritime Society). There was for instance Jacob Hart born in Bethnal Green, East London, who entered the Marine Society on 30 May 1800, aged 13, of 4 feet 4 inches in height, discharged 23 July as servant to Lord St Vincent in his one hundred gun flagship *Ville de Paris.* Hart stayed aboard until 11 January 1801 when he was sent to the 36-gun frigate *Doris,* seeing service in her at the cutting out of the *Chevrette* off Brest the following July. Jews were known to have lived in Oxford since 1733, so it might be possible that the brothers James and William Jacobs were Jewish, aged thirteen and fourteen respectively when joining the Marine Society on 27 August 1795. Within eight days, both were sent to the new thirty six gun frigate *Emerald* as servants to Captain Berkley. William was to stay aboard for two years and James until February 1798. In April 1797 the *Emerald* in company with the *Irresistible* forced two Spanish frigates to strike their colours after an action lasting one and a half hours in Conil Bay near Cadiz. Later they bombarded that port in a small squadron under Commodore Sir Horatio Nelson and took part in the attack on Santa Cruz, where Nelson lost his right arm below the elbow, the following July.[16]

There were, of course, other volunteers, encouraged by generous bounties and the enticement of prize money, but not enough to complete the Navy's manning requirements, so that by March 1795, Parliament passed an Act for each county in England and Wales to raise men for the Navy in proportion to its population. These Quota Men, as they became known, were thus a form of conscript and, although receiving a bounty, were not genuine volunteers. The local magistrates empowered to fill their quotas saw the opportunity to rid the community of petty criminals, tramps and vagabonds. So, by delegating their manning responsibilities, the Admiralty acquired the worst types of men, who were despised by the professional, volunteer seamen. From the register of 3,893 men raised by these means for the Port of London[17] for the six months 26 March to 25 September 1795, six can possibly be noted as Jews.

There was Richard Hart, 21, a servant; Joseph Hart, 28, a shoemaker; William Solomon, 21, a sweep from Bermondsey; Joseph Daniels, 23, a baker from Whitechapel; William Barnard, 21, a bricklayer from Aldgate; and Moses Samuel, 20, an old clothesman from Houndsditch.

Each received a bounty of £5.5s.0d. and a further sum due of £10.10s.0d., entering the Royal Navy as Landsmen. Notwithstanding the Aliens Act, some were of foreign birth. Not for the last time was the Royal Navy to bend regulations to suit its manning requirements. In fact, the number of foreigners was surprisingly high, possibly as much as one-eighth of the total strength by the end of the war.

The foreign seamen could not find employment, trade having been virtually extinguished in the main Baltic and Mediterranean Ports such as Hamburg and Genoa. Provided they had volunteered and had two years continuous service, an Act of 1735 gave them the right to become naturalized. However, the fleet was chronically short of seamen, particularly in the later stages of the war, and foreigners were often pressed on the high seas in spite of their exemption from impressment. Many were Americans, a few were Jews. We find Isaac Levi born and married in New York, pressed aboard *HMS Volage* whilst bound for Boston in 1802.[18] And Nicholas Levy aged fifty pressed from the English merchant brig *Mercury*, put aboard the frigate *Mermaid* on 14 January 1814. He insisted he was French, a native of Dieppe, but to no avail. Apparently, he deserted at Genoa the following July, claiming he had not been given documentation for his pay and prize money after discharge on medical grounds.[19]

Undoubtedly British Jews also found themselves in the Royal Navy against their will, victims of the Press Gang.

The notion which depicts all Jews of the period as pedlars and tailors with bandy-legs, so attracting the attention of the press gang because they had the legs of a sailor, is not based on reality.[20] As we have seen, Jews were already established in many of the sea ports where obviously the press gangs were most active. Jew or not, bandy-legs or not, the press gangs struck. The navy needed to be manned. Impressment was an ugly necessity, supported as necessary for the defence of the country, yet there was sympathy for the press gang's victims. Unlike the popular conception of ruthless and violent gangs, there was control over their activities on land. Primarily, only those "Persons using the sea" could by law be pressed. Those below eighteen and over fifty-five years of age, certain fishermen, watermen and officers in the Merchant Navy were exempt. Foreigners could not be pressed on land. It is possible, as Jews were considered aliens and not seafarers, that they could have avoided impressment if they had wished to.

There was for instance the interesting, but isolated, incident in December 1807 when Lieutenant John Pope pressed some men just about to land from a cross-river boat at Gravesend and took them aboard his ship the frigate *Amelia.* Among those pressed was a shabbily dressed Moses Levy in a coarse greatcoat who, on coming before the First Lieutenant John Bates, was asked if he had any protection from impressment. Lieutenant Bates could not recollect whether Levy told him he was a Jew or not, but suggested that, if he could find two men as substitutes for himself, he would be released, provided he had some security. Moses Levy proposed leaving his watch and greatcoat upon condition it would be returned to him when the substitutes came on board. The First Lieutenant agreed, particularly when a bumboat woman named Cowes said she knew Levy and would be answerable for his return. Levy did not procure two men in his place but instead instigated legal proceedings against Captain Irby in command of the *Amelia* for his watch and coat. When the Admiralty Solicitor, Charles Bicknell cross-examined both Lieutenants, it was stated by Lieutenant Bates that, 'No application was made by Levy for his discharge nor did he even say he was a Jew'. The Solicitor recommended to Captain Irby that he return the watch and coat on the best terms possible as Moses Levy was not a seaman nor by law liable to be impressed.[21]

In fact, a proposal for Jews to be considered among exemptions for impressment had already been wisely rejected by the leaders of the Jewish community in 1778. As far as the Admiralty was concerned nothing was laid down. However, unofficially, "Being a Jew" was a ground for release, although only on specific orders. For instance, the muster of *HMS Victory* for 1805 has the following entry against the name of Moses Benjamin:

> "Discharged from the service on order of Lord Nelson agreeable to orders from the Lord Commissioners of the Admiralty, Moses Benjamin being a Jew".[22]

The Admiralty were not consistent in their attitude towards whether Jewish seamen should be discharged. Other factors appeared to be more important than the seaman's religion. David Goldsmid, a Prussian Jew, applied for discharge in July 1812, on the grounds of being a Jew, whilst serving in *HMS Barfleur*. His application was refused. Apparently his being a foreigner kept him in the Navy, rather than his being a Jew as grounds for release. A man would more readily be released if found not to be used to the sea. This happened to Lyon Hart of *HMS Mulgrave* in February 1813. Nathan Solomons, alias Nathan Williams, tried for release from *HMS Ceres* on various counts in March 1814: being under age; being of the Jewish religion; and not being used to the sea. The Admiralty simply took no action.[23]

Isaac Vallentine, founder of the *Jewish Chronicle*, the oldest Jewish newspaper in the world, was pressed into the Royal Navy around 1812. He eventually obtained his release through the endeavours of the Canterbury Jewish community. Whether it was on the grounds of, "Being a Jew" or because he had been born in Belgium, (foreigners not being subject to impressment on land), is unknown.[24]

From the available evidence it can be seen that any Jew who found himself in the Royal Navy, whether pressed, volunteer, or quota man, hid his religion. He knew that if he revealed it he would be treated with a mixture of contempt, suspicion and aversion. One thing was certain, a man-of-war was no place where he could follow the tenets of his religion. The whole process became a contradiction in practice – only Protestants could join the Royal Navy but the Admiralty did not ask a man's religion, and yet the Jew, knowing his disabilities, still entered the Royal Navy.

Two Jewish brothers, Israel and Benjamin Hart, who as strolling conjurers went aboard a man-of-war in the Downs about 1800 were pressed. We are told that, "Curiously enough the Harts made very good sailors and brave fighting men".[25] Others fell prone to conversion. John Wetherall of the frigate *Hussar* recounts how his shipmate, "John Smith the Jew was baptized married and turned from Jew to Roman Catholic all on a November morning in 1810".[26]

The new entrants' first experience of the Royal Navy was aboard the obsolete men-of-war used as guardships permanently moored in harbour for reception and temporary accommodation until they were sent to ships in commission needed to complete their crews. Here jostled together and overcrowded in deplorable conditions were Englishmen and foreigners, bankrupts and dandies, petty thieves and swindlers, men of trade and occupation and amongst them, the Jew!

Let us follow Richard Barnett from one of these receiving ships. He was drafted aboard *HMS Vanguard* on 28 September 1797, then fitting out at Chatham. His real name was Abraham Barnett, born twenty-two years previously in Berwick Street, Soho, the son of a German Jewish immigrant who had found employment as a gold and silver embroiderer in Maiden Lane off the Strand. Barnett had volunteered, receiving a bounty of £1.10s.0d. In addition he was given two months advance of wages, amounting to a further £2.2s.0d. Slops were supplied for him to the value of £1.6s.1d. and he was allowed 13s.0d. for bedding.

The *Vanguard* was a third-rate of 1,644 tons. The length of her main gun deck was 168 feet and her beam was 47 feet. Built in Deptford in 1787, she was the fifth ship to bear the name and was one of the famous "seventy-fours". Nearly sixty were in the British fleet. They were called that after the seventy-four 32 pounders on her main and lower gun decks. In addition they each had eight carronades, known as "smashers" through the fleet, because their fire power was so destructive to enemy ships' timbers.

Being rated Landsman, Barnett on first going aboard was probably detailed to the after-guard among the other new and inexperienced seamen. These landsmen worked the braces, main-sail and lower stay-sails, manned the capstans and were quartered to one of the guns. The two gun decks was where the vast majority of the crew messed and slept. Between each pair of guns a mess table was lowered. Each normally accommodated eight men. Slung crosswise were the hammocks tied to the deck beams, fourteen inches being allowed to each man. In practice, the actual sleeping space was more, as by the "watch and watch" system, every alternate hammock would be empty. But, with deck space being barely five and a half feet high, it is not hard to imagine the oppressive overcrowding. Fresh air was meant to come in through open gunports in fine weather, pushing the stale air up through the hatchways. For food, the men were victualled with a diet of salt beef or pork, ship's biscuits and sour water from casks, supplemented by a gallon of beer a day, plus a pint of wine or half a pint of rum or brandy. Sweating bodies, foul air, coarse language and brawls were a constant strain on the more sensitive. When fully manned, the ship's company numbered 604 men and 32 boys.

At four in the morning came the shrill Boatswain's call, "All hands – all hands Starboard (or Larboard) Watch Ahoy. Rouse out there, you sleepers, Hey. Out and down here". The day had commenced for the watch below. The seamen hastily threw on any warm clothing they had, to brace themselves for the upper deck and to be mustered. After dawn, the upper deck was either scrubbed or holystoned, then the hammocks were lashed and methodically stowed away in the upper deck nettings, so allowing the lower gun decks to be cleaned. At eight they breakfasted on an awful porridge called burgoo, after which they were employed in general work in the ship until about half-past eleven in the forenoon. Then, if necessary, the hands were turned up to witness the ritual punishment of flogging. At "Pipe to dinner" the seaman reached the best part of his day. It was an opportunity to relax with a great chatter along the gun decks. After the meal, up came the grog. A fifer struck up a ditty and all was merriment until one-thirty in the afternoon when work about the ship continued. The landsmen were drilled at the heavy guns until four. Shortly after supper a drummer beat to quarters, the guns were cast loose, the pumps rigged, lifebuoys moved into position and a minute inspection made to see that everything was in order. At eight the first night watch was set and the watch below went to their hammocks until midnight. The four hour watch and watch about system came round with the hours between 4 pm and 8 pm split into two dog watches. This made seven watches in each twenty-four hours, which ensured that a man would not always have the same periods of duty. Even during his four hours off watch, the seaman was liable to be called. Every Monday there was gun drill; every Tuesday, sail drill; on Wednesdays, boat drills; on Thursday afternoons, hands were sent to make and mend clothes; on Fridays, the boats' crews were armed and exercised with cutlasses and muskets; and on Saturdays, hammocks were changed and scrubbed and the lower deck washed down. This routine was broken on Sundays. Then, divisional inspections were held. The ship's company was summoned aft for prayers and a short address (read by the Chaplain). If there was no Chaplain, as in the smaller frigates, then the Captain would sometimes hold a form of service or just read the Articles of War! Sunday afternoons was spent visiting each other's ships when in harbour. These same conditions and routines were carried on throughout the fleet.

Religious service for all was compulsory. Arthur Anderson, later to become a founder of the Peninsular and Oriental Steam Navigation Company, who served in a man-of-war as a Captain's Clerk, related:-[27]

> We had prayers regularly read every Sunday on board, the captain officiating, for the law, having taken precedence of the gospel, deprived us of the valuable services of the chaplin, who was captured by a bum-bailiff the night before we sailed. A rigid attendance was expected from all hands at prayers; and, in order that no laxness, in this respect, might take place, two elders of the kirk, in the shape of a master at arms and a boatswain's mate, used to go round the ship to see that there were no backsliders. One Sunday morning an

> unfortunate wight, who, it appears, was troubled with a conscience, was found sitting alone in his berth, with a small book in his hand. The elders accosted him thus: 'Holloa! what are you skulking there for?' 'I'm of a different persuasion,' muttered the man. 'I'm a dissenter.' 'You be blowed, you skulking son of a sea-cook, what business have you to be a dissenter? Start up on deck, and be d . . . d to you.' – giving him a cut with a rope's end, and away went the poor non-conformist.

It was only a few months before Barnett joined the *Vanguard* that the seamen had won for themselves better pay and rations through the mutinies at Spithead and the Nore. The relatively simple and ill-educated British seamen were willing to accept the iron discipline together with poor food and unhealthy conditions as a necessary part of their life. Some of the more educated and articulate quota men gradually made them understand how they were being exploited. The seamen came to realise that certain other unpleasant factors in their living conditions were considered unnecessary evils. Better food and treatment of wounded were asked for and removal of inhuman officers too quick with the lash and sadistic in its application. The lack of understanding in the seamens' welfare by those in authority ashore and afloat was a flaw in the Royal Navy's achievements during the Napoleonic Wars.

By the end of 1797 the war had not been going well for England. She now stood alone against Bonaparte who was seeking to expand his conquests as far afield as India. The Commander-in-Chief, the Earl of St Vincent, Sir John Jervis, blockading off Cadiz, asked for his protégé, the newly promoted Rear-Admiral Nelson, to take command of a squadron in the Mediterranean to scotch the French plans. The *Vanguard* was chosen as Nelson's flagship (under Captain Edward Berry).

It transpired that Richard Barnett now began to keep *"A Journal of Remarkable Occurences on Board HMS Vanguard. Commencing December 24 1797, ending January 31 1800"*. The eleven separate octavo sheets were in bold clear hand, with an irregular use of capitals and erratic punctuation.[28]

The first entry recorded was 24 December 1797. *HMS Vanguard Commissioned.* The date of commissioning was really 19 December. By March, *Vanguard* had left Chatham for Portsmouth to provision an ammunition ship and, on the 29 March, Nelson hoisted his flag at Spithead, the ship sailing with a convoy to Lisbon on 10 April. The journal now closely follows the actual log of the ship, which possibly indicates that Barnett was by now one of the Captain's Clerks. The

*Vanguard* parted from the main fleet under Lord St. Vincent, reaching Gibraltar on 4 May; she left four days later in company with two other seventy fours, the *Alexander* and *Orion,* and four frigates. The Royal Navy was back in the Mediterranean after a lapse of more than two years. On 17 May she: *"Took a Privateer of 6 guns and 64 men and sent her to Gib also sprung our Foretop Mast and refitted a new one".* (This recorded the capture of the small French corvette *Le Pierre* by one of the escorting frigates *Terpsichore,* Nelson obtaining intelligence that Bonaparte had arrived with troops at Toulon intending to sail shortly). On 21 May they were hit by a: *"Severe gale in the Gulf of Lyon, 3 masts and 3 men lost".* As the *Vanguard* lay dismasted, the French sailed and all contact with them was lost. After repairs, the *Vanguard,* now reinforced with a fleet of fourteen "seventy-fours" sailed east in search of the French. A chase started on 7 June which was not to end until 2 August, culminating in the Battle of the Nile. During this time, Barnett noted on 10 June that: *"The Orion took a Genovese Pallacre with silks etc. and the Alexander took a French packet of 16 guns and 182 men laden with silks, etc."* and on the 16 June *"The Captain of the Culloden went on board the Mutine Brig into Naples with Dispatches for the King and returned."*

The 1 August 1798 saw the British Fleet off Alexandria. Early in the afternoon *HMS Zealous* flew the signal "Enemy in Sight". Thirteen ships of the French fleet were at anchor, protected by shoals and a battery on Aboukir Island. Nelson quickly realised that, as the enemy had room to swing at a single anchor, there must be room between them and the shoal for his own ships to pass inside the line. With only two hours of daylight remaining, the French did not expect to be attacked. Up went the signal from the *Vanguard,* "Attack the enemy's van and centre". The British Captains – Nelson's band of brothers – knew exactly what course of action to take. Barnett recorded that at: *"20 minutes past six the French Fleet hoisted their Colours and Commenced Firing on our van ships".* One by one, the British ships *Goliath, Zealous, Orion, Audacious* and *Theseus* crossed the enemy's van and passed inside the French line and anchored. The French were now in a cross fire as the *Vanguard, Minotaur, Bellerophon, Defence* and *Majestic* engaged from the seaward side. Within two hours the first five ships in the French line took a terrible beating and struck their colours. The French flagship *L'Orient* blew up at 10 o'clock, a decisive moment of the battle. The French were now beaten, losing eleven ships in all. Two more French ships, the *Franklin* and *Tonnant,* were eventually captured after a heroic struggle.

The British fleet had won an audacious victory. Bonaparte's power at sea and ambitions in Egypt had been checked. In his journal, Barnett recounts the battle, giving a list of the French ships, number of guns, men on board and their fate, whether captured, dismasted or destroyed. On the back is drawn a battle plan. He also set down a list of killed and wounded aboard the *Vanguard*, numbering 105.

*Battle of the Nile. 1 August 1798. HMS Goliath (far left) crossing head of French line. Rear Admiral Nelson's Flag Ship HMS Vanguard right of centre. (from a coloured aquatint). National Maritime Museum.*

The *Vanguard* left Aboukir Bay with the badly damaged *Culloden* and *Alexander*, together with some frigates, on 19 August, making their slow way to Naples for repairs. During the voyage Barnett continues:

*"Intercepted several Boats loaded with Mellons and Grapes that Bonaparte had sent for the French Fleet, also 2 small Bullocks"*. 11 September: *"Came to anchor at Messina, obtained various kinds of fruit, Holystones, Bibles, etc."* 22 September: *"Arrived at Naples where we were received in the greatest Friendship imaginable and was visited by the King of Naples and his suit, also His Excellency Sir William Hamilton and his Lady before we let go our anchor or had time to prepare for their Reception"*. 15 October:*"Weighed Anchor and Departed on a Cruize the King prince Nobles and their Suits Breakfasted*

*on board as also did Sir William and Lady Hamilton and took an affectionate leave of us at Naples we got a New Foremast Bowsprit and fitted our Main and Mizen Mast and received Bullocks Poultry Sheep Fruit Hogadent etc."* The *Vanguard* with a small squadron were bound for Malta. Barnett's next entry of note was when in Naples Bay again, 18 November: *"Came on board the Admiral accompan'd by Sir William and Lady Hamilton also took in Field Ordnance and Camp Equipage"* After visiting Leghorn back again to Naples. 21 December: *"Came on board his Majesty the King of Naples his consort the Princes and Princesses and their Suits also the Admiral Sir William and Lady Hamilton".* 26 December: *"Arrived at Palermo in the Island of Sicilly where the People seemed happy to receive their King who went ashore to receive his People about 9 o'clock in the morning accompan'd by the Admiral and received ashore with shouts of apparent joy from a Numerous and polite Concourse of People there being a vast quantity of Carriages which followed the King in Procession and about 12 o'clock Sir William and Lady Hamilton went ashore and we moord Ship".* Four days afterwards they,*"Discharged all the Maltese that were willing to go".*

No further entry was noted until 14 June 1799 when they, *"took in troops belonging to his Sicillian Majesty and came to see Admiral Duckworth's Squadron in company".* This was the reinforcement for Nelson following the French slipping the British blockade of Brest and getting twenty-five sail of the line and five frigates back into the Mediterranean. The *Vanguard* arrived at Naples on 24 June to find it retaken by the Neapolitans. On 13 July,*"the French surrendered the Castle of St. Elmo"* and the day following,*"fired a grand salute on the occasion".* Nelson had in fact already shifted his flag from the *Vanguard* to the *Foudroyant.* After seeing further service off Malta and Minorca, the *Vanguard* was ordered home. It had been decided that the repairs carried out at Naples after the Battle of the Nile had not been sufficient to keep her in the fleet. Barnett notes the voyage home. "7 *November "Gibraltar". 30 Anchored at Lisbon and moor'd ship. 12 December saw Cape Finister"* and the very last entry was for 25 December *"Left the Powerfull in the Channel also spoke a Danish Vessel but last from Rochford bound to Opporto".*

The *Vanguard* arrived at Spithead on 5 January 1800 and by the 25 January was lashed alongside *HMS Ganges* in Portsmouth Harbour. On 2 February the ship's company was paid off, each man receiving £4.14s.0d. prize money for their share in the Battle of the Nile. So ended a famous commission.

Another possible Jewish volunteer aboard the *Vanguard* with Richard Barnett was an Isaac Samuel of about the same age, born at Chatham, who also served as a Landsman.

Many of the ship's company were discharged into the guardship *Royal William,*[29] including Barnett. He was to stay there until 16 March, when he was sent to the thirty two gun frigate *Ceres*. She was of 692 tons with a complement of 121 officers and men. Barnett found himself back in the Mediterranean, as the *Ceres* was bound for Malta with a contingent of soldiers. On 1 September 1800 Richard Barnett was rated Able Seaman, but on 11 March 1802 he deserted from the ship at Portsmouth.[30] It was at this time that about 500 men were deserting every month.

Unlike John Levy, flogged round the fleet for desertion, Richard Barnett was not discovered. Apparently he took on shoemaking, married and had seven children. He died in 1821. On 27 March 1802 within a few weeks of both Levy and Barnett leaving, the short-lived Peace of Amiens was signed. The Royal Navy's strength was summarily reduced from 100,000 to 56,000 men.

Throughout the war, it had been customary at the Great Synagogue, Duke's Place, City of London, to record in the marriage registry the name of the eldest brother of the bridegroom. Against one entry is found, "His brothers are at sea, in the King's ships".

A Jewish tradition of service on the lower deck of the Royal Navy had been founded.

Seaman 1802

# CHAPTER 5

## The Loyal and the Not so Loyal

*"Better to suffer an injustice, than to do an injustice"*

Jewish Proverb.

By the end of the eighteenth century, the majority of London Jews lived within a square mile east of the Great Synagogue in Duke's Place. It was the oldest Ashkenazic synagogue, having originally been established in Mitre Square about 1690. Another place of worship was the Hambro Synagogue in Magpye Alley, off Fenchurch Street, dedicated in 1725 and taking its name from the Jews of Hamburg. The New Synagogue was founded in 1760, later to establish itself in Great St Helens. There was also Bevis Marks in Heneage Lane, which served The Sephardim. However, by 1796, when the Western Synagogue was founded in Denmark Court in The Strand, the migration from the City synagogues to more westerly parts of London had started.

*The Great Synagogue, Duke's Place, London, in 1809. (from an engraving Ackerman's Microcosm of London).*

Decorum in the synagogues was at a low ebb. Those that did attend came and went as they pleased during the services. They were not spiritual by modern standards. As one congregant complained, 'The house of prayer was converted into an exchange or mart for the discussion of news or carrying out of commercial transactions'. Such conduct was possibly brought about by a void in ecclesiastical leadership, there being no spiritual head of The Sephardim between 1784 and 1804; not until the Ashkenazic Rabbi, Solomon Hirschell, became the first Chief Rabbi of England in 1802 did religious observance begin to improve, with better relations between the Sephardim and Ashkenazim.

The fashionable area was Goodmans Fields, with the wealthy living in the private mansions of Prescott, Mansell, Alie and Lemon Streets, soon to be supplanted by Finsbury Square. Here lived the few wealthy Jewish families whilst the rest, mainly poor German and Polish immigrants, eked out a living east of the Minories. The social gulf was wide. The poor were only given mitzvot (synagogue honours) on unimportant days, since they were unable to pay seat rentals. In 1804, a small synagogue was built for some virtually destitute, newly arrived Polish immigrants, in Cutler Street, Houndsditch, through the generosity of the Keyser family (a descendant, Private Leonard Keysor, was the first Australian Jew to win the Victoria Cross for conspicuous bravery and devotion to duty at Gallipoli in 1915).

Education was virtually non-existent for the poor until the establishment of the Jews' Free School in Ebenezer Square in 1817, whilst the wealthy sent their children to an "Academy" in Highgate. The Sephardim were better provided for, having already established their first school as early as 1664. There education ended, as Jews were not admitted to the great public schools. Cambridge University allowed Jews to become undergraduates but excluded them from taking degrees, whilst Oxford University refused their admission altogether. No member of the Jewish community could hold civil or municipal offices, nor become a Member of Parliament. Being a Freeman of the City of London was also closed to him, which meant Jews could not open retail shops within the precincts of the City. Yet a limited number of twelve influential and wealthy Jews had been admitted to the Royal Exchange a hundred years before. When one of their number died his place was taken by a co-religionist who had to pay as much as £2000 for the medal that entitled him to the privilege.

In spite of their disabilities, the loyalty of English Jews was real, if only because they could follow the free exercise of their religion without hindrance. Even with a modicum of toleration, the Jews felt they had a stake in England and were ready to live and die for their country. The martial ardour of the ancient Israelites was re-awakening after centuries of oppression.

The collapse of Holland and the evacuation of the British army in April 1795, meant the French controlled the whole length of continental coastline, to threaten England. The least militaristic country in Europe turned itself into an armed camp by means of improvisation. Three hundred thousand volunteers responded from the length and breadth of the country. They were formed into local regiments, vying with each other as to who were the best turned out and the most efficient.

On 28 November 1796 after a meeting at the Beneficial Society Hall, Portsea, books of enrolment were opened. They had to recruit enough to form at least two companies of sixty men into the Portsea Loyal Independent Volunteers. On turning out for the oaths of allegiance to be administered in April 1797, the men were very smartly attired in round black hats with bands of bear fur, white feathers with red tops, black cockades and stocks, scarlet coats with gold wings, blue collars, and button holes edged with gold. The Portsmouth Volunteers had even finer costumes, being given the nickname "The Golden Goldfinches".[1] This show of loyalty was denied to the Jews of the Borough of Portsmouth. It was a snub deeply felt, as evident in a plea to the Secretary of War by Jacob Levi, a grocer and pawnbroker of 103 Queen Street, Portsea, on 4 May 1798. It is here recorded in full together with the subsequent reply:[2]

> Sir,
>
> I beg leave to address you on behalf of myself and Bretheren the Congregation of Jews residing within the Borough of Portsmouth, since the notice you gave to the Public directing all good subjects to train themselves to arms and thereby become enabled to stand forward in the Defence of their King and Country we the Jews have offered our services to enter the Different Voluntary Corps but our offers are not accepted by the Governor or Mayor alleging for a reason tis not usual with Government to enroll Jews. We feeling ourselves greatly hurt by such refusal, with utmost respect we crave your opinion and advice. Assuring you we have collectively and individually on all occasions afforded our best means and endeavour towards the support of Government. I may with truth assure you there exists not within His Majesty's Realm a more Loyal People than the Jews that since their establishment they have been drawn and served in the Militia equal with other subjects the present area is perhaps the greatest wherein

man may evince his attachment to Government and at such a time should we become proscribed would generally hurt our feelings and perhaps endanger our personal safety. Jews are now and have been prior to your last notice admitted and enrolled in the several Corps at Dover, Bristol, Plymouth, Exeter, Liverpool, Gosport and many other Towns which causes us to feel the greater disappointment. The Majority of us may boast the right of Native and many (without presuming of any consequence therefrom) are Freeholders. For our Moral Character as well as our Fealty, we humbly refer your enquiry to the Mayor and Justices of this Borough. Should we ultimately be refused we beg you make it known to the Public that we wish to do our Duty as good Citizens and that we have used our best endeavours to obtain leave so to do.

I have the Honour to be
Sir
Your most Obedient Humble Servant

Jacob Levi
May 4 1798 Grocer 103 Queen Street Portsea

The letter was passed to the Garrison Commander, Sir William Pitt, who replied from the Governor's House, High Street, Portsmouth on 1 June 1798 to the Right Honourable Henry Dundas:-[3]

Private

Dear Sir,

I have been honoured with your Private letter of the 29th past, enclosing a representation from the Congregation of Jews residing in the Borough of Portsmouth. In answer to which it is necessary to inform you that some months ago, upon application being made to me by the Commanding Officers of the Volunteer Companies relative to the propriety of enroling Jews into their Corps I discouraged it on account of there being a great number of suspicious itinerant Jews at that time in the Town of Portsmouth, all of whom have since been found out and removed from hence by the activity and vigilence of the Magistrates. There still remains however a considerable number of that sect who I find have been long residents of this Town and of Portsea, many of them very respectable Tradesmen, and are considered as Loyal good subjects, but they never made an offer of their services to me until yesterday when three of their Principles came with proposals for the Jews being enrolled into any of the Companies that may be inclined to receive them; I propose to them the forming of a Company entirely of their own sect, as they have sufficient numbers for it but that they declined, they are therefore to bring me a list of such whose Principles and Conduct they will be answerable for, they shall then be distributed into the different Corps, which I hope will meet with your approbation.

I have the honour to return you herewith the letter from Mr Jacob Levi and have the honour to be

Dear Sir
With the greatest Regard
Your most obedient humble servant

W. PITT

It was of course true that the itinerant Jews were to many a nuisance, travelling from town to town in single-horse carts purchasing goods off those who embezzled the King's Stores from the dock-yards. As Patrick Colquhoun, the London Police Magistrate and Sociologist remarked in 1795 on the problem of the Jewish poor: 'They keep alive a system of fraud and depredation, which perhaps is generated in a greater degree by their peculiar situation than by an actual disposition on their part to pursue these nefarius practices.'

Some of the most disreputable associated themselves in the thoroughly disgraceful activity of "crimping" much to the detriment of their fellow Jews. A crimp made it his business to persuade seamen to desert from a ship by devious means in order to deliver him to another ship, usually a merchantman, for payment.

Crimpage is not to be confused with those who discovered and handed over concealed Royal Navy seamen to the authorities for a reward of £3.0s.0d. for Able Seamen and £2.10s.0d. for Ordinary Seamen. By Royal Proclamation it was quite legal for persons to procure the voluntary enlistment of any man to enter aboard one of His Majesty's Ships of War provided the seaman was not a deserter. A reward of £3.3s.0d. was by 1809 paid for procuring an Able Seaman, £2.2s.0d. for an Ordinary Seaman, and £1.1s.0d. for a Landsman, with in addition a travel allowance of one penny a mile to the nearest ship or rendezvous (recruiting centre). Sometimes difficulties arose over proving the Certificates of Procuring Seamen made out by the receiving Captains when presented to the Clerk of the Check in the Dockyards for payment. Sampson Levy of 37 Whites Row, Portsea, having not long moved from

Plymouth in 1809, was refused his bounty as a William Saunders, procured and put aboard the sloop *Hound,* turned out to be a foreigner. In the following year confusion arose whether two men were already impressed or had volunteered aboard the sloop *Rattler.* Eventually David Lazarus a Constable of Portsea was given the benefit of the doubt receiving £5.10s.0d. as the Admiralty still wanted him to go on procuring seamen.[4]

So the demands for seamen continued unabated for both the Royal Navy and Merchant Service and, as is so often the case when demand exceeds supply, the unscrupulous move in. Many crimps were keepers of seamen's lodging houses or taverns in the busy ports where access to liquor made it easy to make the seamen drunk and then hand them over to the merchant shipping owner, often for the seaman's first month's pay. The authorities closed their eyes to these practices as the merchant service virtually relied on the crimps, in the same way as the Royal Navy used the Press Gang, to complete the ship's complement, though with one important difference - enticing seamen to desert the Royal Navy was an indictable offence leading to a prison sentence.

For the Admiralty Solicitor to obtain a conviction was not easy as the testimonies from many of the illiterate and inarticulate seamen could not altogether be relied upon, often unsupported by corroborative evidence. Lord Nelson, in a memorandum to the First Lord of the Admiralty, Earl St Vincent, in 1803, delved to the root cause of the problem. 'A sum of money and liquor held out to a seaman are too much for him; he allows himself to be seduced and hid, he first becomes fearful of apprehension and then wishes and exerts himself to get out of the country in the Merchant's employ.' [5]

Lord Nelson went on to disclose one of the many deceptions practised. It involved a merchant vessel from London which cleared at Gravesend for her voyage to India, with all her manning papers in order. Her crew were protected from impressment. The captain, or owner, then arranged for the crimps to supply deserters when the ship called in at Portsmouth. These deserters then took up the names and places of the original crew who landed and made off to repeat the deception on board another ship. Bounties were paid, the money finding its way into the hands of the crimps. Since East Indiamen were the finest ships in the Merchant Service, carrying cargo and passengers and armed as warships, they were a lucrative source for the crimps.

The East India Company's Offices were in an imposing building in Leadenhall Street on the Eastern side of London. Here the crimps would bring the seamen off the mean streets bordering the Thames to sign papers. The area teemed with lodging houses, inns and run-down tenements in narrow, dark alleys frequented by prostitutes, pickpockets, vagrants and seamen. The times were corrupt, with thousands driven to crime. Liquor was plentiful and easy to obtain – 'drunk for a penny, dead drunk for tuppence', went the saying.

The crimps would rely on young boys acting as their servants to make the first approach to seamen, who could not be mistaken by their dress and general demeanour. It was impossible to tell whether they belonged to a King's ship or not as uniform dress for the Royal Navy was not officially regularised until 1857 with the establishment of a standing navy. The "Barkers" as the boys were known, would accost the seamen. 'Do you want lodgings?' or 'Do you want a ship?' they would enquire. The seamen would then be taken to a lodging house where they would be plied with drink, made insensible, and put to bed. Next day, in the company of other seamen in the same plight, they were given food and more drink, then, half drunk, taken to India House, calling at public houses on the way. The papers were signed, with the crimp taking a slice of the seamen's pay, as well as the crimpage bounty. Back at the lodging house, the seamen would be kept virtual prisoners with their clothes taken from them whilst asleep, until the crimps were ready to take them in a boat down the Thames to the Indiamen lying at Gravesend.

The Admiralty relied on informers to help track down the crimps. Jeremiah Barber, formerly a Pilot in the King's Service, gave information to Vice-Admiral Stanhope at Sheerness which led to Goodman Levi of 4 Bury Court, Saint Mary Axe, being charged in March, 1810, for conveying six seamen of His Majesty's Navy aboard an Indiaman. Apparently, as Barber was passing over London Bridge early on the morning of 23 March, he met six seamen who stopped him and enquired whether any Indiamen were going out. Barber suggested they went to India House. Suspecting the seamen were King's men, he followed and near India House saw them directed by some Jews to Goodman Levi's house. A few hours later Barber maintained he saw Levi and another young Jew drive off in two post-chaises with the same seamen towards Cornhill. Charles Bicknell, the Admiralty Solicitor, did not pursue the matter because there was no evidence that the seamen actually belonged to the Navy, or even if they did, that Levi was acquainted with the fact.[6]

In his testimony Barber was under the impression that Goodman Levi had a contract with the East India Company to supply seamen to the

*Canton.* Just a week after Goodman Levi was charged, Asher Nathan of Portsmouth was also accused of supplying Royal Navy seamen to the same ship, the *Canton.* This suggests that information was passed from Goodman Levi to Asher Nathan about when to expect the *Canton* at Spithead, the East Indiamen's last port of call before leaving the English Channel for the East. Counsel's opinion was taken by Charles Bicknell but the charge was dropped, there being no evidence to corroborate the seamens' testimony.[7]

In addition to the crimpage bounty, some slopsellers pressed unwanted clothes upon seamen, taking their two months advance wages in payment. Abraham Franklin and Daniel Jacobs, slopsellers on The Point, Portsmouth, employed young Jewish boys as their servants to accost the seamen and bring them to their shops. The easy-going seafarers were then duped with the offer of clothes and made intoxicated. In December, 1808, Franklin denied the charge of enticing the seamen to desert and board the Indiaman *Warren Hastings* (1,064 tons) but accepted that his servant Benjamin Hart had brought three seamen from the *Dromedary* to be fitted out with clothes amounting to £8.2s.0d. On enquiry, the Admiralty Solicitor dropped the prosecution as the seamen were not in His Majesty's service, but men hired for the voyage. The *Dromedary* turned out to be a privateer.[8] The same occurred in October, 1810, when "Levi, a Jew" was accused at Deptford of crimpage. However, it transpired that the seamen hired for the voyage did not belong to the fleet.[9]

There must have been some truth in these accusations. They give an insight into the activities of the Jewish and non-Jewish crimps working like parasites on the credulous seamen. It was between 1808 and 1810 that the Jewish crimps were most active, organising themselves into gangs. Although it was an indictable offence to crimp Royal Navy men, any merchant seaman crimped was not protected by the law at all.

Royal Navy ratings of a more recent age remember, 'The run ashore, up the line to Smoke', referring to the short leave from Chatham Dockyard or Barracks by train to the attractions of London. So it was in the Napoleonic Wars except that there was no Union Jack Club nor railway line. But there were the crimps!

What was the "run ashore" like in those days? On the last day of January, 1808, the eighty gun *Pompee* paid off at Chatham with many of her crew being sent to the *Victory*, giving an opportunity for the more trusted seamen to be given ticket-of-leave for fourteen days.[10] Some came ashore at Chatham on Sunday afternoon, 31 January, and made their way to London in groups, dressed in their short, blue jackets with bright buttons, flowing blue, white or striped trousers, checked or striped shirts, tarpaulin hats and black or coloured kerchiefs loosely tied round their neck. Most were in their early twenties.

A small group of shipmates walked the eight miles to Gravesend with others who had taken the coach from Chatham, they boarded a passage boat to Billingsgate that same evening. Apparently, four other seamen managed only as far as an ale-house in Gravesend, before falling foul of two crimps who treated them to plenty of food and drink. Then, in a state of intoxication, they were carried overnight on board an Indiaman, the *Ceres* (1,180 tons) lying in the river at the Lower Hope, off Gravesend. In fact, eleven Indiamen were fitting out ready to assemble at Portsmouth by 15 February. They were to sail in convoy under the protection of the sixty four gun *Lion.* In addition to their cargoes, they were carrying the Seventeenth Regiment of Light Dragoons and other recruits for Madras.[11]

*Gravesend circa 1828. (from an engraving by J. Rogers).*

By the following Thursday, the 4 February, just five days after coming ashore, the money was running out for those seamen who had reached London. Able Seaman Richard Teazle had three shillings left, so he went down to Billingsgate to catch a Gravesend boat, meaning to return to the *Victory* at Chatham. Some more of his shipmates turned up at Billingsgate and boarded the passage boat *Sir Francis Burdett.* Little did they realise that George Martin, her master, was in the pay of regular crimps for whom he had occasionally worked before – Lewis Lazarus of 3

Bury Court, St Mary Axe, William Phipps of the White Swan, Leadenhall Street, and two others, Phillips and Mitchell of Walworth. Martin was to receive ten guineas for bringing these unsuspecting seamen into the Downs for the Indiaman *Exeter* (1,200 tons).

Before sailing at seven that evening, Lazarus brought on board a number of drunken seamen with the help of five or six other Jewish crimps including Samson Samuel, a servant to Henry Nathan – a partner of Lazarus. Within the hour, a stop was made down river at Blackwall, when Nathan himself boarded with another batch of seamen, who he had previously approached at a public house frequented by the passage boat crews. There were now eleven seamen from the original "run ashore" aboard the *Sir Francis Burdett* as it sailed off back to Chatham via Gravesend. All were in various states of intoxication. Nathan got to work offering each a £5.0s.0d. bounty and £4.10s.0d. advance of wages to join Indiamen. All refused.

By the time Gravesend was reached, many were asleep. Another sixteen seamen, not only from the *Pompee,* were put ashore with Lazarus and rowed out to the *Ceres* as it lay at the Lower Hope, and to other Indiamen, including the *Calcutta* (819 tons). The *Sir Francis Burdett* left Gravesend that night with a pilot, Robert Grundy, also in the pay of Nathan. Next morning, Friday 5 February, the remaining *Pompee* seamen were surprised to find themselves in the Downs and asked to be put ashore. Instead, Nathan attempted to get alongside the Indiaman *Exeter* (1200 tons) but was told to keep off. The press boat out of Deal with a press gang aboard had swung under the stern of the *Sir Francis Burdett.* Nathan told the Pilot and Master that he was just taking the men to Deal and that he would not show the officers the protections against impressment he had for the seamen as they were in possession of their own leave tickets. The Master now realised he had men-of-war's men aboard so refused Nathan's request to make sail and avoid being inspected. Nathan became alarmed – the game was up!

At noon, the press boat escorted the *Sir Francis Burdett* to the Guardship *Princess of Orange* (74 guns) lying in the Downs and put all the seamen and crew aboard, including Henry Nathan and Sampson Samuel. Here they joined other seamen from the *Pompee* who had already been taken out of the *Ceres.* The "run ashore" was over. But Henry Nathan's tribulations were just beginning. He was locked in the Gun Room with a sentry over him. He requested to see the Captain, but was refused. "We will hear you speak at the Old Bailey." However, Nathan was permitted to send a letter to William Phipps at the White Swan,

Leadenhall Street, to see if he could get himself and Sampson Samuel cleared.

That Saturday, Captain Horton, in command of the *Princess of Orange*, examined all the seamen of the *Pompee*, together with the Master and crew of the *Sir Francis Burdett*, but not Nathan who was kept under guard. Captain Horton in his report felt that if Sampson Samuel was handed over to the civil powers he would give a lot of information as to how the crimps carried on their nefarious practices. The Master, George Martin and Pilot, Robert Grundy, taken off the *Sir Francis Burdett*, declared the agreement made with the Jews was in the customary mode of employ to carry seamen down to Indiamen, but if they had known the seamen were men-of-war's men then the *Sir Francis Burdett* would not have been taken to the Downs. Samuel and Martin went on to give the names of known crimps, many of them Jews and accomplices of Nathan, living in London:-

Samson Samuel and Ilyath Isaacs, both of 102 Rosemary Lane.
Lewis Lazarus, David Levy and his brother Moses, of 3 Bury Court, St Mary Axe.
William Phipps, White Swan, Leadenhall Street.
George Childers, Private house in White Chapel.
Clark at the Jolly Sailor, Lower East Smithfield.
Mitchell and Phillips of Walworth.

The report and testimonies were sent by Captain Horton on Sunday, 7 February to the Commander in Chief Downs, Vice-Admiral Rowley, for consideration. Meanwhile, Nathan wrote again to William Phipps at the White Swan:-

> I am very Uneasy in my mind god Nows what the Consequence will be for I am Innocence – their has been an Information sent Down to the admirall from London two days before we arrived and they were Looking out for us. Tell George Childers to go to my wife and Not to tell her what suitavasion that I am in but I shall be home very soon and let her have what money she wants. I think it would be best if you would go to Mr Isaacs the Attorney in the Mitre Court and get him to move me from the ship to London with abeus corpus.

Then to his wife Mrs Nathan at 2 Lion Square, White Chapel, Near the Church, London:-[12]

My Dear Deal.

This comes with my kind love to you and hopes you are well the Same as I am at Present and Dont be Uneasey bout my Staying for I am waiting to get the men clear which was prest from me and if you want any money go to george Childers and he will give you some I shall be home as soon as Possible so no more at Present.

From your Loving Husband

H. Nathan

Sunday Morning
ten o'clock.

The same day Captain Bazley, in charge of the Impress Service at Deal, informed William Pole, First Secretary at the Admiralty, that two crimps, Henry Nathan and Sampson Samuel, were impressed at the same time as taking out the *Pompee* men. Back came the reply, 'Convey to Plymouth, put aboard the first ship going foreign'. Pole obviously felt the best and only way to deal with crimps was to get them out of the country.[13]

However, a day later the First Secretary had received Vice-Admiral Rowley's letter with Captain Horton's report and testimonies of those held aboard the *Princess of Orange*. Matters were held up until Charles Bicknell, the Admiralty Solicitor, had seen the papers. By 15 February, Bicknell communicated that there was sufficient evidence to convict Henry Nathan of unlawfully enticing Able Seaman Robert Teazle, Ordinary Seaman William Hart, Landsman William Porter and Armourer's Mate John Stubbs to desert His Majesty's Service. It was on these four seamen's testimonies that he could most rely to get a conviction.[14] Next day, Nathan was removed from the *Princess of Orange*[15] to the gun brig *Blazer* for a passage to The Nore, then by further transfers to the small twenty eight gun frigate *Enterprise*[16] acting as Guard Ship off the Tower of London. From there he was eventually handed over to the Thames Police on 5 March.

The trial came up for hearing five months later at Maidstone Assizes on 10 August before the Right Honourable Lord Chief Justice Ellenborough and a special jury.[17]

The indictment against the defendant Nathan, a Jew Crimp, was for seducing eleven seamen to desert from His Majesty's Service in order to get them aboard an Indiaman.

Bicknell had mainly to rely on the evidence of just Teazle, Hart,

Porter and Stubbs, as some seamen he wanted to see as witnesses had already returned to the *Victory,* having left Chatham the previous April for the Baltic as Flagship of Sir John Saumarez. This was just one of the difficulties of bringing civil cases in the courts where seamen were involved. John Stubbs, aged forty seven, had come ashore alone from the *Pompee* without a leave ticket the day before the others to see his brother. On the Monday morning whilst his shipmates were enjoying their first day in London, Stubbs was passing India House about 10 o'clock when Henry Nathan and others accosted him. He was taken to a private house in St Mary Axe where he was given grog but tried to escape, later being forced into a coach and then aboard a passage boat as far as Gravesend. By 8 o'clock the same evening Stubbs was being offered £5.0s.0d. bounty and £5.0s.0d. crimpage aboard the Indiaman *David Scott* (1200 tons), not being released until the Friday when the boatswain from the *Pompee* came aboard.

Lieutenant Anderson of the Deal Impress Service stated he had received intimation that the seamen in question were on board a Gravesend boat at the Nore. He therefore went in pursuit of them and saw the *Sir Francis Burdett* Gravesend boat, hovering about an Indiaman at the Nore. He hailed and obliged her to bring to. On getting aboard, Nathan met him and showed a protection against impressment for ten men for the *Dorset* East Indiaman. Anderson refused to look at it and went below, finding the seamen. Each produced his liberty tickets, none of which were expired. He then put all the seamen and Nathan aboard the *Princess of Orange.* The seamen recounted how after the money had run out whilst on liberty, they just wished to return to their ship, having no desire to sign for an Indiaman, and were enticed by Nathan into a state of continual intoxication aboard the *Sir Francis Burdett* until found by Lieutenant Anderson.

Nathan's Counsel contested that the seamen had imposed themselves upon the defendant, and that they had represented themselves as foreign seamen. To prove this he called a Mrs Damsey and her daughter who kept a sailor's lodging house at Wapping. She stated that the seamen employed Nathan to give them a ship, and gave an absent bond to repay him his advances. William Hart, being shown the bond, denied he had ever set his mark to any paper. Hart was then asked whether one of his shipmates named Farrier could write. 'Yes, he knew he could write in French or a foreign lingo, but not sure whether he could write in English, and had never seen him sign his name.'

After a trial lasting six hours, Henry Nathan was found guilty and received sentence in the next Michaelmas Term of Kings Bench. He was to pay a fine of £50 and to be imprisoned in Newgate Jail for one year, or longer if the fine was still unpaid. The punishment was relatively light. Nathan was prepared to abandon a legal action commenced against Vice-Admiral Rowley for keeping him in irons for a month whilst aboard the *Princess of Orange* and others of his Majesty's ships.

As for Sampson Samuel, he had also ended up in the *Enterprize* at the Tower of London but was discharged on 28 March by Admiralty Order. Two further Jews, Jacob Moses and Solomon Hyams were convicted of being the keepers of the ale-house in Gravesend who enticed Ordinary Seaman Alexander MacDonald and Carpenter's Mate William Williams to desert the *Pompee* and put them aboard the *Ceres* on 1 February.

The example of Henry Nathan shows how the seamen of the day were ill-used. Already addicted to drink from rum, beer and wine aboard ship to wash down the salty provisions, it was not surprising that the easy-going sailors went off with the crimps who paid for their liquor and gave them lodgings.

The Jewish crimps outside East India House, Leadenhall Street, were a public nuisance and as late as November 1810 were still active. Samuel Solomons was taken into custody for being the leader of a gang of up to fifty who caused an assault and riot in Leadenhall Street when physically attacking Captain White, forcing him to release a boy apprentice. The Lord Mayor observed at the Mansion House hearing that the conduct of these gangs were a serious disgrace to the City and would be punished with the utmost severity.[18]

Royal Marine 1805

# CHAPTER 6

## The Goldsmids – Bullion, Benevolence and Lord Nelson

*There are those who gain eternity in a lifetime, others who gain it in one brief hour.*

*Talmud*

The activities of the Jewish crimps and the criminal classes of the Jewish poor in general had always been an embarrassment to the wealthier Jewish élite. At the turn of the nineteenth century, a wide ranging system of Jewish hospitals, asylums, schools and workshops under the supervision of a Charitable Board was proposed, to take the Jewish poor off the parish. However, as the Sephardim were unwilling to join the scheme and to thus be associated with the mainly German Jewish poor, the Bill before Parliament had to be abandoned, much to the disappointment of Abraham Goldsmid, a member of the leading family in the Jewish community.

In the annals of Anglo-Jewish history, the Goldsmid family is one of the most distinguished. The founder, Aaron, settled in London as a merchant about 1743. He originated from Amsterdam, but was of German origin. He had four sons and four daughters. The two youngest sons, Benjamin (born 1755) and Abraham (born 1756), entered into partnership as loanmongers, branching out from the bullion brokers Mocatta and Goldsmid. A legacy from an uncle and their wives' dowries gave the brothers Goldsmid capital to expand their business, backed by financial genius of the highest order. Millions of pounds passed through their hands in the sale and purchase of bullion, navy and exchequer bills, and the negotiation of foreign bills of exchange. By 1795, the brothers breached the ring of the old established banking houses, causing the average rate of issue to rise by at least three per cent, to the advantage of the Treasury. They moved their offices from Whitechapel to the City and became members of the Stock Exchange, assisting in the huge government loans to finance the struggle against Bonaparte. Bullion was moved between London and Hamburg in 1797 to ease the pressure of a run on the Bank of England. Stability returned, but two years later the Hamburg merchants needed to buy gold in London to bolster their own dwindling reserves.

The London merchants rallied round and, with the permission of the Bank of England, a large sum of silver and gold bullion was ready for shipment. The Treasury instructed Admiral Lord Duncan, Commander-in-Chief, North Sea Fleet on 9 October, 1799, in his flagship *Kent* lying in Yarmouth Roads, to send a brig or cutter to Gravesend for the service of receiving on board some bullion and conveying it to the Elbe. The armed cutter *Nile* was dispatched. Her captain, Lieutenant J. Wood, sailed from Gravesend on 14 October. 'Having received on board the Bullion from the House of Messrs Goldsmid and Co. and there being no post to-day from London I have judged it for the good of His Majesty's Service to proceed with the said Bullion to the place of consignment.' The *Nile* got through but Lieutenant Wood was reprimanded for having left Gravesend without definite permission from the Admiralty. Perhaps he had been under private pressure from the Goldsmids to set sail.[1] Certainly, Admiral Lord Duncan was being pushed. The London merchants were asking him to convey bullion as quickly and safely as possible. The cutter *Courier* was made ready, but Duncan changed his mind for a more heavily armed and fast frigate when learning of the very high quantity of bullion, in addition to what had already been sent in the *Nile*. Duncan wrote to the Admiralty on 9 October, 'The merchants interested in making remittances to the continent for the support of their credit having made application to me for a King's Ship to carry over a considerable sum on account of there being no pacquet for that purpose I complied with the request and ordered the *Lutine* to Coxshaven'.[2]

Originally French, *La Lutine* had been captured by Admiral Hood off Toulon in 1793 and re-named *Lutine*, of 900 tons and thirty two guns, manned by a crew of over 200. The *Lutine* (Captain Skynner) sailed from Yarmouth Roads in the early hours of 9 October. On board was Joseph Schabracq, originally from an Amsterdam Ashkenazic family, a distant relative of the Goldsmids. Schabracq was employed to act for the Goldsmids in his capacity as a notary to look after the legal documentation in the transfer of the bullion.[3]

The *Lutine* made good progress across the North Sea, but by afternoon a strong nor' nor'-wester was blowing. The weather deteriorated and on approaching the Dutch coast the wind had got up to a full gale. The *Lutine* was driven on to the outer bank of the Fly Island Passage between the Dutch Islands of Vlieland and Terschelling. A strong lee tide did the rest. The sloop *Arrow* (Captain Portlock) was in the vicinity, her log reading on the night of Wednesday, 9 October: 'At Fly Island Anchorage. Wind WNW to NW. Strong gales and squally employed variously at half past nine heard the report of some guns in the NNW. Saw rockets and fires from a ship making signals of distress. Sent a cutter to their asistance.' Then next morning: 'At half-past seven the cutter returned without being able to afford them any assistance, at ten came alongside a schooner with 2 men, one dead the other to all appearances dead but by the exertions of the surgeon he recovered. She proved to be HM Ship *Lutine.* She went all to pieces and all but one of her crew drowned.'[4]

The single survivor died before reaching England. One report said it was Joseph Schabracq who supposedly was able to relate just a few words about the *Lutine's* valuable cargo.[5]

Lloyd's of London paid the insurance on the bullion cargo. Some of it was recovered in 1858, with a few gold bars having the letter mark "G" for Goldsmids. As a reminder of the tragedy the *Lutine's* bell hangs in the Underwriters' Room in Lloyds where it is rung on special occasions, once for bad news, twice for good.

At the end of the eighteenth century the Goldsmid brothers occupied as powerful a position as the Rothschilds were to fill soon after them. Benjamin became the personal friend of Pitt, whilst Abraham was on intimate terms with George III who spoke of him as, 'My friend Abraham!' The brothers were as distinguished in philanthropy as they were in finance, their charities not just being confined to their co-religionists.

At Roehampton, Surrey, in 1792, Benjamin acquired a burnt out ruin of a house with some stables on a 150 acre site. Here, in its place, he built a princely mansion on two floors, with ornate furnishings of the latest taste. The ground floor consisted of drawing rooms, a large dining room, a music room, a library and a ballroom which stretched from front to the rear of the house, leading on to a magnificent terrace with a heavy columned portico. Stables, a farm, a dairy and gardens tended by twelve men completed the mansion. One apartment was fitted for use as a synagogue. Benjamin's ambition had been achieved. He felt himself an English nobleman with his own aristocratic country residence. Here he entertained on a lavish scale. Pitt, Dundas, the Duke of Cambridge and Lord Nelson were among his visitors.

It was said the celebrations held at Benjamin's house on the news of Nelson's victory at the Battle of the Nile were unequalled throughout the land. Festivities went on for almost a whole day with music, dancing and masques and a splendid firework display illuminating the mansion. Thanksgiving prayers were held at the Great Synagogue, Duke's Place, where both Goldsmid brothers in turn served in executive offices. A special form of Service was printed for the occasion:-

> A Form of Prayer, Praise, Thanksgiving, and Laud to be chanted in the German Jews Synagogue in London. With the voice of joy and gladness on Thursday the 29 November 1798 being the 21st day of Kislav, Anno Mundi 5559, the day that His Majesty our Gracious Sovereign hath commanded us to give thanks and praise to the Almighty God, Who is tremendous in works, for the great success of Admiral Nelson, his officers, pilots and seamen on board the ships of our Sovereign Lord the King.

It was composed in Hebrew by the Reverend Moses Myers and translated into English by order of the Presidents of the Ashkenazic Synagogues by David Levy. It ran to twenty octavo pages.[6]

This was not the first special prayer recited in the London Synagogues with naval connotations. A General Thanksgiving for the many and important Victories to His Majesty's Fleets in the course of the present War had been declared in 1797. It was during Chanucah week, in fact Tuesday 19 December 1797, that a Special Service was held at Bevis Marks to give thanksgiving for the victories at sea of Admirals Sir John Jervis and Adam Duncan. The service opened with versicles sung by Reader and Congregation and by passages to be read and sung. Then followed the prayers in Hebrew specially composed for the occasion. First was described the abortive attempt of the French invasion of Ireland in December, 1796, under General Hoche. It was rebuffed by the spirited action of Sir Edward Pellew in the *Indefatigable,* and eventually dispersed by a severe storm. Such phrases as, 'When our enemies came against us in ships from across the sea . . . as they rowed to approach the shore Thou didst cast a whirlwind upon the sea, turn back their wisdom, bring to nothing their knowledge and on them didst Thou fulfil the verse. Thou dost scatter them and the wind beneath them away and the storm disperth them.' Prayers continued, alluding to the victory of Sir John Jervis off Cape St Vincent: 'the enemy vessels out numbered ours.' Then mentioned Duncan's victory at Camperdown, with prayers signifying: 'This victory finally put an end to all danger of an immediate invasion of England by France and Holland'. The service concluded with a moving appeal for peace.[7]

It was particularly well timed to hold this Thanksgiving Service during the Jewish Festival of Chanucah. It is a celebration of the restoration of the Jerusalem Temple Service in the year 164 B.C., following the military prowess of those great Israelite warriors, the Maccabeans.

The war at sea had brought its casualties. After the Battle of the Nile and towards the end of 1798, an Andrew Thompson advertised for subscriptions to a charity under the patronage of the Duke of Clarence called the "British National Endeavour". The Institution was established at Clarence House, Paddington Green, for the education, maintenance and apprenticing out the orphans of soldiers and sailors who had fallen or who may fall in the defence of their King and Country.

The charity appealed to the public and large sums were subscribed with particular support from Admiral Lord St Vincent and City merchants. Something like £1,700 came into Thompson's hands. It was later found that the Duke of Clarence had not given his name to the venture. Suspicion began to grow that Thompson was defrauding the subscribers and a meeting was convened at Clarence House, Paddington on 5 December, 1800, with Prince Augustus Frederic in the chair. At another meeting eight days later, a committee was formed which included Jacob Franco, a convert from the Jewish religion, well known in London society. It was decided to confine the activities of the institution to the children of sailors only as the government was about to establish a Military Asylum at Chelsea.

As for Thompson, he was put into custody as apparently he had charged for articles which were never purchased, and charges appeared for others which were consolidated in subsequent accounts. For instance, he manufactured an account for furniture amounting to £179.17s.11d. but in effect the supplier was paid a sum of £40.9s.6d. against an actual bill of £69.8s.0d., the balance of £28.18s.6d. being unpaid. As in all frauds, the exact sum which found its way into Thompson's pocket is difficult to establish, but must have been in the region of £1,000 – a not inconsiderable sum.[8]

The committee now made efforts to put the institution on a better footing, the name being changed from the "British National Endeavour" to the "Naval Asylum". A donation of twenty guineas constituted a Life Governor, entitling the subscriber to three votes on all questions relative to the charity, whilst at the other end of the scale an annual subscription of one guinea resulted in a single vote. The First Lord of the Admiralty, the Earl of St Vincent, was approached to see that boys sent from the

Asylum into the Royal Navy would be placed in more respectable positions than those from the Marine Society. Immediately after the Battle of Copenhagen in April, 1801, advertisements were placed in the morning papers inviting funds from the general public to support the "recently established Naval Asylum". The stigma of Thompson had been erased.

However the fifty-one boys and eleven girls were poorly accommodated at Clarence House, Paddington Green, with bad food and clothing. To assist the Institution in raising badly needed funds to improve the orphans' support an approach was made to the City merchants. An Anniversary Dinner for the 1 June to commemorate the Earl of St Vincent's famous victory of the First of June 1794 was held at the London Tavern. An invitation was sent to Benjamin and Abraham Goldsmid who attended with their friends; £379.1s.0d. was collected, this sum being made up to 1000 guineas by the Goldsmid brothers and a John Glenny.[9]

In fact, the Goldsmid brothers had also been benefactors to the Marine Society donating twenty guineas each in 1794. At its inception in 1756 Sampson Gideon donated £50. His son, Sir Sampson Gideon, no longer of the Jewish faith, was to donate £580 between 1773 and 1782. It was to the building fund of the Marine Society in 1779 that wealthy Sephardic Jews gave their support, notably Isaac Baruch Lousada, Abraham Furtado, (a Lloyds underwriter), Ralph and Jacob Franco, and Michael Adolphus whose brother Isaac was secretary of the Marine Society in the early 1770s, when the offices were over the Royal Exchange.[11]

Following the Goldsmids successful support of the Naval Asylum at the Anniversary Dinner, both brothers were invited to join the Institution's committee in July 1801. For doing so, they each had the privilege of nominating a child into its care. Benjamin put forward a John Slipe aged five and a half years, whose father was killed when the *Invincible* was wrecked in the previous March off the coast of Norfolk, whilst in the following October, Abraham nominated James Dickson, also the orphan of another sailor lost aboard the *Invincible.* The committee, with the Goldsmids as members, held regular meetings at the Crown and Anchor Tavern in the Strand and by the end of 1801 accounts of the Institution were available and published in the morning papers the following March.

It was at this time that Lord Nelson gave over his nomination to Benjamin Goldsmid who nominated a poor boy William Hart to the Institution. He was the son of a deceased sailor and was admitted after attending before the committee with his mother. William Hart later left the Asylum in November 1803 to join the Royal Navy.[12]

The Anniversary Dinner of the Naval Asylum for 1802 was held at the London Tavern on 2 June with the Goldsmid brothers acting as stewards. About two hundred attended, including Admiral Sir Hyde Parker and Lord Nelson. Sir Sidney Smith gave an impassioned speech, with numerous toasts drunk, including that for the Earl of St Vincent and the Wooden Walls of Old England. The evening finished with the children singing "Rule Britannia" and "God Save the King". £1,317.10s.0d. was collected.[13]

The Goldsmid family figured in the subscription lists of many charities of all denominations. Benjamin was the more flamboyant of the two brothers, with social aspirations extending to the Royal Family. The visit by the King's brother, the Duke of Gloucester, to the Great Synagogue on 10 April 1801 was at the Goldsmids' instigation. It was the first royal visit ever to an Ashkenazic Synagogue.

The King inspected a general review of volunteers in Hyde Park on 26 October 1803 with several hundred Jews present. On hearing the roll call of an East End regiment, it is said he expressed some amusement to hear such names as Fox, Wolf, Bear and Lyon, more familiarly borne by wild animals.[14] It is possible this regiment comprised some of the Whitechapel Volunteers which Abraham Goldsmid helped to raise the preceeding August.[15] *"The Times"* of 3 November 1803 reported how, the day before, the Whitechapel Volunteers assembled at their parade ground soon after six in the morning, arriving at Epping Forest about four hours later for, 'A grand field day and sham fight'. Breakfast was served at the "Bush and Green Man" with a marquee to accommodate all the volunteers. At eleven the drum beat to arms. A general action now ensued with Captain Goldsmid in charge of the light company. 'The day passed without accident, the firing and discipline of the Whitechapel Volunteers was excellent. To conclude the day the Officers entertained the regiment at dinner at the "Green Man and Bush".' Apparently a good time was had by one and all.

From both the Jewish and Protestant fraternity, there was now an awareness of Jews in the Navy, Army and Volunteers. England's first Chief Rabbi, the much respected Solomon Hirschell, preached in the Great Synagogue on 15 August 1803, that it was a duty to take up arms in the defence of King and Country. Hirschell pointed out that unless the situation demanded it then Judaism with its ritual precepts, such as the keeping of the Sabbath, was not to be ignored.

RECEIPTS AND EXPENDITURE OF THE NAVAL ASYLUM from 5 December 1800 to 31 December 1801[10]

| Receipts | £ | s | d |
|---|---|---|---|
| Balance on hand 5 Dec. 1800 | 445 | 19 | 9 |
| Sale of a cow, 2 pigs and a quantity of waste paper found on the premises 5 December 1800 | 18 | 15 | 10 |
| Collection after Bishop of London's Sermon at St. George's Church Hanover Square 1 June 1801 | 132 | 4 | 6 |
| Collection at Anniversary dinner held at London Tavern 1 June 1801 | 211 | 14 | 0 |
| Donation of A. and B. Goldsmid and their friends at Anniversary Dinner held at London Tavern 1 June 1801 | 379 | 1 | 0 |
| Committee at Lloyds' Coffee-house donated from the fund subscribed for the Sufferers in Lord Duncan's victory | 245 | 0 | 0 |
| Collection Paddington Church 18 August 1801 | 18 | 1 | 3 |
| Collection Wapping Church 22 Nov. 1801 | 14 | 0 | 0 |
| Sundry Benefactions and Subscriptions 5 Dec. 1800 to 13 Dec. 1801 | 976 | 0 | 10 |
| Balance due to Accountant | 138 | 8 | 9 |
| | 2579 | 15 | 11 |

| Expenditure | £ | s | d |
|---|---|---|---|
| Workmans Bills for alterations and fitting the house and premises | 219 | 7 | 7 |
| Furniture and Bedding | 114 | 18 | 2 |
| Advertisements, paper, printing, stationery previous to 5 Dec. 1800 | 123 | 0 | 0 |
| Provisions to Xmas 1800 | 179 | 11 | 9 |
| Salaries and Wages left unpaid at Xmas 1800 | 37 | 10 | 6 |
| One years provisions for 50 children, Master, Matron and 2 servants at an average of 3/7 a week | 506 | 14 | 10 |
| 5 Quarters rent and 1 years land tax | 101 | 16 | 0 |
| Clothing and Household Linen | 200 | 12 | 3 |
| Coals, candles, laundry expences and sundry contingencies in the house | 107 | 4 | 3 |
| Salaries and wages to Officers and servants | 116 | 0 | 0 |
| Gratuity and allowance to Mr Cuppage for his extraordinary trouble and attendance from 5 Dec. to 1 Jan. 1801 (re Thompson) | 21 | 0 | 0 |
| Mr Baker for medicines | 4 | 1 | 0 |
| Advertisements, printing circular, lists of subscribers, stationery, school books, messengers, expenses etc. | 133 | 10 | 1 |
| Purchase Exchequer Bill £500 plus interest | 514 | 8 | 7 |
| Purchase Exchequer Bill £200 | 200 | 0 | 11 |
| | 2579 | 15 | 11 |

*Author's note:*
*There is a discrepancy of ten shillings on the receipts side.*

A week before the King's inspection of the volunteers in Hyde Park the previous October, there was a large church parade in the City. It was said 300 Jews were to take the oath, a contemporary news-sheet reported:-

> By an order from the Jews High Priest they were prohibited from attending in our churches during the time of Divine Service. The High Priest, however, expressed his highest concurrence to their taking the oaths of fidelity and allegiance to our king and country. These gentlemen accordingly took the oaths, either upon the drilling-grounds of their respective corps or in the vestry room of the churches as circumstances required. They were sworn upon the Book of Leviticus instead of the New Testament.[16]

Meanwhile the "Goldsmid Friends" continued to support the Naval Asylum with the treasurers entry of £162.5s.0d. in 1803. Some were partners of the Goldsmids – David Mocatta, Daniel Eliason and Thomas Moxon, whilst others who became members of the Institution were Nathan Salomons (financer and lay head of the New Synagogue, Leadenhall Street), Joseph Hart Myers (a physician), Eleazor Solomons, Gabriel Brandon, Solomon Levein, Moses Zuntz, Joseph Cohen, Lyon and Samuel Levy. Another member was Joseph Cohen, an East India broker in the City and warden of the Great Synagogue. It was possibly through him that early one August during this period, Captain (later Admiral) Sir William Sidney Smith, called upon Joseph Cohen's father, Levi Barnet Cohen, a merchant of the highest standing, at his home at 11 Angel Court, City. Sir Sidney may well have been seeking funds for the Naval Asylum. He was intrigued to see the family seated on low chairs. Judith, one of Levi Barnet Cohen's daughters, later to become Lady Montefiore, explained, 'This is the anniversary of the destruction of Jerusalem which is kept by conforming Jews as a day of mourning and humiliation. We treasure the memory of the unavailing valour exhibited by our ancestors as a bright example to ourselves how to fight and sacrifice our lives for the land in which we were born and which gives us shelter and protection.' It was the Fast of Tisha B'Av. Apparently Sir Sidney Smith and the others were pleased with the explanation, observing: 'It was a most noble feeling which prompts the true patriot to mourn for the brave – the struggles of the Jews in Palestine remain the rightful masters of the Land which God has apportioned to them as an inheritance – it was a glorious monument to their dauntless valour and fervent devotion to a good and holy cause.'[17]

The Goldsmid brothers were again stewards at the Anniversary Dinner in June 1804, the *Naval Chronicle* reporting:-

> The Anniversary Dinner of the Naval Asylum, for the education of the Orphans of British Sailors and Marines, was held at the London Tavern, his Royal Highness the Duke of Cumberland in the chair. The institution now maintains 36 boys and 8 girls. The claimants would be as many hundreds if there were funds. An apology was made for the absence of Lord Melville; Earl St Vincent gave a donation of £1000 to the fund. It has hitherto been chiefly supported by the liberal exertions of Messrs Goldsmids and their friends of the Jewish persuasion. Out of £725.17s.0d. collected no less than £650 was paid in by them.[18]

Later that same month, Abraham Goldsmid was examined under oath, before the Commissioners of Naval Enquiry, into irregularities in the Office of Treasurer of the Navy. The Tenth Report, as it was known, did not appear until February, 1805. It showed that one of the Paymasters had ten years previously speculated with £20,000 of public money, apparently with the connivance of the Treasurer of the Navy, later Lord Melville, First Lord of the Admiralty. The scandal was to force his resignation.

This Tenth Report did show how, at the end of each year, Messrs Goldsmid rendered accounts to the Navy Board of the Exchequer Bills which they negotiated, deducting their commission of one-eighth per cent together with the loss upon sale, if any. In the year 1797 for instance £27,309 was paid to Messrs Goldsmid out of the monies voted for the service of the Navy. Out of this report an Act was passed in 1807 wherein the Treasurer of the Navy could only apply to the Bank of England for money immediately required for the Naval Service thus restricting the involvement of Messrs Goldsmid.[19]

The brothers were not always popular, it being said of Abraham Goldsmid by William Cobbett in his *Weekly Political Register*, "A man acquiring such immense wealth, must see that something was necessary to keep the public from grudging – he merely tossed back to the miserable part of us in the shape of alms, the fraction of pence, upon the immense sums of money that he got by his traffic in loans, bills and funds." And yet Abraham had I.O.U.s which were in effect gifts, amounting to over £100,000. He was the more popular of the two brothers, with a country seat at Morden Hall in Surrey, close to his brother and a near neighbour of Lord Nelson at Merton Place.

It was on 13 September 1801 that Nelson purchased for £9,000 the 100 year old Merton Place. It lay in about 70 acres of delightful grounds on either side of Merton High Street, a short distance from what is now South Wimbledon Underground Station. Here, after his famous victories of the Nile and Copenhagen, he hoped to lead a family life with Emma Hamilton and their newly born daughter, Horatia. Nelson took up residence in October. The villagers had erected a triumphal arch in front of the spacious house. It was a mansion eminently suitable for Emma's taste for entertaining. Before Nelson was to return to sea in May 1803, he was to have many contacts with his Jewish neighbours.[20]

*"Tea in the Drawing Room at Merton Place" circa 1803. Admiral Lord Nelson is at the centre, Lady Hamilton at the piano, with John Braham the celebrated Jewish tenor standing with sheet music. (from an artist's impression – Navy and Army Illustrated 21 October 1897).*

Card evenings were played at Abraham's. Nelson made use of a special rack which he could more conveniently use with his single arm. On one occasion, besides Nelson, there were present the Duke of Sussex, Daniel Mocatta, (who had married into the Goldsmid family), and the singer John Braham. The latter had been brought to the Goldsmids as a young Jewish boy. He had a beautiful voice and sang in the choir of the Great Synagogue during the mid 1780s. He was to become one of the best known English tenors of the period and to gain international status. Nelson had met Braham during one of his singing tours in the Mediterranean, once at Leghorn and again in June 1799, on board his flagship, the *Foudroyant*, when Braham sang before the Queen of Naples. Braham was a promoter of patriotic songs, particularly those with a nautical flavour, one of his better productions being ,*"The English Fleet in 1342"* performed at Covent Garden in 1803, "with unprecedented applause". It was an historical comic opera on the Battle of the Sluys, altered in part to the contemporary naval scene. The music-loving and attractive Goldsmid daughters sang and played with Emma Hamilton who in turn had lessons from Braham. In a letter to his wife on 20 March, 1802, Lord Minto, recently returned from being British Ambassador in Vienna, remarked that: 'Braham, the celebrated Jew singer, performed with Lady Hamilton. She is horrid, but he entertained me in spite of her.'[21] Another visitor to Morden Hall was Doctor Lettsom who recalled in a letter to the Reverend J. Plumtree, 'I may notice a fine concerto I lately witnessed at my friend and patient's Abraham Goldsmid, the rich Jew, where Lady Hamilton, Braham and others were of the party.'

*The Seat of Abraham Goldsmid, Morden, Surrey. circa 1798. A neighbour of Admiral Lord Nelson of Merton. (from a print).*

The entertaining and visiting continued. It is purported that one card evening when Nelson revoked, 'Excuse me Mr Mocatta,' he said, 'but I have the French Fleet on my mind all the time.' On another occasion, in 1805, George Matcham, Nelson's nephew, was a guest at Abraham Goldsmid's. His sketch diary noted, 'Went to Mr Goldsmid's . . . Fine House. Saw his sons . . . After breakfast row'd in the Boat. Horace shew'd his skill. Grounds poor. Very polite. Did not like their dinner; Jewish. The Hall, the height of the house, very gaudy; as are all the rooms; but tasteless.'

Lord Nelson also visited another Goldsmid brother, Asher, where it is said that at a dinner party he met the young Moses Montefiore who chanted the long grace after meals in Hebrew, supposedly much appreciated by the Admiral.

Sir William Sidney Smith, the hero of the defence of Acre, was also on the most friendly terms with the Goldsmids. In another letter Doctor Lettsom described a party at one of the Goldsmids, sometime during 1805.

> At Goldsmid's ball I met a man I had wished much to know Sir Sidney Smith, so I told him, and he assured me he had a similar penchant. We ate a sandwich together; and then hob-a-nob'd our glasses of porter. He was very conversible and tout eveille; although he had been detained at supper by the Duke of Sussex till four in the preceeding morning; he then met the King at Woolwish [sic] and was on horse-back the whole afternoon. At half past one in the morning I left him dancing with a Jewess. He told me he was on shore to have a little rest, but I could not see much rest would result from such exertions.[22]

Sir William Sidney Smith was a great supporter of the Naval Asylum where the demands upon the Institution were growing daily. Clarence House, Paddington Green, could only accommodate seventy children and it was decided to transfer the establishment to Greenwich under the aegis of a Royal Foundation. So by Royal Warrant dated 25 July 1805, Commissioners were appointed to prepare a report with Rules and Regulations for the proper government of the Royal Naval Asylum to accommodate up to 700 boys and 300 girls. Abraham and Benjamin Goldsmid took no part whatsoever in this Royal Foundation but at the winding up of the old Committee, held at the Duke of Cumberland's on 14 November 1805, the minutes read:-[23]

> It was afterwards resolved that the thanks of this Committee be given to Abraham and Benjamin Goldsmid Esq., and their friends for their most zealous munificent and unremitting support of this Institution and that the same be communicated to them by letter.

The Royal Naval Asylum was now on a proper financial footing with an annual Parliamentary grant of over £20,000, plus donations including £40,000 from Lloyds Patriotic Fund. In 1806 the Goldsmid brothers made another effort among the Jewish community, with £2,600 donated. By 1825 the Asylum was amalgamated with the existing Greenwich School to become the Royal Hospital Schools, housed in what is now the National Maritime Museum. The school moved to its present home at

Holbrook in Suffolk during 1933.

Many boys have entered the Royal Navy from the school and what was started by an adventurer to defraud the patriotic zeal of the subscribers developed, with the help of charity, into a national institution. Jewish involvement at a critical financial stage was to go unrewarded as far as Abraham and Benjamin Goldsmid were concerned. Whatever they did with their wealth and influence could be misconstrued. By charitable action the public were warned by pamphleteers and others that wealthy Jews never parted with a farthing without some potent reason. If they had kept their wealth this would have been worse. Suffice to say the Goldsmids interested themselves in a worthy cause for the benefit of the Royal Navy.

After the long and disappointing chase of Villeneuve's Fleet to the West Indies, Lord Nelson returned to England and was back at Merton Place on 20 August 1805. His stay was to be short lived. Early on 2 September, his trusted Captain, Henry Blackwood of the frigate *Euryalus,* brought the news that the combined fleets of France and Spain were at Cadiz. The Admiralty immediately gave Nelson orders to resume command of the Mediterranean Fleet. All was now hurry and bustle. On Thursday 12 September Lord Nelson bade farewell to the Prince of Wales at Carlton House, returning to Merton Place in the late afternoon, where Lord Minto had been waiting to take final leave of him. The story can now be taken up from the unpublished diary of Benjamin Goldsmid's youngest son, Lionel, born in 1797, and written in later years:-[24]

> Thursday 12 September
>
> I remember Lord Nelson slept at our house (Thursday 12 September) the night before he left England on his last fatal mission – he was walking the last morning arm in arm with my mother up and down the drawing room – a large room with two immense glasses – then a rarity – from the top to the floor of the room at the upper end, and my youngest sister and myself on the side of his armless body and each time he told us two to look at that old fellow Lord Nelson and see what a funny-looking fellow he was, he was dressed in a naval coat, white naval breeches with naval buttons at knees, silk stockings, invariably hanging on as if not pulled up, too large, and shoes rather high in the quarters large and with buckles. He was kind in the extreme and we all loved him. I particularly wished to go to sea with him – I was too young . . . One day, my dear mother near the fireplace, one end of the large

room and two of my brothers looking out of the centre bay window with a large telescope – the servant brought my mother a letter and soon she screamed out, 'Children, Lord Nelson is killed.'

Lord Nelson wrote in his own private diary, Friday Night 13 September:–

> At half-past ten drove from dear dear Merton, where I left all which I hold dear in this world, to go to serve my King and Country. May the Great God whom I adore enable me to fulfil the expectations of my Country; and if it is His good pleasure that I should return, my thanks will never cease being offered up to the Throne of His Mercy. If it is His good providence to cut short my days upon earth, I bow with the greatest submission, relying that He will protect those dear to me, that I may leave behind, His will be done: Amen. Amen. Amen.

By noon on the Saturday, 14 September, Nelson's flag was again hoisted on board the *Victory*. He sailed the following morning in company with the *Euryalus*. The course was set to join the blockading fleet off Cadiz – and Cape Trafalgar.

Early on 19 October, the frigate *Sirius* close inshore gave the long awaited signal that the combined fleets of eighteen French and fifteen Spanish ships of the line were coming out. Over the horizon Nelson waited his opportunity. At day-break on 21 October, both fleets were in sight of each other. The British fleet bore upon the enemy in two columns. The weather division of twelve ships of the line led by Nelson and the lee division by Collingwood with fifteen ships of the line. At 11.45 the immortal signal from the *Victory, 'England Expects that Every Man will do his Duty,'* was hoisted. It was immediately followed by Number 16 *'Engage the enemy more closely'*, hoisted at the topgallant mast-head, where it was to remain until shot away.

Let us try and follow those Jews in the British fleet on that historic day.[25]

From the Muster Roll of the *Victory* it has already been noted how, against the name of Moses Benjamin and dated 20 August, 1805, appears:

> Discharged from the service on order of Lord Nelson agreeable to order from the Lord commissioners of the Admiralty, Moses Benjamin being a Jew.

In fact the order was not complied with before the *Victory* left Portsmouth on 14 September. Moses Benjamin simply went from the main to the Supernumerary List, receiving victuals and wages only. He was therefore at the battle, but did not receive the government grant or prize money. However, his son John Benjamin was permitted, in later years, to trade in the City of London, under the law granting special privileges to the families of men who had served in the forces. Also aboard the *Victory* and a possible co-religionist of Moses Benjamin was Boy Third Class Joseph Moss, born at Newington, Middlesex.

As the *Victory* bore on to the heart of the enemy's line, bearing the brunt of a withering fire, it is likely, as he was only fourteen years of age, that Joseph Moss supplied one of the guns with cartridges from the magazine, one slung to each shoulder. There he would be running to and fro over the bloody and splintered deck, with the ship shuddering from her own broadsides and those of the enemy. Above all there would be the devastating noise. By 1 pm the action had become general with the *Victory* dropping alongside and locked into the French seventy four gun *Redoutable.* The sharpshooters in the fighting tops now wreaked havoc on the crew of the *Victory's* upper deck. The French thought they could board but the curve of both ships' hulls did not allow for it, added to which men from the *Victory* came from below to secure the upper deck. Although wounded, Captain Lucas of the *Redoutable* collected his men together and lowered the main yard to form a bridge across to the *Victory.* This attempt was forestalled as the British ninty eight gun *Temeraire* (Captain Harvey) next in line to the *Victory* came up on the *Redoutable's* disengaged side. The Frenchmen received a terrible hammering and did not make any further resistance. At about 1.15 pm Lord Nelson had been hit by a mizzen-top marksman. With a bullet lodged in his spine he had been carried below to the cockpit.

The *Temeraire* had already been in action with the Spanish flagship *Santisima Trinidad* and was now looking a cripple, or so it appeared to the French seventy four gun *Fougueux.* Captain Harvey held his fire. Then at point blank range successive broadsides crashed into the surprised *Fougueux.* "Away Boarders!" as the two ships crashed into each other and within ten minutes it was all over.

The British hoisted their colours on the *Fougueux.* As Admiral Collingwood was to write to Captain Harvey "Nothing could be finer – I have no words in which I can sufficiently express my admiration of it." Aboard the *Temeraire* was the twenty three years old Londoner, Midshipman Benjamin da Costa, probably a member of a well-known and respected Jewish Sephardic family, who had volunteered for the Royal Navy the preceeding June.

*Battle of Trafalgar 21 October 1805. Situation of HMS Temeraire at 3 p.m dismasted (at centre) with British colours hoisted on the* **Fougeux**. *Midshipmen Benjamin Da Costa of an old Sephardic family served aboard HMS Temeraire from June 1805 to January 1806. (from an engraving by J. Bailey).*

Lord Nelson's plan of breaking the line to split up the enemy's ships and cut them off from one another was proving successful as each ship of the British weather column followed the *Victory* and *Temeraire* into action. Sixth in line and flying the flag of Rear-Admiral the Earl of Northesk, third in command, was the one hundred gun three-decker *Britannia* (Captain Charles Bullen). On the gun decks below were four London Jews, all in their early twenties and all volunteers. It is possible they were known to each other, as all were drafted to the ship on the same day, 1 September 1804. Joseph and Nathan Manuel could have been brothers. The other two were Henry Levi and Benjamin Solomon. We can picture them stripped to the waist with black silk handkerchiefs bound tightly round their ears to help keep out the noise. With the guns loaded and run out they waited at their gun stations. Into range came the Spanish seventy four gun *San Francisco de Asis*. "Fire!" The heavy breeching rope stopped nearly three tons of recoil as the fifteen men of the 32-pounder gun crew worked feverishly to reload. Two would sponge out; two more load and ram home the shot; then others run out the gun to the firing position by means of hand-tackles; the handspikeman trained and elevated, directed by the gun captain, who eventually fired by means of a flint-lock and lanyard. It was possible for a smart crew to get off a round every two minutes. At any time, two of the gun's crew could be detailed off as boarders or sail trimmers and two always stood by as firemen with buckets of water and swabs at each gun. So the battle continued as *Britannia* got off her broadsides with the ship keeling under sail. The acrid stench of powder smoke was so thick that a lantern was required to see the priming of the gun. Above all was the terrifying din. Then another three-decker, the *Rayo* of one hundred guns came into range, with action continuing for a short time, *Britannia's* log reading: '1.50 observed the ship we were engaging on our larboard quarter totally dismasted – continued our course in order to break through the centre of the enemy's line, engaging on both sides in passing between their ships. At 3 passed through the line. 4.30 hauled to the wind on the larboard tack per signal. 5.30 ceased firing.'

*HMS Britannia lying at Portsmouth after the Battle of Trafalgar. Four London Jews were part of the crew of about 900 officers and men. (from a print by G. F. Bragg after R. H. Nibbs). National Maritime Museum.*

Vice-Admiral Collingwood leading the lee column in his flagship, the one hundred gun *Royal Sovereign* ,eventually broke the line between the *Fougueux* and the massive one hundred and twelve gun *Santa Anna* and by 12.10 pm was heavily engaged. Within twenty minutes the Spanish *Santa Anna* struck her colours, but the *Royal Sovereign* was in such a sorry state that by 5 pm, she had to be towed away by the *Euryalus*. Aboard the *Royal Sovereign* was a John Benjamin of London, aged thirty four, having only just joined the ship at Portsmouth. Another sailor, and probably a Jew, was Philip Emanuel. He was aged twenty one and also from London, serving aboard the *Colossus*. It was the sixth ship in the lee column and came to the assistance of the *Bellerophon* at about 12.30 pm. The *Colossus*, of seventy four guns, had spirited actions with the French *Swiftsure, Argonaute* and the Spanish *Bahama* with two of them surrendering. The *Colossus* suffered more heavily in killed and wounded combined than any other British ship in the fleet. But Philip Emanual survived.

*Battle of Trafalgar 21 October 1805. **HMS Colossus** (far left) coming to assistance of **HMS Bellerophon** (centre) heavily engaged on both sides at about 1.15 p.m. **HMS Colossus** was to suffer the most casualties of any ship in the British fleet with 200 killed and wounded. Philip Emanuel of London was the only known Jewish seaman aboard **HMS Colossus** who survived. (from an engraving by T. Sutherland).*

James Brandon, quite probably of the Jewish faith, a Landsman aboard the seventy four gun *Revenge*, was not to be so fortunate. Against his name in the Muster Book is noted: 'Born London. Age 20 – D.D. (Discharged dead). Killed in action 21 October 1805.' He had joined only five months previously.

The *Revenge*, of seventy four guns, (Captain Robert Moorsom), being eighth in Collingwood's column, joined the action late, but was soon heavily engaged between 12.45 and 1 pm. In attempting to get through the enemy's line, she passed down the side of the French *Aigle* delivering a couple of broadsides. Then standing on, she was suddenly fired upon by the *Principe de Asturias* of one hundred and twelve guns who, in conjunction with three two-deckers, hemmed in the *Revenge*.

This British ship took a terrible beating until relieved by the *Dreadnought* and *Thunderer*. Twenty eight of her crew were killed, including James Brandon.

By the late hours of the afternoon the outcome was clear. The Royal Navy had won a devastating victory over the combined French and Spanish fleets. By the time the battle ceased, seventeen enemy ships had been taken and one blown up. Bonaparte's bid for maritime ascendency was over; Lord Nelson had died in the cockpit of the *Victory* at 4.30 – his work completed.

News of the battle reached London on 6 November; it was met with rejoicing but sobered by a real sense of loss with the death of Nelson. Abraham Goldsmid illuminated his house but is reported to have said with a heavy heart, 'I rejoice for England, and I mourn for my friend.' Both Abraham and Benjamin were the recipients of memorial rings, with the former a mourner at Nelson's funeral at St Paul's.[26]

Thursday 5 December was appointed a General Thanksgiving for the victory, the *Annual Register* reporting, 'All the Churches and Chapels were crowded, all distinctions of sects were done away and Christian and Jew, Catholic and Protestant, all united in the expression of one feeling of piety and gratitude to the Almighty.'[27]

This feeling of one nation even spread to the otherwise separate and at times poor relationship between the Sephardim and Ashkenazim, with their respective ecclesiastical chiefs, Raphael Meldola and Solomon Hirschell, combining for the very first time to prepare jointly, "The Order of Service and Special Prayer of the Hebrew Thanksgiving", to be said on 14 Kislev 5566 (the Hebrew corresponding date to 1805) in all the London Synagogues. It was striking in composition, with the divine deliverance granted to those seamen who go in constant danger of their lives.

> We prostrate ourselves in Thy holy temple to acknowledge Thy name for all the goodness Thou hast shown unto us. When the strong vessels of the enemy were in sight a spirit of valour clothes our captains and sailors to do battle against them. They drew up their vessels in aray against the enemy, line against line. Then wast Thou our helper. Our choicest ships were there with admirals and commanders swifter than eagles, stronger than lions. Where the foe went there went they, and when he stayed then stayed they to make an end to the vengeful enemy. Thou didst deliver them into our hands – some to death, others to captivity. Our flag Thou didst set on high. Thou didst give us the shield of Thy salvation and Thy right hand supported us. From the wild

> and tempestuous winds Thou didst deliver us; from the destructive fire Thou didst save us . . .[28]

Rabbi Solomon Hirschell preached the sermon which became the first address delivered in the Great Synagogue to be published. As *The Gentleman's Magazine* remarked on its content, "A strain of true piety, a great loyalty and universal benevolence." Here are some of the passages:–

> A more important cource of rejoicing, and thanksgiving, may be found in the conviction which this glorious victory must impress on our minds, of the justice of our cause, and of its rectitude in the sight of God; whence we may form every reasonable hope of ultimate and complete success . . .
>
> Now, as it is well known that in this battle we were much inferior in number, and no very extraordinary stress is laid on the manoeuvres we employed; nay, as it even appears that the enemy had address enough to oppose two ships to one of ours (which, however, drove off her opponents, and ultimately took them), it is evident the victory cannot be ascribed to either of these two causes. Now, as we have already remarked, that miracles have ceased, since we have ceased to deserve them, there only remains one way probably to account for it, viz. from that increased energy which the consciousness of a right and just cause infuses into man, and which, under God's providence, inspired our seamen with a double portion of courage on this occasion . . .
>
> . . . The fall of Lord Nelson is a severe evil; a loss not easily repaired. His piety made him favoured of God; and his courage, his skill, and his activity, made him the darling of his country. While his successes have been the pride of his countrymen, his name the terror of the enemy. 'Alas! how are the mighty fallen in the midst of battle! (Second Book of Samuel, Chapter 1. Verse 25). O, Nelson! thou wast slain in thine high place!' Let us then here regard the hand of God, and not be extravagant in our exultation; but still remember, that all is in the hands of him who causeth death, and who bringeth again to life. Thus whilst he has permitted us to triumph over our enemies, he has deprived us of our leader; our mighty one! His will be done. 'The Lord has given; the Lord has taken; let the name of the Lord be blessed.' (Book of Job. Chapter 1. Verse 21). We have not only lost a good and pious man. All his hope, all his dependance, was on God; and to God did he, with due humility, ascribe the victory of the Nile. His language was modest, his conduct religious, and his humanity exemplary. Such a man was worthy of the favour of Providence; nor did it ever fail him. May his successors imitate his example, and thus prove deserving of the protection of Heaven, and like him become invincible . . .

> . . . On no occasion can charity be so well timed, and on no persons can it be so properly bestowed, as on those in whose behalf it is now to be collected; and so impressed am I with its being an imperious duty incumbent on us, that even if the plan had not already been set on foot, and arranged by the public at large, we ought spontaneously to have come forward, and brought our aggregate subscription to that noble institution, the Patriotic Fund.
>
> What ought we not to do for those brave men, who, disregarding all endearing ties at home, disregarding of all personal danger, boldly advance to chastise the enemy . . .
>
> Powerful, therefore, is the claim which the poor widow and the orphan must have on us, who are protected by the valour and loyalty of the fallen husband and father. In our cause, and for our safety, he died; the wife, the child, crieth to us for bread; shall we dare to withhold it? If, as men, as citizens, we must attend to such solicitations, how much more ought we, as Jews, who are cherished and protected in this happy country, even as its own children! Cast out from the land of our forefathers, we find this land congenial to us, surely then, its cause is our cause; and we ought, on every occasion, to evince ourselves grateful for its fostering protection.[29]

Prayers continued for King George III and for the Royal Navy, the service ending with a prayer for peace and welfare of the country.

Notwithstanding their disabilities and long before the Jews of England enjoyed the privileges of their fellow citizens, their patriotic spirit manifested itself in many other ways. After Nelson's death at Trafalgar, Nathan Vallentine, whose son Isaac was to find himself at sea in the Royal Navy, produced in Hebrew and English, "The discourse of the three sisters, respecting the fall and murder of Admiral Nelson". John Braham, the Jewish tenor, produced, "The Death of Nelson" which Lady Hamilton saw time and time again, bursting into public tears at the appropriate moment, as if to get into the act.

In the centre of the stage would be a marble tomb surmounted by a figure of Britannia, her head bowed in grief, holding a wreath of laurels. The audience would rise and cheer, silenced only when Braham, dressed as a British sailor, sang the opening words of the recitative, "O'er Nelson's tomb . . ." Ladies sobbed, strong men shed tears. There was tumultuous applause and the whole had to be repeated again and again:–

*Twas in Trafalgar's bay*
*We saw the Frenchmen lay;*
*Each heart was bounding then;*

*We scorned the foreign yoke,*
*For our ships were British oak,*
*And hearts of oak our man!*

*Our Nelson marked them on the wave,*
*Three cheers our gallant seamen gave,*
*Nor thought of home and beauty,*
*Along the line the signal ran:–*
*"England expects that every man*
*This day will do his duty."*

*And now the cannon's roar*
*Along that frightened shore:*
*Our Nelson led the way:*
*His ship the Victory named.*
*Long be that Victory famed!*
*For Victory crowned the day.*

*But dearly was that conquest bought,*
*Too well the gallant hero fought*
*For England home and beauty.*
*He cried, as midst the fire he ran:–*
*'England expects that every man*
*This day will do his duty.'*

*At last the fatal wound,*
*Which spreads dismay around,*
*The hero's breast, the . . . hero's breast received:*
*'Heav'n fights up – on our side! The day's our own, he cried.*
*'Now long enough I've lived.*
*In honours cause my life was passed.*
*In honours cause I fall at last, For England home and beauty.'*
*Thus ending life as he began, England confessed that every man that day had done his duty.*

The song[30] had no great originality and was full of cliches but sung with conviction by a fine tenor voice it moved an emotional audience. In fact it became Braham's signature tune, particularly as the public knew the singer had been a friend of Lord Nelson. Sung at every opportunity it was in part a debt of honour for it was said Nelson made Braham promise to play music at his funeral.

Towards the end of 1805 Lionel Prager Goldsmid recalled in his diary:–

> Lady Hamilton, who was received everywhere and known as Lord Nelson's most attached friend, received visitors of condolence upon the death of our beloved Hero just after or at the time of the funeral. I was eight years old and was allowed to accompany my mother and those of the family who made up the party from our house. I was a great favourite of Lady Hamilton's and bathed in tears at times as she talked over his virtues and exhibitied the various gifts he had made her on different occasions . . .
>
> . . . The very coat in which the dear old admiral was dressed in the fatal battle, and received his death wound was on the outside of the bed – the hole where the bullet passed through stiffened with congealed blood.[31]

It was Lord Nelson's wish for Lady Hamilton to be, 'a legacy to my King and country, that they will give her an ample provision to maintain her rank in life'. However, this did not come about. With the period of Nelson's mourning over, the bills mounted and many conveniently forgot her. She turned, among others, to the Goldsmids for encouragement and financial assistance. Abraham arranged a loan to tide her over and wrote on 8 April 1806[32] by way of condolence, 'It is our duty to content ourselves, and on mature reflection you'll be convinced that it was done for the good of those he esteemed, and his time was to die, and if not by shot you might have lost him by sickness, and then his feelings would not have been fulfilled according to his own wishes'.

Her financial position failed to improve. Merton Place had become a liability. It just had to be sold. This time it was Asher Goldsmid who came to the fore, relieving Emma of the declining property which was encumbered with debts, and purchasing it for £12,930. 'I am glad to hear a Goldsmid has purchased Merton rather than a stranger', wrote Nelson's sister, Mrs Bolton, to Lady Hamilton. By November 1808, the sale was completed. Emma Hamilton informed Charles Greville, 'At a moment of desperation when I thought they neglected me Goldsmid and my city friends came forward and rescued me from destruction – Goldsmid has been and is an angel to me, and his bounty shall never be abused.' Asher Goldsmid preserved some of the rooms as they had been in Nelson's time.

Abraham Goldsmid found time in June 1806 to arrange with the Admiralty for the body of Benjamin Chapman to be removed from the grounds of Haslar Hospital, Gosport, for burial according to Jewish rites. In the original application, Goldsmid referred to Chapman being killed by an accident caused by one of the guns aboard *HMS Captain*. Yet the ship's log recorded on 10 June 1806, whilst in Portsmouth Harbour, 'A.M. Cloudy. Convicts employed stowing the hold, hoist and striking down. Benjamin Chapman fell into the Main Hold and departed this life'. Here was another case of name changing by a Jew. He was only eighteen years of age, having only just joined his first ship, the *Captain*, after volunteering at Gosport the month before his fatal accident.[33]

Disaster was now to overtake Abraham from which he was never to recover. His brother and partner Benjamin took his own life on 15 April 1808, at his Roehampton home. The jury returned a verdict of lunacy after learning he had suffered from long periods of depression and severe attacks of gout.

Apparently, the Goldsmids were not always efficient in their accounting as by a letter George Rose M.P., Treasurer of the Navy, wrote to the Navy Board on 8 February 1808, which declared that £3,880 was still outstanding from 1804, for interest on Exchequer Bills.[34]

Two years later far worse was to follow. The banking houses of Baring and Goldsmid were contractors for a government loan of £13,400,000. The boom years were over, the market fell and a 3½% discount had to be quoted. Suddenly Sir Francis Baring died and the scrip fell further to a 6½% discount. Panic began to grow. The East India Company claimed £35,000 outstanding to them on Exchequer Bills. Now Abraham really missed his brother Benjamin during this period of crisis – like him he suffered from long fits of depression. He could not face the possibility of a fast approaching financial crash, which in the event may well have been avoided. It was too late. Abraham took his life on 28 September 1810.

An era was over. The Goldsmid brothers had done much to improve the position of English Jews on the long road to emancipation. Other leaders were to follow. Already the young Nathan Rothschild was one of the wardens of the Great Synagogue when Abraham Goldsmid arranged for three of George III's sons to attend sabbath eve service on 14 April 1809.

Lord Nelson's victory at Trafalgar did not see the end of the war at sea and, before the peace was signed ten years later, many actions were to follow, albeit much smaller than the last great naval battle under sail. Those of Jewish birth were to see further service in the Royal Navy in many parts of the world, and some instances are worth recording.

One of the most evenly matched frigate actions of the whole war took place on 23 January 1814 off the Cape Verde Islands, when two British 18-pounder thirty six gun frigates, the *Creole* and *Astrea,*[35] chased and engaged two French forty gun frigates, the *Etoile* and *Sultane*. The *Astrea* in particular put up a gallant fight, after catching fire and losing part of her masts. She lost nine killed, including her captain, with thirty seven wounded. Fortunately, the French frigates, also in a sorry state, gave up the action after three hours. Aboard the *Astrea* was Ordinary Seaman Daniel Levy, a cook, aged thirty, from London, who went to the *Creole* after the action. Another possible Jew, Ordinary Seaman John Daniels, aged twenty six, from Canterbury, was a shipmate of Levy. Emanual Isaacs of London, aged twenty two, was severely wounded when the thirty eight gun frigate *Macedonian*[36] surrendered to the forty four gun heavier *United States* after an action lasting two hours on 28 October 1812. Another British frigate to surrender was *HMS Ceylon* of thirty guns; whilst on passage from Madras to assist in the capture of the Isle of France, she met and engaged a superior force of two French ships, the *Venus* (44 guns) and *Victor* (18 guns). The muster book of the *Ceylon*[37] discloses a number of possible British Jews, Leven Benson from Stepney, Joseph Diamond from Exeter, a Jacob Davis and John Braham (alias Wilson). All suffered wounds. Ordinary Seaman Anthony Meyer was in the carpenter's crew of the thirty six gun frigate *Ethalion* at the capture of Martinique in February, 1809. Landsman John Cohen of the forty eight gun frigate *Loire* (Captain Alexander Wilmot Schomberg) and Landsman Samuel Daniel of the seventy four gun *Sceptre* were present at the capture of Guadaloupe early in 1810. Ordinary Seaman Manuel Joseph of the eighteen gun brig *Harpy* and Landsman Joseph Myers of another eighteen gun brig *Hecate* were both at the capture of Java a year later. David Barnard was a carpenter aboard the small sixteen gun brig *Sparrow* at the capture of San Sebastian, Northern Spain in 1813. For these various captures all six seamen were awarded and received the belated Naval General Service Medal in 1849.[38]

The Battle of Waterloo on 18 June 1815 and the peace signed in Paris the following November brought a decisive end to Bonaparte's ambitions. Long neglected political and social reforms could now commence. Throughout the rest of the nineteenth century Jewish disabilities in England were slowly to diminish. The foundations for emancipation had been laid in part by the contribution made by the Goldsmids and their wealthy brethren, together with those poorer Jews who had served in the Royal Navy and Army during the long Napoleonic Wars.

Paid off, and in many ways cast off, the sailors returned. Some of those wounded or grown old in the service were admitted into Greenwich Royal Hospital on the recommendations of senior and influential officers. Many of the seamen were disappointed as the waiting lists grew. Wren's masterly design was enlarged to take the maximum number of 2710 pensioners by 1814.[39] That July Thomas Levy of Chatham, aged fifty, was entered after thirty seven years in the Royal Navy, surely the longest serving Jewish man-of-war's man. Before him was William Myers, born in Whitechapel and aged fifty nine when entering the Hospital in October 1803, after seventeen years service in the King's ships.[40]

In fact the Hospital was a large self supporting almshouse with its own pension scheme subscribed to by the seamen because they had sixpence per month deducted from their wages during their merchant and naval careers; unclaimed prize money also went to the hospital. The lucky ones who secured a place would relinquish their out pension of £18.5.0d. a year and in return had their board and keep free, receiving a shilling per week pocket money. Every alternate year a complete suit of clothes was issued and annually a pair of trousers, cocked hat (worn on Sundays and on ceremonials), round hat, three pairs of stockings and four pairs of shoes. Shirts were supplied as they wore out. At the start of the nineteenth century their diet was one loaf of bread of sixteen ounces and two quarts of beer every day, a pound of mutton on Sunday and Tuesday and a pound of beef on Monday, Thursday and Saturday with pea soup, cheese and butter on Wednesday. Religious toleration was strictly observed with Catholics and others who dissented from the Established Church able to obtain permission to attend their respective places of worship.[41] In after years the *Jewish Chronicle* reported how, "Many years ago there was a Jewish pensioner in Greenwich Hospital. He retained affection for his religion, notwithstanding his naval vicissitudes and went to the home of some friends regularly at the recurrence of Passover!"[42]

As the old pensioners strolled in the quiet courts, colonnades and along the piazza known as Smoker's Arcade, there was much talk of their experiences. Perhaps Thomas Levy or William Myers would have recounted the fate of their co-religionist Landsman Isaac De Costa, of the seventy four guns *HMS Resolution*, who had fallen from the mizzen topsail yard and drowned on the 22 May 1806, about forty five miles from the Texel. He was a young man of twenty and like William Myers was born in Whitechapel.[43]

Falling from the rigging was just one of the hazards seamen had to face as there were more fatalities from accident, disease and shipwreck than from death in action. The every day hardships of poor food, low wages, little or no shore leave, floggings for small offences against the rigid discipline would suddenly fade in the seamen's minds as the drums beat to quarters. Enemy in sight. The guns were run out. Confidence returned. The Royal Navy seamen knew they belonged to the foremost sea-service in the world. Here was an opportunity to earn some Prize Money.

Seaman 1805

# CHAPTER 7

## "Prizes, Grants and Wages"

*In all labour there is profit.*

Proverbs 14:23

Prize money is practically as old as the English Navy itself, with all rights thereto belonging originally to the Crown. To give encouragement to the seamen, the Crown by very ancient grants ceded a portion of those rights, which gradually increased over the years. The fundamental basis for the law of prize is found in the Cruisers Act of 1708, laying down the process and regulations of prize-taking from capture, through adjudication in the High Court of Admiralty, to distribution of the prize proceeds.

On hostilities commencing, the whole system could only be put into operation by Royal Proclamation, with the recruiting posters loudly acclaiming the opportunities for prize money. A lucky capture, or series of captures, might bring untold wealth, particularly to the Officers, who received the largest shares. When for instance the Spanish treasure ship *Hermione* was captured in May 1762 by the *Active* and *Favourite,* the Commander-in-Chief for the Mediterranean, Admiral Sir Charles Saunders, received £64,963, every Lieutenant £13,000 each, whilst the share of every seaman and marine was £485. Such large sums from a single capture were unusual. It was the seizure of neutral vessels for their contraband which became the main source of prize money.

During the Napoleonic Wars, the High Court of Admiralty in London adjudicated over disputes as to legal prizes, whilst the Vice-Admiralty Courts performed virtually the same function in Dover, Portsmouth, Bristol, Hull and Plymouth. Many prizes were brought into naval ports overseas, and so Vice-Admiralty Courts were also found in Malta, Bermuda and Halifax. Bringing a captured prize into port could herald the start of endless litigation to satisfy both international and national law. Stringent rules were laid down as to procedure, leaving much scope for legal argument. The sheer number of prizes caused administrative problems aggravating the delays in payment to the capturing crews.

Prize money was not divided throughout the fleet, but only to those crews who were actually present at the capture of the prize. There could therefore accrue to individual Officers and men a number of prizes in which they were interested, but it would take years before the actual prize money was received. When the Officers and often illiterate seamen were at sea, they could not possibly deal with the legal and financial formalities in obtaining the prize money due to them. So grew up the practice of Prize Agency.

Admirals' Secretaries, like George Hulbert, Secretary to Sir John Borlase, Commander-in-Chief of the Halifax and Bermuda station in 1807, became Prize Agents. So did lawyers and, in particular, merchants with some legal training. James Sykes was an example. He traded with Madeira, the Azores and South America while combining the business of Prize Agency. The firm became Thomas Stilwell and Sons in 1816. It was eventually taken over by the Westminster Bank in 1923 and to this day the National Westminster Bank at 26, Haymarket, London is still known as the Navy Branch.[1] Many Prize Agents established themselves in The Strand area of London and were in effect bankers to the Officers of the Royal Navy. Open house was kept for their client naval Officers who became the Prize Agents' confidants and friends. During the Napoleonic War, vast sums of money passed through their hands. Toasts were raised between the Prize Agents and lawyers, *"May we never see another war"*, which was really interpreted as "may the war never end". In Plymouth between 1793 and 1801, nearly 1,000 captures were sold off. Abroad, huge sums accrued from prizes. One firm alone, Messrs Wills and Waterhouse, Merchants and Prize Agents of Jamaica and London, reported proceeds of £2,145,000 from about 1,400 captures.

Of the main Prize Agents during the Napoleonic Wars based in London, numbering some thirty or so, there was only one Jew in the business and only to a very small degree. He was Isaac Levy of 14, Mount Place, Whitechapel Road.

On 19 May 1808 Levy was appointed lawful Attorney and Agent by the Officers and crew of His Majesty's Bomb Vessel *Fury* (325 tons) under the command of Lieutenant J.S. Gibson. It was armed with twelve small guns and was, at the time, lying at Yarmouth Roads when it was ordered to join Vice-Admiral Sir James Saumarez in the Baltic. The *Fury* was destined to be involved in a number of skirmishes and captures. During the summer of 1808, off the Norwegian coast, she took as prizes ten small Danish gunboats. One was the Danish brig *Vigilentia,* loaded with timber on passage from Norway to Jutland, taken prize on 26 November. On the last day of 1808, after closing a convoy of Danish vessels, the Fury took possession of another, the *Corroborata.*[2]

Meanwhile, under section 57 of the Act for the Encouragement of Seamen 1805 (45 George III Chapter 72), Isaac Levy had on 15 December 1808 lodged a bond for £5,000 with the High Court of Admiralty, together with his letter of Attorney from the Officers and crew of the *Fury*. His two sureties by this joint and several bond were a Jewish merchant, David Solomon Aaron of Fenchurch Buildings, Fenchurch Street, London, and a William Jenkins, clerk in the Navy Office for seamen's wages.[3]

As soon as the captures were made, it was important for the Officer in charge of the boarding party to see that none of his men plundered the prize in any way, and to secure the prize's ship's papers. At the earliest opportunity, a Prize List was made out by the Captain of the capturing ship, setting out all the members of his crew. Here was detailed in duplicate against the list of names their qualities, (whether rated Landsman, Ordinary or Able Seaman, Petty Officer, and so on) stature, complexion, colour of eyes and hair, together with such other particulars as may serve to make identification possible, as in a lot of cases the seamen were unable to sign their names. One list was sent to the Prize Agent, the other to the Navy Pay office, both being signed by the Captain. With a copy of the Prize List to the Agent was also dispatched details of insuring the prize and, where possible, a copy of the prize's manifest. This document was carried by all the merchant ships and gave details of her tonnage, master's name, cargo carried, names of shippers, consignees and other relevant information.[4]

On the arrival of the prize in port, the Prize Agent, or his representative, took possession and sent the preparatory details with the prize's manifest to the Registrar of the High Court of Admiralty. Lengthy legal proceedings were then gone through, with the rights of neutrals to be heard and appeals considered. The High Court of Admiralty, through its Prize Courts and the Lord Commissioners of Appeal, had the sole and exclusive jurisdiction over the question of prize or no prize, and who the captors were. On passing a sentence of condemnation to the actual captors, the authority of the Court ceased, and the property vested absolutely in the captors. The Prize Agent could now, and only at this stage, sell the prize, unless the cargo had been perishable, and only then upon representation by affidavit.[5]

Under section 67 of the Act for the Encouragement of Seamen, 1805, the Prize Agent, after compulsory advertisements in *The London Gazette*, announced he was about to lodge in the High Court of Admiralty an attested copy of his detailed accounts, together with vouchers verified on oath. By long usage, a 5% fee was deducted by the Prize Agent from the net sum after deduction of all the legitimate expenses. Interested parties could object and, on the accounts being passed by the court or amended, the monies in the hands of the Prize Agent were ready for distribution. First however, and within ten days, under an Act of 1806 (46 George III Chapter 100) £1.13s.4d. per cent had to be paid over to the Royal Hospital, Greenwich, as part of their income for the day-to-day running of the Hospital. In addition, and at the same time, a further £3.6s.8d. per cent was sent to increase the Greenwich Chest, out of which the Greenwich Hospital Pensioners were paid (46 George III Chapter 101). After the final 5% deduction by the Prize Agent, the Officers and seamen received their shares, as laid down in the various prize proclamations. The divisions being:–

<table>
<tr><th>CLASS</th><th>RANK</th><th>PRE-1808</th><th>POST-1808</th></tr>
<tr><td>1.</td><td>Flag Officer</td><td>One eighth of Captain's share</td><td>One third of Captain's share</td></tr>
<tr><td>1.</td><td>The Captain or Commander</td><td>Three-eighths share</td><td>One-quarter's share</td></tr>
<tr><td>2.</td><td>Lieutenants, Masters, Physician, Captains of Marines equal shares in</td><td>One-eighth share</td><td>One-eighth share</td></tr>
<tr><td>3.</td><td>Principal Warrant Officers, Masters Mates, Chaplin, Lieutenant of Marines equal shares in</td><td>One-eighth share</td><td>One eighth share</td></tr>
<tr><td>4.</td><td>Midshipmen, Inferior Warrant Officers, Principal Quarter Masters Mates, Master at Arms, Marine Sergeants equal shares in</td><td>One-eighth share</td><td rowspan="2">One-half share</td></tr>
<tr><td>5.</td><td>The remainder of the crew – Seamen, Stewards, Trumpeters, Cooks, Marines, shares in</td><td>One-quarter share</td></tr>
</table>

The distribution of prize money is best explained by a typical example. The following is taken from the accounts of J.S. Hulbert, Prize Agent for the crew of His Majesty's Sloop *Dotterel* in the capture of the American Schooner *Dart*, dated 4 September 1813:–[6]

| | £. s. d. | £. s. d. |
|---|---|---|
| Net amount of proceeds for schooner and her cargo | 8487. 13. 5. | |
| Interest gained on exchequer bills purchased | 61. 13. 9. | 8549. 7. 2. |
| Various agreed expenses listed | | 229. 10. 10. |
| | | 8319. 16. 4. |
| Prize Agent's fees 5% of 8319 16. 4. | | 415. 19. 10. |
| | | 7903. 16. 6. |
| Greenwich Chest £3. 6. 8% of 7903. 16.6. | 263. 9. 2. | |
| Greenwich Hospital £1.13. 4% of 7903. 16. 6. | 131. 14. 7. | 395. 3. 9. |
| | | 7508. 12. 9. |

| | |
|---|---|
| Captain received one-quarter share of 7508. 12. 9. of which one third of the Captain's share went to the Flag Admiral:– Flag Admiral (Class 1) | 625. 14. 4. |
| Captain (Class 1) | 1251. 8. 8. |
| 3 Commissioned Officers equally divide one-eighth share of 7508. 12. 9 (312. 17. 2. each) Class 2 | 938. 11. 6. |
| 5 Warrant Officers equally divide one-eighth share of 7508. 12. 9. (187. 14. 4 each) Class 3 | 938. 11. 6. |

At this stage one-half of the 7508. 12. 9. had been distributed leaving the other half of 3754. 6. 2 to be shared by the remainder of the crew. This was again divided according to quality (i.e. rank) into shares:– (Class 4 and 5)

4½ shares to each Midshipman and First Class Petty Officer
3 shares to each Second Class Petty Officer
1½ shares to each Able and Ordinary Seaman
1 share to each Landsman and Servant
One half-share to each Boy
The number of men in each quality was known making it possible to calculate the grand total of shares required. This total divided into the sum left for distribution gave the equivalent of one share. It was now possible to calculate each individual's share:–

| | |
|---|---|
| 14 First Class Petty Officers at 4½ shares each equals | 63 shares |
| 7 Second Class Petty Officers at 3 shares each equals | 21 shares |
| 51 Able and Ordinary Seamen at 1½ shares equals | 76½ shares |
| 29 Landsmen at 1 share each equals | 29 shares |
| 15 boys at ½ share each equals | 7½ shares |
| Total shares required | 197 |

197 shares divided into the total for distribution of 3754. 6. 2. equals 19. 1. 1. being the value of each single share. Each quality therefore received:–

| | |
|---|---|
| 14 First Class Petty Officers: 85. 14. 9. each | 1200. 6. 6. |
| 7 Second Class Petty Officers: 57. 3. 2. each | 400. 2. 2. |
| 51 Able and Ordinary Seamen: 28. 11. 7. each | 1457. 10. 9. |
| 29 Landsmen: 19. 1. 1. each | 552. 11. 5. |
| 15 Boys: 9. 10. 6. each | 142. 17. 6. |
| Fractions retained by Prize Agent | 18. 3. |
| | £7508. 12. 9. |

It can be seen how the Prize Agent had accounting and legal procedures to negotiate and sometimes travelled to superintend the prize concern when not using sub-agents or correspondents on the spot. In the case of one of the *Fury's* prizes, the *Corroborata,* Isaac Levy travelled up to Berwick-on-Tweed on the express wish of her captain, Lieutenant J.S. Gibson. The *Corroborata* had in fact been beached about ten miles away on Holy Island and was a complete wreck. Levy spent from February to June 1809 in Berwick dealing with the salvage and shipment of the cargo to London. His advertisement lodging the prize accounts in the High Court of Admiralty did not appear in *The London Gazette* until July 1810. The prize and cargo had been sold for £2008 but outgoings were heavy, amounting to £1561. This left just £447 of which Levy's fees were £22.6s.10d. plus all his expenses. The crew of the *Fury* were to fare better with the *Vigilentia* prize, with no wreck or salvage and a valuable cargo of timber. The net proceeds for distribution amounted to £2,612 with Isaac Levy receiving a fee of £154.[7]

Distribution of the prize money to the *Fury's* crew for all their captures was made at Isaac Levy's offices in Commercial Chambers Minories, where he had subsequently moved on 23 August 1810. Recalled every Tuesday and Thursday for three months. In other words, as required by section 75 of the Act for Encouragement of Seamen 1805, applications could be made after 23 August for another three months to the Prize Agent. By section 80 of the same Act, within four months after distribution all unclaimed prize money then had to be sent to the Royal Hospital Greenwich. He also had to send full accounts under oath and the Prize Lists showing what payments had been made. The fine for failure to comply was £100. Seamen could then apply to Greenwich Hospital for their unclaimed prize money up to six years after distribution. They could claim on the grounds that they had not been in England or that they had been left off the Prize Lists by design or accident. A certificate of service had to be produced with a petition, which could result in the Hospital prosecuting the Agent on behalf of the sailor. Otherwise, all unclaimed prize money, together with that belonging to seamen who between the time of capture and distribution had deserted (marked 'R' for run, on the Prize List which information had been taken from the Ship's Master Books) would go to the Greenwich Hospital.

The legislature thus intended that seamen should be notified and should secure their prize money as an incentive to serve in the Royal Navy. This was the theory, but in practice it was a different matter. Albeit, Greenwich Hospital improved their funds from the unclaimed shares and those disqualified through desertion. Between 1807 and 1811, the unclaimed shares were thought to be over £1,000,000, of which, at a modest estimate, it was said one quarter would remain in the Hospital's hands. The Treasurer at Greenwich had to inform the Navy Pay Office of all shares paid by the Prize Agents. This, in turn, was a check on Greenwich for the benefit of the seamen, who could inspect the lists on every week day at the Navy Pay Office, Somerset House.

To make effective Britain's blockade policy, certain goods were legally proscribed as contraband with the right of British warships to search and bring into port all neutrals before a prize court for adjudication. If found to be contraband, it was sold and added to the prize funds for distribution. This type of capture gradually produced the largest source of prize money. Valuable cargo carried in merchantmen were all-important to the Officers and men of the Royal Navy.

Clearly, some Captains saw it more profitable to go chasing after enemy and neutral merchantmen than to seek out the enemy's men-of-war. The authorities realised this temptation to leave station and so came into being "Prize Bounty" or "Head Money" as it was known. Originally, through the Cruisers Act of 1708, £10 was paid for every gun in an enemy ship captured or destroyed. In practice this was a poor inducement, and so was later improved by substituting £5 for every member of the enemy's crew instead of by the gun. A seventy four gun ship would then yield £3,000 instead of £740. Hence the term "Head Money" – a matter of counting "Heads". The Prize Courts were more rigid over Prize Bounty than prize money, the grantees having to be content with what was actually given and no more, being divided in the same proportions as prize money.

"Head Money" was in addition to prize money paid by the Navy Board for captured Spanish and French warships, which were often of superior build to the British. A fair price was paid by the Navy Board, who always received first refusal from the Prize Agent. It was rarely declined, with 83 ships of the line and 450 other captured enemy warships increasing the strength of the British fleet by about 25% during the Napoleonic Wars. Yet paradoxically, it was still more profitable to capture a fully laden merchantman.

The Prize Agent also collected freight money for his clients. Unlike prize money, the carrying of specie was not governed by any statutes, but by ancient usage. Only Flag Officers and Commanders of the warship involved were entitled to a gratuity. Nathan Rothschild paid a half per cent. For instance, he sent £100,000 in gold coin to Viscount Wellington via Lisbon in October, 1812. It went in various consignments, some in foreign coin, in different frigates, one of which was the *Stag*. Captain King of the seventy four gun *Venerable* received £572.10s.0d. freight money from Rothschild's for the delivery of specie from Deal to Walcheren during the expedition to the Scheldt in 1809.[8]

The final financial inducement was the Government Grant made to the participants after every major naval battle. £300,000 was voted for the British Fleet which took part at the Battle of Trafalgar. The Grant and Prize Bounty was paid to the various Prize Agents and distributed in the same way as prize money. In the case of the *Victory*, Captain T.M. Hardy received £2,389.7s.6d. grant and £973 Prize Bounty whilst the seamen and marines received £4.12s.6d. and £1.17s.8½d. respectively.[9]

Setting aside the prospect of promotion for the Commissioned Officers in a naval action, one glaring financial fact emerges: the great gulf between what the Admirals and Captains received compared to the ordinary seamen. For the small *Aurora*, captured by the *Fury*, Isaac Levy advertised in *The London Gazette* for the shares to be paid on 3 December 1811 as £19.10s.8d. to the Captain; £5.9s.10d. Commissioned Officers; £2.3s.9d. Warrant Officers; £1.1s.0d. First Class Petty Officers; 14s.1d. Second Class petty Officers; 7s.0d. Able Seamen; 4s.8d. Landsmen; down to just 2s.4d. for each Boy Seaman.

The main Prize Agents opened accounts for the Officers by virtue of letters of Attorney collecting on behalf of their principals all wages, prize money, prize bounty and other income. Loans were made pending such payments to enable the Officers to purchase their sea-going outfits and subsist. A charge of 5% was made by the Prize Agents. They were in effect bankers for all Lieutenants upwards, dealing with their financial affairs whilst at sea.

The pecuniary advantage for the Prize Agents was with the Commissioned Officers, not the men of lower rank whose prize distributions often amounted to less than a pound. Prize money for the class 3, 4 and 5 men was duly advertised and that more or less was that. The seamen had to seek out what was due to them, as the Prize Agents were not interested. The clamour made by the seamen on recall days was a nuisance, and is best summed up by Thomas Rowlandson's contemporary drawing of Agents pushing seamen out of their offices. One was on crutches, another had lost a leg and a widow was holding a baby in her arms – pushed out and to where?

The seamen turned for assistance to the only link they knew between themselves and those in authority ashore, the tradesmen in the naval towns. As Commissioned Officers had their Prize Agents, so the seamen their Navy Agents. Historically, Naval Agency grew out of the financial transactions between the traders and Royal Navy seamen.

From long usage, traders boarded the warships on pay days only, as the seamen were not allowed ashore for fear of desertion. When the seamens' services were no longer required by the Navy, they were discharged with wage tickets which were later discounted at large profits by traders, publicans and brothel keepers. A pamphlet giving a description of Portsmouth in the early eighteenth century and before the Jews settled in the naval town recorded; *"Our gains from trading are constantly laid out in buying up sailors' tickets whom we make pay thirty or forty per cent discount, besides oblige them to take parcels of our heavy wares, by way of acknowledgement for the favour we show them"*.[10] It was not until an Act of 1792 (32 George II Chapter 33) that the more regular payment of seamen returning from foreign service was implemented. No longer was it necessary for the seaman to await the return home of the different ships on which he had served overseas before being paid. Outstanding wages could now be collected from the Pay Offices at Portsmouth, Plymouth, Chatham, Sheerness and the nearest revenue office to the seaman's home. Therefore, by the start of the Napoleonic Wars, the traffic in wage tickets had been reduced.

It was much simpler for the easy-going seamen not to wait for wage tickets but to accept a small sum for their anticipated wages and prize money by legally signing them over to third parties. Often this was transacted under the influence of drink, much like the crimps pursued their unfortunate victims. Wills were also made in favour of third parties to the detriment of the seamen's families. These practices were stopped by the establishment of the Inspectors Branch of the Navy Pay Office in 1786. From this date all Wills, Warrants of Attorney or Orders for the payment of wages and prize money by seamen and marines had to be attested by the Inspector, which could only be executed on board one of His Majesty's ships or in Hospitals witnessed by the Commanding Officers. Wills could also be executed before the Clerks of the Treasurer of the Navy at Portsmouth, Plymouth, Chatham and Sheerness. Third parties could still benefit under these Wills and Powers of Attorney, provided the correct procedure was followed. But in particular no letter of Attorney was valid unless declared to be revocable. By 1807, after a period of 21 years, the Inspectors Branch had investigated 57,718 Powers of Attorney; 27,763 Wills and 39,941 Petitions or Applications from next of kin.[11]

By a further Act in 1792, (32 George II Chapter 34) Inferior Officers, seamen and marines could grant Orders instead of Powers of Attorney in cases where the wages due and payable to them did not exceed £7. These had to be witnessed by the Commander or Lieutenant on board of the ship where the seaman had served. The Order was then submitted for inspection and stamped for payment at the Navy Pay Office, London. The Navy Agent could legitimately buy such Powers of Attorney and Orders, often in kind and not cash, for the seamen's wages. It is important to note that this Act did not apply to seamen's prize money.

As for the seamen's families, it was not until an Act of 1795 (35 George III Chapter 28) that Petty Officers, seamen and Marines could voluntarily allot part of their wages to the maintenance of their wives, children or mothers. Every Petty Officer could allot one half of his wages; Able Seamen 5d; Ordinary Seamen or Landsmen 4d and Marines 3d per day, which sums were slowly allowed to be improved upon. 29,937 families were being supported by this means in 1801. So came into being the allotment system which, with its variations over the years, was to become so important to the Royal Navy and naval traders of future generations.

Sadly, in a dishonest age the whole system was open to abuse, wills and letters of Attorney were forged, false oaths were taken in order to obtain Probate or Administration, Seamen and next of kin were impersonated and women impersonated wives of seamen to obtain their allotment. Not least, orders to obtain prize money were also forged. In many cases the penalty was death. During the 21 years between 1786 and 1807 of the 40 charges instigated, 12 persons were convicted. Of this number a James Walsh and Joseph Moses had joint warrants issued against them in 1791 for procuring another to take a false oath, but they absconded and were never found. On 15 October 1798, Joel Emanuel and Emanuel Levy were discharged by magistrates for want of evidence after being accused of forging a certificate and letter of Attorney.[12]

A little earlier in, February 1795, Gershon Woolfe, a navy agent and silversmith of The Hard, Portsea, was conveyed to London with some other Jews having been found in possession of a quantity of forged official stamps from various ports.[13] There was also a legal action brought by Peter Williams, late gunner of the *Eurus*, against Judah Jacob, slopseller of Portsmouth, in the Kings Bench Division before Lord Ellenborough and a Special Jury on 11 December 1802, to recover the sum of £282.10s.6d. prize money. The case created a lot of interest being reported in *The Times* and *Portsmouth Telegraph*, with a full report in the *Naval Chronicle*:–

> Opening the case Mr Erskine for Williams the plaintiff, made a number of observations upon the various frauds which were practised

upon careless seamen, more particularly by a number of Jew slopsellers and dealers, who invariably pillaged the poor fellows of almost all they earned by their labour, or acquired by their bravery. He contended the plaintiff had only received from the defendant £27.10s.0d. yet by some trick or other the defendant had obtained receipts of £250 and £204. Erskine then pronounced "The knavish Jew defendant had somehow duped the poor sailor, but he insisted that by the accounts it must be evident those sums had never been paid".

In evidence William Hill, a clerk in the dock-yard at Woolwich proved the signature of a power of attorney dated 28 November 1798. The power of attorney purported to be in consideration of £250 paid by the defendant to the plaintiff, the receipt for which being endorsed on the back. Then a John Lawson stated in April 1800 he had received £282.10s.0d. from the main prize agent for Peter Williams' share of a prize taken by the *Eurus* for a Danish ship in October 1798. Lawson paid the £282.10s.0d over to Judah Jacob, who had a power of Attorney to receive it. another receipt from the plaintiff to the defendant was also produced dated December 1800, by which Williams acknowledged to have received from the defendant £204 in full for his prize money, and acquittance of all demands. John Hector, an attorney, stated he was employed in Michaelmas Term 1800 to recover some money from a person of the name of Cave for Williams, and that he did obtain £67 which he paid by Williams direction to the defendant Jacobs. Williams at the same time telling him he owed Jacobs a great deal more money.

For the defence David Lazarus, a Watchmaker and Silversmith, was next called who said that on the 27 October 1801 he went to see the plaintiff then on board the *Roebuck* lying off Woolwich. Lazarus showed Williams the receipts in question who acknowledged them to be his hand-writing, and told him he did not want to go to law with Jacobs but had been persuaded to do so.

The son of the plaintiff, a lad of fourteen, was also examined, who said, he was present when the warrant of attorney was signed, and that his father received at the time some slops and some money he believed about forty or forty-five shillings, but certainly not such a sum of £250, or he would have seen it.

Mr Garrow made a very able defence, in which he warmly combated the prejudices against Jews, which if followed by juries would lead to the greatest injustice. He called upon the jury to examine attentively all the papers; and say whether they would venture to pronounce them forgeries.

Lord Ellenborough in his summing up observed that though the case consumed much time it was one which deserved great attention.

> The defendant had admitted receiving £282.10s.6d. but he had given notice of a set off amounting to £250 and £204 cash advanced, for which plaintiffs receipts were produced; plus commission £14 and other small items including sums recovered on behalf of one Cave amounting in total to £538.11s.6d. With respect to the power of attorney endorsed for £250 it appeared that it was given in the prospect of the plaintiffs share of prize money. And yet the prize was not then condemned so was it probable that the defendant would advance the plaintiff such a sum upon the bare prospect of being repaid when the prize money should be received; and that the money was actually advanced did not appear from any evidence but the receipt of the defendant. Whether that receipt was fraudulently obtained was for the jury to determine. It was also remarkable that in the receipt for £204 was stated to be in full for the balance of prize money. How could that be? It did not square with the defendants own accounts. The whole of the prize money amounted to £282.10s.6d. Of this £250 had been paid, how then could Jacob's pay at a subsequent period the sum of £204 as a balance between former advances and amount of prize money? If Jacob's accounts were correct then instead of their being a balance due to the plaintiff in April 1800 when he professed to pay £204 as a balance then the plaintiff would have owed money to the defendant.
>
> The Jury withdrew for about half an hour returning a verdict in favour of the plaintiff to his full demand of £282.10s.6d. less the £27 he had admitted to have been paid by Jacob.[14]

More of Judah Jacob later. For David Lazarus, an elder of the Portsmouth Synagogue, a disappointment, knowing the adverse publicity it would bring his community.

By the turn of the nineteenth century, the Jews of Portsmouth had probably grown to about 50 or so families, the majority originating from Germany, some from Holland and a few from other parts of Europe. The early generations born in Portsmouth were now taking an active part in the town and synagogue, some had joined the Royal Navy either as volunteers or pressed men. The prosperity brought about by the Napoleonic Wars and the expansion of the Fleet, the Dockyard and Military Garrison attracted the Jewish dealers and pedlars from London and elsewhere. In 1801 *Mottley's History of Portsmouth* recorded "The Jews having considerable privileges in this town have so far availed themselves of such a favourite opportunity as to occupy houses and shops in the first style of mercantile consequence". They lived mainly in Portsea divided by the long Queen Street extending from the Dockyard to Lion Gate. On the north side of

Queen Street, with its shops, were private houses in Daniel, Cross and Cumberland Streets. The long and confined Frederick Street led to the water's edge and a rope walk. To the south of Queen Street was White's Row, with the synagogue, and several other streets, Union, Bishop and Hanover, leading down to Ordnance Row and The Hard with its embarkation to the ships in reserve. High Street, Portsmouth extended the length of the town with its "George" and "Fountain" Inns, leading to Broad Street and The Point:–

Hail! Place of noise, distraction, fun!
Hail! Point of wide-spread fame!
To every nation fully known,
Which knows the English name!
Here oft in midnight revelry,
The violin and song,
Conjoined with mirth and jollity
Exhilarate the throng.

Here taverns numberless indeed
In long succession rise;
And the gay shops of Israel's seed
Entice the seamen's eyes.

*Portsmouth Point. The well-known etching by T Rowlandson circa 1799. There was never a Moses Levy on the point but the artist obviously knew of the Jewish presence. (National Maritime Museum)*

To George Pinckard, writing in 1795 during a visit to Portsmouth, the town verified everything he had heard about it. It was unpleasant, vulgar and immoral. It was a town of dirty streets and languid dullness, which would burst into life and activity whenever a fleet docked or was about to sail, then fall back into its calm torpor.

Everything changed in wartime. The sleepy streets, where the grass grew to a height, were full of the sound of boots. The rent of houses and apartments rose considerably. They even had their own war price and their peace price, both distinctly fixed. The price of food rose, of beer in the taverns, of stables, indeed, of every item and service.

It was the general poverty of the town which struck Pinckard as leading people, especially the women, into immorality. He wrote:

> 'In some quarters Portsmouth is not so filthy, and crowded, but crowded with a class of low and abandoned beings, who seem to have declared open war against every habit of common decency and decorum. The riotous, drunken and immoral scenes of this place, perhaps, exceed all others. Commonly gross obscenity and intoxication preserve enough of diffidence to seek the concealment of night . . . but here hordes of profligate females are seen reeling in drunkenness, or plying upon the streets in open day with a broad immodesty which puts the great orb of noon to the blush.

*Portsmouth Point. The Long Room. Scenes of all night drinking and debauchery. (from an engraving by G. Cruikshank). National Maritime Museum.*

To form to yourself an idea of these lanquishing nymphs, these lovely fighting ornaments of the fair sex, imagine a something of more than Amazonian stature, having a crimson countenance and warlike features . . . then add to her sides a pair of brawny arms, fit to encounter a Colossus, and set upon two ankles like the fixed supporters of a gate.

Afterwards, by way of apparel, put upon her a loose flying cap, a man's black hat, a torn neckerchief, stone rings on her fingers, and a dirty white, or tawdy flowered gown, with a short apron, and a pink petticoat; and thus will you have something like the figure of a 'Portsmouth Poll'.

Callous to every sense of shame, these daring objects reel about the streets, lie in wait at the corners, or, like the devouring Kite, hover over every landing place, eager to pounce upon their prey; and each unhappy tar, who has the misfortune to fall under their talons, has no hope of escape till plucked of every feather. The instant he sets foot on dry land he is embraced by the neck, hugged round the waist, or hooked in the arm by one or more of these tender Dulcineas; and thus poor Jack, with pockets full of prize money, or rich with the wages of a long and dangerous cruise, is, instantly dragged (though, it must be confessed, not always against his consent) to a bangio, or some filthy pot-house where he is kept drinking, smoking, singing, dancing, swearing, and rioting, amidst one continual scene of debauchery, all day and all night, and all night and all day, until his every farthing is gone. He is then left to sleep till he is sober, and awakes, to return, pennyless, to his ship . . .'

Then before the Fleet sailed:-

'The general crowd and confusion was increased by multitudes pressing into and overflowing the shops; people running against or tumbling over each other upon the streets; loud disputes and quarrelling; the sadness of parting; greetings of friends unexpectedly met and as suddenly about to separate; sailors quitting their trolls; drunkards reeling; boatmen wrangling; boats overloaded or upset; the tide beating in heavy spray upon the shore; persons running and hurrying in every direction for something new or something forgot; some cursing the boatmen for not pushing off with more speed, and others beseeching and imploring them to stop a minute longer . . .'

Yet in the Portsmouth Synagogue all was exemplary – decorum reigned supreme. No one was allowed to talk, or to leave his seat, and the children sat under the charge of their Hebrew teacher. Even outside the synagogue, religious control was kept over the members by a system of fines. In 1807 the minute book recorded one of £4.17s.6d. on a congregant for going two or three times on Sabbath aboard a man-of-war, whilst in 1810 the same fine was imposed for boarding a boat and publicly breaking the Sabbath.

Inspired by traditional Jewish attitudes towards charity the Portsmouth Hebrew community, from an annual income never exceeding £700 during the early nineteenth century, granted pensions to widows of former paid officials. The Hebrew Benevolent Society, founded in 1804, looked after the Jewish poor, so that they were not a burden on the rates. There was an active Ladies' Guild subscribing £14.0s.0d. for the purchase of a Sepher Torah and coverings, two candlesticks, curtain, and an embroidered mantle for use on Sabbath. During Passover in 1813 eighty-two ladies gave a crimson velvet curtain for the Ark. The entry in the minute book concluding "All these ladies contributed to the best of their ability according to the blessing wherewith the Lord blessed them". Between 1814 and 1833 contributions of £86.0s.0d. were made by the community in aid of poor Jews in Palestine. Then, as announced in the contemporary *Naval Chronicle* of 1812 under a heading "Good Samaritans":[15]

> At a Meeting of the Congregate body of Jews, at their Vestry Room White's Row, Portsea on 29 January 1812:-
>
> Resolved 1. That the distress of the widows, orphans and suffering relatives of the crew of His Majesty's Ships *St George, Hero and Defence* lately lost, be of a serious consideration. 2 Resolved therefore that a sum of thirty pounds be voted towards their relief. 3 That the said sum be paid into the hands of the Worshipful the Mayor of the Borough of Portsmouth.
>
> Signed L. Lazarus. President.
> G. Levi. Elder.

The money had in fact been raised by a tax on each seat rental of the synagogue. A few months before the Committee Room at Lloyd's Coffee House had written:- [16]

> 13th Sept 1811
>
> Gentlemen – I am directed by the Committee to acknowledge the receipt of £20. 3s. 6d. being the amount of a Collection made at the Synagogue at Portsmouth towards the relief of the British Prisoners in France.

The Committee also direct me to return their thanks to you and the other Contributors for the humane attention paid to the suffering of our unfortunate Countrymen Prisoners in France – I have the honour to be, Gentlemen, your obedient servant

For Thos. Ferguson *secretary*

Messrs Barnard and Lazarus *elders.*

In difficult circumstances the community had tried to keep to the high standards set in the Portsmouth Synagogue Seals. One dating from 1747 made by the celebrated engraver Elias Levi showed a lion for strength; scales for justice and fair dealing; and a slab and crown for the ten commandments, signifying "With all thy strength do right and above all keep the torah". But all the Jews of the naval towns were stigmatized in some naval literature and by certain historians in a cruel and humiliating manner, becoming the objects of prejudiced stereotyping.

The mistaken belief that only Jewish traders in large numbers were grasping extortionists came about more from the fact that the seamen looked upon all tradesmen as petty bankers, giving them the nickname "Jews". From their travels the seamen had found Jews dealing in money, hence the nickname. Much in the same way as a chaplain was called a "Mufti" or "Padre", nicknames picked up in the Levant and Spanish Ports. Mathew Baker (The Old Sailor) in *Jem Bunt,* a tale of the land and ocean, relates:-

'The Point was also famous for the dwellings of those kind-hearted children of Israel, who supplied the wants of the seamen at the moderate interest of about five hundred per cent. Talk of your London Jews – keen as they are – a Point Jew would have cheated a dozen of them in an hour. The sea-line of this neck of land was prepared as a fortification, and its semicircular arches used to remind me of an enormous mouse-trap'.

Naval ballads also depicted the Jews unfavourably. *The Sailors Garland or The Ticket Buyers Lamentation* was an example showing on the one hand a trio of impecunious tars and on the other the usurers who had given advances at an exhorbitant discount and now seem likely to be shorn of their ill-gotten gains:-

A usurer in Lothbury, a Jew of high renown
Hearing the sailors would be paid strait hosted up to town;
All in his hall the clerks amazed and agents, frightened sore,
'Adieu', cried out 'forty per cent, Adieu for evermore . . .

Yet Isaac Levy was the only Jewish Prize Agent.
Mathew Baker again in his book of Greenwich Hospital:-

> 'Ha, ha, ha! chuckled Sam Halliards; Haugh, haugh, haugh! roared Tom Pipes, on seeing an ancient Israelite with his shop i.e. his petit bijoux box, on his back, advancing from the college towards the Prize Pay Office. They remeber'd old times, when these rats practised their arts, and nibbled up the hard-earned substance of all jolly tars, under the moderate advantage of shent per shent.'[17]

Against this background of preconceived opinions, the true correlation between the Jewish traders and seamen was reluctantly admitted by the author of *A Naval Sketch Book* in 1834. 'It is one of the many odd traits which make up Jack's character that though his dislike of Moses exceeds all the bounds of decorum it is to him he confides his grievances and by his advice most of his actions are governed'.[18]

Seaman 1806

# CHAPTER 8

## Jack! How Much for Your Prize Money?

*When in Plymouth Sound our ship appeared.*
*By all the others she was cheered;*
*And visitors from noon till night*
*Flocked off, to ask about the fight;*
*And girls and Jews came off to try*
*For Sailors Love and Agency.*

(The Adventures of Johnny Newcome in the Navy – A.J. Burton 1818)

The seamen were a class apart, out of touch with ordinary life ashore, and so disposed to take their own life as it was. Uninhibited, predictable, suspicious of land-lubbers they were intensely loyal to each other. As for prize money, to the seamen it was a lottery, some gambling the prospect away against their grog. If the prize money was won the seaman's cheery, philosophic nature led him not to expect very much. 'I had £70 coming to me when I belonged to the *Le Loire* and it was so long heaving in sight, I gave it up for a bad job and was obligated at last to sell it to a Jew on The Hard for a suit of mustering rigging, a thundering old turnip, and a bladder of gin.'[1]

It had of course suited the Treasury to defer payment of the seamen's wages and, as prize money was an inducement, the authorities were not that concerned if the seamen actually received their shares or not. The legal framework for payment of prize money was provided for. How distribution worked in practice the Admiralty felt was not their concern. As long as the recruiting posters loudly proclaimed opportunities to earn prize money, helping keep the fleet manned was all that really mattered. Reforms were slowly enacted for the prompter and more regular payment of seamens' wages, but with the distribution of prize money it was even more protracted.

Admiral Sir John Jervis, Earl of St Vincent, had remarked in August, 1797: 'You may rest assured the civil branch of the Navy is rotten to the core.' When St Vincent became first Lord of the Admiralty in February, 1801, he entered into reform with zeal. The intention was good, but the result brought conflict between the Admiralty and Navy Boards. Little was gained, particularly as it was wartime.

It was in 1803 that St Vincent achieved a Royal Commission to inquire into the irregularities, frauds and abuses practised in the naval departments and in the business of Prize Agency. The fourteen reports between May, 1803, and June, 1806, exposed incredible corruption and fraud. Accounts for both cash and stores had remained uncleared for years. The financial manipulations in the dockyards for private gain were a disgrace.

The Fourth Report concerned Prize Agency, its enquiry had been conducted between March and July, 1803. Vice-Admiral Lord Viscount Nelson in his examination before the Commissioners remarked:

> Prize money does not get into the pockets of the captors so expeditiously as it ought, and in many instances, not at all; great sums of money having been lost by the failure of agents.

Complaints were levelled mainly against the delays and in particular the shady practices of some overseas Prize Agents. Captain Alexander Cochrane in his evidence stated, *'Agents abroad are in general more attentive to their private interest than to that of their constituents; and I have not the least doubt that in many cases where appeals are entered it is done by the contrivance of the agents in order that they may keep the proceeds in their own hands.'* It was not until the major consolidating and reforming Act of 1805 (45 George III Chapter 72) that anything was done, including establishing the bond for £5,000 that each Prize Agent had to enter into. The new Act did not go far enough. There were too many fingers of consequence in the prize money pie.

The report was illuminating in its findings relating to the Prize Agents and Navy Agents. It was as if the latter were taking the blame for the failings of the system:- *'The mischief in the present system of prize agency, of which we had had proof in the course of the inquiry, fall under the description of abuses and irregularities, rather than fraud. We find no reason for subjecting to general censure of involving in general dispute, the persons concerned in this business . . .'*

Then as to the agents for seamen the findings continued . . . *'But we are satisfied that there exists a set of men, who take advantage of the unsuspicious character of the indiscretion and extravagance which prevail among seamen; and who, in time of war, earn a scandalous livelihood, by supplying them with liquor, clothes, and trifling sums, and getting from them wills and powers of attorney for their prize money . . . It should be remembered that many of the frauds by which they suffer do not so much arise in the business of prize agency, as in the tricks and impositions of persons not engaged in that business, and consequently not within the scope of our enquiry.'*

The Prize Agents were virtually exonerated, very few cared about the seamen. However, the commissioners did recommend: *'Sailors are often cheated by way of anticipation of all their future prize money, leads to suggest, that possibly this might in some measure be prevented, if it were enacted that no transfer by deed, will, or otherwise by agreement for a transfer of any share of prize money executed or made before notification of distribution of the prize, upon any consideration whatever, should be valid. By such a provision; the sailor would at last have an opportunity of knowing the amount of what he gives in exchange for what he receives.'* The recommendation was partially enacted in 1805.

A general Prize Office was also proposed, but never evoked, mainly because of the cost. Admiral Sir Charles Pole, M.P., Chairman of the Enquiry, observed as the 1805 Bill was going through parliament, that the seamen would *'continue to employ the mean characters by whose villany they constantly suffer,'* and knew there would be prolonged delays in examining documents at the Inspectors Branch of the Navy Pay Office regarding their prize money. Even the clerks in the Navy Pay Office went slowly about their work in order that they could transact their own private agency direct with the seamen, much against the regulations of 1796 forbidding such activities.

As noted, the main Prize Agents, a preponderance being based in London, acted for the Officers and crew under a single Power of Attorney. They dealt with the prize concern from capture, acquittal or condemnation in the High Court of Admiralty, final adjudication and sale, to distribution, with unclaimed and forfeited shares paid over to the Royal Hospital Greenwich. They distributed the shares to the Commissioned Officers, probably keeping their accounts of income and disbursements, giving loans, and acting in the form of bankers. But what about the seamen, how did they obtain their prize money, if at all?

Under a statute of 1793 subsequently consolidated in the Act of 1805 (section 73 George III Chapter 7) Prize Agents were bound to advertise details of the distribution of prize money in *The London Gazette.* In particular, they had to state when and where the prize money was to be paid. Where possible, Prize Agents preferred to await the arrival of the capturing warship at one of the Out Ports: Portsmouth, Plymouth, Chatham or Sheerness, in order to make the first payment on board. This was to prevent demands from the holders of authorities which may have been revoked. More often than not, distribution would be made at the Prize Agent's office. Sometimes another agent or intermediary would deal with the whole distribution at the port.

A James Poulain of 3, Salters Hall Court, Cannon Street, London, was one of these specialist Agents. He was paid ½% commission by the main Prize Agents, with a charge of £10.10s.0d for payments made aboard ship at Plymouth and £5.5s.0d at Portsmouth. Unclaimed shares could be applied for on certain days up to three years from the first distribution. These were known as recalls.

The method of payment was unsatisfactory. Frequently, the seamen had been moved aboard another ship when the distribution was made and could be on foreign service for many years. True, they could apply to the main Prize Agent after, or Greenwich Hospital on their return, but that meant journeys at an expense often more than the prize money itself. The seamen just did not have the aptitude to pursue what was due to them. How much easier then for the seamen to give powers and orders to the tradesmen they knew to collect their prize money as agents. It was on these authorities that the Prize Agent paid the prize money to third parties. Stamp duty of fifteen shillings was charged, which could be more than the prize money due, so the seamen gave general instead of special powers for each separate capture with which they were involved.

It was these general powers for all captures which gave rise to confusion and abuse. Upwards of 200 seamen could join in one Power of Attorney for receipt of their prize money. Then each individual seaman could claim shares under different prize distributions. In the meantime, the so-called Agents, who were often publicans and brothel-keepers, did nothing in the execution of their powers, whilst itinerant hawkers and slopsellers received the money and disappeared. Seamen continued to be impersonated and defrauded. The general public only really became aware of these practices as a result of the 1803 enquiry, and it was recognised by the authorities in 1805. By section 92 of 45 George III Chapter 72, all future Powers of Attorney relating to prize money (as distinct from wages) had to be executed on a statutory form. The order had now to specify the name of the particular prize and the name of the capturing ship. It had to include a full description of the seaman giving the order and be signed by the Captain and one other Commissioned Officer of the ship in which the seaman was serving when the capture was made. Or if discharged from the service, then the order with the same description had to be witnessed by the Minister and Churchwardens of the Parish in which the former seaman resided. (see illustration)

An easier way for the seamen to benefit from prize monies was to volunteer for service in a privateer. Discipline was less severe than the Royal Navy, with the crews virtually free from impressment. As a general rule, the privateersman drew no regular wage and looked solely to his share of prize money. But it was far greater in proportion to what he could possibly receive in the Royal Navy. Sailing under a letter of marque granted by the High Court of Admiralty, the armed merchantman would go on a cruise with the sole object of enriching the owners and ships' companies at the expense of their country's enemies. The prospect of prize money was the great attraction. It was alloted according to a definite scale agreed beforehand. Under the Prize Proclamation, all prizes taken by ships and vessels having commissions of letters of marque could be sold and disposed of by the merchants, owners, and others, for their own use and benefit, after final adjudication in the High court of Admiralty, not before. Often more than one merchant shared ownership of a privateer. They dealt with the distribution of prize money after deducting expenses which included fitting out, victuals, ammunition and repairs. In effect, there was no Prize Agent as such, no Admiralty bureaucracy, no deductions from the seamen's prize money going to Greenwich Hospital, and fewer delays. But the seamen still needed a Navy Agent or, to be more precise, a Privateersman's Agent. Fortunately, some of the papers of one of these Agents is to be found in the City of Liverpool Record Office, that of Joseph Joseph, a Jewish silversmith and jeweller.

Liverpool, where many of the privateers sailed from, saw its first Jews forming a community about 1750. Superseded by further settlers some thirty years later, 'the immigrants then consisted of persons engaged in vending clothes, watches and jewellery to the seafaring population . . . These early Jewish inhabitants were mostly Germans and Poles, and, with their characteristic zeal for the religious observance of their forefathers, they soon assembled for religious worship (in the year 1780), in a small house in Turton Court near the Custom House. In 1789, a house was acquired and converted to congregational requirements in Frederick Street.

Joseph Joseph settled in Liverpool about 1796 as a goldsmith and jeweller. He lived at 71, Cable Street and had a shop at 1, Pool Lane

(South Castle Street). Later he appears at 36, and subsequently at 37, Castle Street as a silversmith and bill discounter within the business district among about 100 Jews living in the area at that time. With the expansion of trade in Liverpool, the small synagogue in Frederick Street became too small for the increased number of Jews arriving from other parts of the country. The foundation stone of the Seel Street Synagogue was laid on 1 April, 1806. The site was obtained free of cost from the Corporation on a perpetual lease, provided the building to be erected remained a house of worship. Soon after the consecration of the building on 16 September 1808 the Seel Street Synagogue was the first in Anglo-Jewry in which sermons in English were preached. The congregation stayed until 1874 when it moved to the still existing and imposing Princes Road Synagogue.

*Pool Lane, Liverpool circa 1798. The upper portion looking down to the shipping in the old dock. Joseph Joseph, Privateers Agent, had his shop at No. 1 Pool Lane. (from a drawing by W. G. Hardman).*

As in the naval ports, Joseph Joseph was not a seamens' Agent when he first settled in Liverpool but a silversmith and jeweller, gravitating in effect to become a money lender to the seamen of the port. This had the full blessing of the Liverpool Merchants and Ship Owners, enabling them to pay their crews on how successful or otherwise they may have been in capturing prizes.

The privateersmen received an advance on commissioning which went some way towards their needs, but nowhere near far enough, relying mainly on the prize money they might hope to receive in the future. So on signing on, the privateersmen turned to the tradesmen for ready cash, particularly to the slopsellers, jewellers and silversmiths. During 1793, at the start of the Napoleonic Wars, 120 privateers were fitted out in Liverpool, manned by 8,754 seamen. The Jewish slopsellers, including Josiah Lemon and Ralph Samuel, together with the silversmiths and jewellers, and in particular the "Josephs" in Castle Street and Pool Lane, were about to have a renewed demand for their goods. There was no need, at this time, for the small Liverpool Jewish community to consider continuing their migrations to Dublin or perhaps America. The slopsellers and jewellers now became Privateers' Agents as their co-religionists in the naval towns were Navy Agents. They were primarily tradesmen becoming agents to the seamen as a means of increasing their incomes.

Joseph Joseph would give loans at 5% interest against the security of a deed whereby the seaman handed over all his rights to wages and prize money to Joseph. The same document gave Joseph a Power of Attorney to act as the seaman's legal representative with the seaman receiving any balances after Joseph had deducted the original loan plus interest and expenses. Seamens' wills would be drawn up in the same way in favour of Joseph who acted as executor. Alternatively, Joseph would purchase the seaman's share of prize money outright by agreement. Copies of all the documents would be lodged with the seaman's shipowning employers for eventual payment of wages and prize money to Joseph. For the shipowners, this offered a means of settling aggregate sums to the seamens' Agents instead of having to deal with a lot of small amounts with all the attendant clamour from the seamen.

It can be seen from the examples to follow how Joseph dealt with the seamen in various ways. He granted loans against their future prize money; purchased their shares in prize money outright and acted as their Agent by collecting prize money and wages. He would pay their outgoings and accounting costs for a fee with interest charged on the money lent. Alternatively, he would sell silverware and jewellery against their accounts for prize money and wages held. Sometimes there was a combination of these various dealings, always secured by means of powers of Attorney, assignments and indentures in Joseph's favour drawn up by his solicitor, Richard Rowlinson, of 3, Mathew Court, Liverpool.

In October, 1803, the Liverpool privateer *Ainsley* (Captain Every), brought into the Mersey one of the most valuable prizes of the Napoleonic

Wars. It was a large French Indiaman, the *L'Amiable Lucile,* bound from the Isle of France to Bordeaux when captured, and valued at £80,000. For this capture the surgeon of the *Ainsley,* William Homer, gave Joseph a power of Attorney dated 1 March, 1804, to acquire his eight shares in the prize. Homer had in fact already received a loan of £40 from Joseph. Other crew men of the *Ainsley* were also given loans by Joseph. For example, Edward Bennet, an ordinary seaman, obtained a loan of £14 with interest and reasonable charges against his single share, sealed in the presence of the Mayor, on 15 December, 1803. There was hardly time for the *L'Amiable Lucile* to be condemned in the High Court of Admiralty, and sold off with her cargo. Here lay the risk to Joseph. He immediately informed the owners of the *Ainsley,* Messrs Fisher Brocklebank and Company, of the assignment and that all prize money should be paid to him sending a copy of the indenture entered into. This procedure of informing the owners was always followed.

Joseph was careful to see he obtained receipts duly witnessed and signed:-

> Received this twentieth day of September 1805 from Mr Jos. Joseph the sum of six pounds, sixteen shillings and 6d being the purchase money paid by him to me for all my rights title and interest of in and to my share or shares of Prize Money which I'm or may be entitled to as Gunner on Board the ship *Crescent* of Liverpool, Captain Leigh Lyon, for the capture of the *Charles Carter* and *Hunter* on her late voyage. I say Received the sum in full of all claims and demands whatsoever.
>
> Witness William Brooks
> his X mark

When a large sum was granted by Joseph, as in the case of James Wingett of Liverpool, he would arrange for the seaman's will to be made out in his favour and witnessed by his solicitor. In this case, Wingett was aboard the London ship *Endeavour* which had captured two Spanish merchant vessels, for which he received £40 from Joseph.

One of the most famous Liverpool privateers of the period was the *Kitty.* Joseph dealt with some of the prize money for her crew in 1804 when capturing the *Le Jeune Amelia.* The prize was later to become the *Kitty's Amelia* serving as the last Liverpool slaver. Joseph expended £334 in purchasing the right to the prize money of 11 members of the *Kitty's* crew, ranging from £12 for a boy's share to £95 for that of a second mate.

MR GEORGE LYON
(account made up to 24 February 1806)

Dr.

| Date | | Item | £ | s | d |
|---|---|---|---|---|---|
| 1803 | | | | | |
| October | 31 | To Watch | 12 | 19 | 6 |
| | | Gold Chain | 5 | 15 | - |
| | | Gold Seal | 2 | 17 | 6 |
| | | Gold Key, pin, 2 silver pencil cases | 3 | 7 | 6 |
| | | Gold chain, ring pocket book, strong silver set of tea-spoons | 3 | 6 | 6 |
| | | Silk umbrella, razors and knife | 3 | 5 | 6 |
| | | To cash advanced | 20 | - | - |
| | | Interest to this day (on £20 from 31 Oct. 1803 to 24 February 1806 @ 5%) | 2 | 6 | 3 |
| | | Cost of Assignment, copy notices and Power of Attorney with stamp duty | 5 | 5 | - |
| 1804 | | | | | |
| March 29 | | To Cash advanced | 1 | - | - |
| | | Interest to this day (on £1 from 29 March 1804 to 24 February 1806 @ 5%) | | 1 | 10 |
| April | 4 | To Cash advanced | 2 | - | - |
| | | Interest to this day (on £2 from 4 April 1804 to 24 February 1806 @ 5%) | | 3 | 8 |
| 1805 | | | | | |
| August | 24 | To 1 pair candle-sticks | | 10 | 6 |
| | | 1 pair silver tongs | | 14 | 6 |
| | | 1 set knives and forks and tea caddie | | 12 | 6 |
| | | 1 pair steel snuffers and stand | | 5 | 6 |
| 1806 | | | | | |
| February | 9 | Watch glass, gilt chain | | 7 | 6 |
| | | To seal and key | | | |
| | | Commission on receiving £72 and attendance @ 5% | 3 | 12 | - |
| | 24 | To Balance owing | 7 | 5 | - |
| | | | 75 | 15 | 9 |

Cr.

| Date | | Item | £ | s | d |
|---|---|---|---|---|---|
| 1804 | | | | | |
| July | 11 | By: received on 4 shares @ £10 per share | 40 | - | - |
| | | Interest paid from 11 July 1804 to 24 February 1806 on £40 @ 5% | 3 | 4 | 9 |
| 1805 | | | | | |
| April | 15 | By: received on 4 shares @ £3 per share | 12 | - | - |
| | | Interest paid from 15 April 1805 to 24 February 1806 on £12 @ 5% | | 11 | - |
| 1806 | | | | | |
| January | 12 | By: draft due 12 March 1806 | 20 | - | - |
| | | | 75 | 15 | 9 |

On another occasion Joseph advanced £40 to William Rochester, prize master of the *William,* for the Dutch ship *Nord Holland* in September 1803. Three years later Rochester had to write regarding the balance of his prize money, apparently amounting to £20, not minding whether Joseph sent him cash or a single cased gold watch. There was some delay in payment, but nothing compared with two other seamen of the same ship and prize who did not receive the balance of their money amounting to £4.7s.0d. until May 1816. Joseph Joseph had died about the year 1811, and the money was paid by his widow.

It is possible in the case of Rochester that Joseph was holding an account for him as it transpired he had one with another seaman, George Lyon, also of the *William,* for the *Nord Holland.*

Some interesting points come out of this statement of account. Before receiving any prize money, Joseph allowed Lyon goods to the value of £31.11s.6d. from his shop and advanced £23 in cash between 31 October 1803 and 4 April 1804. Joseph would have first taken a Power of Attorney in his favour as security. He would have seen Lyon's numbered certificate from the owners of the *William,* S. McDowal and Co., to verify that he was aboard the vessel at the time of capturing the *Nord Holland* and the number of shares he was entitled to on the Articles. Joseph could, at the same time, with the co-operation of the owners, gauge how much the prize may eventually produce. With as much information as possible, and his own knowledge, Joseph should have been able to tell how much each share was worth and act accordingly. The prize money was distributed in two parts, one of £40 in July, 1804, for the cargo, and a second of £12 for the ship itself the following April. Joseph then had money in hand for his customer and sold him some further goods, leaving a balance in Lyon's favour of £7.10s.6d. Joseph charged 5% on the actual prize money received and for collecting a draft on Lyon's behalf.

Joseph Joseph could hardly be accused of gross over-charging and even paid interest at 5% on the monies he was holding on Lyon's behalf. In fact, this was the same percentage he charged before the account came into credit. In effect Joseph earned £3.12s.0d. commission less £1.4s.0d. net interest paid but, and this is important, he sold goods to the value of £34.2s.0d. He was therefore more interested in selling his gold and silverware – hardly the grasping seaman's Agent of popular belief, unless of course the goods were foisted on Lyon at enhanced prices. As a general practice, Joseph tended to hold the money to credit until he was asked for it, in the hope of being able to sell more goods.

Other members of the Joseph family lived in Castle Street and Pool

Lane. They were also jewellers as was a Morris Mozley, whilst the slopsellers included Josiah Lemon of South Dock and Ralph Samuel of Bridge Street. No doubt this trading with the seafarers indirectly helped to finance the building of the Seel Street Synagogue in 1807.[2]

*Know all Men by these presents that we Isaac Myers No 60 St Mary Street, Portsmouth George Blake of Ordnance Row Portsea and James Dunstan of High Street Portsmouth. . . . . . are jointly and severally held and firmly bound to our Sovereign Lord George the Third of the United Kingdom of Great Britain and Ireland. King Defender of the faith & in the penal sum of Two Hundred Pounds of lawful British Money to be paid to our said Lord the King, his Heirs or Successor. For which payment to be well and faithfully made we bind ourselves and each of us by himself for and in the whole our and each of our Heirs, Executors and Administrators and every of them firmly by these presents Sealed with our Seals. Dated the twenty eighth day of September in the Forty ninth Year of the Reign of our said Lord the King and in the Year of our Lord. One thousand Eight hundred and Nine.*

*Whereas the above bounden Isaac Myers. . . . . . hath applied to the Treasurer of His Majesty's Navy for Licence to act as one Agent for the receipt of Wages Pay, Prize Money, Bounty Money and other allowances of Money for and in respect of the Services of Petty Officers and Seamen, non commifsioned Officers of Marines and Marines and other Persons done on board His Majesty's Ships, pursuant to the directions of an Act of Parliament made and pafsed in the 49th Year of the Reign of His Majesty King George third intituled. 'An Act to explain and amend an Act made in the forty fifth Year of His present Majesty for the Encouragement of Seamen and for the better and more effectually Manning His Majesty's Navy during the present War and for the further Encouragement of Seaman and for the better and more effectually providing for the Interest of the Royal Hospital for Seamen at Greenwich and the Royal Hospital for Soldiers at Chelsea and to extend the provision of the said Act to cases arising in consequence of Hostilities commenced since the pafsing of the said Act; which Licence the said Treasurer hath agreed to grant on this present Bond being entered into with such Condition as hereinafter mentioned.*

*Now the Condition of the above written Obligation is such that if the above bounden Isaac Myers . . . . do and shall from time to time and at all times demean himself properly as such Agent as aforesaid and also duly account to all Persons for whom or for whos use any Wages, Pay, Prize Money, Bounty Money or other Allowance of Money shall have come to his hands for or on Account or in respect of the Services of any Petty Officer or Seamen non-commifsioned Officer of Marines or Marine or of any non commissioned Officer or Soldier of the Army or other Person done on board any of His Majesty's Ships or on any conjunct Expedition of the Navy and Army as in the said Act is exprefsed and pay over the same Wages, Pay, Prize Money, Bounty Money or other Allowances of Money or so much thereof as shall appear to be justly due and owing on every such Account without Fraud or Delay then the above written Obligation to be void or else to be and remain in full force and Virtue.*

*Sealed and Delivered*
*being first duly Stampt by*
*the above Bounden*

Isaac Myers — Myers
George Blake — G Blake
James Dunstan — James Dunstan

*in the presence of*

of Mr Taylor, clerk to the
Treasurer of the Navy – Portsmouth.

*Example of Bond to act as a Licenced Navy Agent as submitted to the Treasurer of the Navy by Isaac Myers, dated 28 September 1809. (reproduced by permission of the PRO ADM 49-72).*

As the seamen were better off as privateersmen, so were their Agents. They were not governed by any of the Acts for 'The Encouragement of Seamen . . .' which referred only to seamen serving in the Royal Navy. One glaring example in Joseph Joseph's accounts was that he charged 5% commission, whereas agents for Royal Navy seamen could obtain only 2½% as laid down in the Act of 1758 (section 30 George II Chapter 10). However, as the Privateersmens' Agent lent money before any prizes were captured and condemned, it can be said that he was entitled to a higher return for the greater risk he took than the Navy Agent, as will become apparent.

Subject to legal restraints the Navy Agents for seamen acted in a similar way as Joseph Joseph the Privateer's Agent, but the process by which the seamen serving in the Royal Navy received their prize money was different.

It was not until 1809 that the first attempts were instigated to regulate the activities of the Navy Agents. These were the result of efforts made on the seamen's behalf by the Right Honourable George Rose M.P., who had become Treasurer of the Navy in April, 1807, and remained so for over ten years. Against opposition, Rose had a genuine concern for the seamen, although he knew it was impossible to stamp out the abuses entirely. As long as there was no proper Prize Office established, the seamen would go on giving powers to third parties in return for small sums advanced.

On 20 June, 1809 another Act was passed 'For the encouragement of Seamen' - (49 George III Chapter 123), which was mainly concerned with Greenwich Hospital and Prize condemnations. However, at the end under Section 35 *'And whereas it has frequently happened that frauds have been practised upon Petty Officers and Seamen in the Navy and on Non Commissioned Officers of Marines, and Marines, by Persons of bad Character who have been authorized by them to receive Wages, Pay, Prize Money and Bounty Money . . .'*

At last the abuses had been officially recognised with a system of licensing devised whereby before any person (except a close relative of a seaman) could act as an Agent for receiving Wages, Prize and Bounty Monies for Petty Officers, Non-commissioned Officers, Seamen and Marines, that person first had to take out a licence from the Treasurer of the Navy. A bond had to be given with two sureties, the applicant undertaking to act properly and account for all monies coming into the Agent's hands, or face a penalty of £200. The licence continued in force for three years and was renewable by application. The Treasurer of the Navy had wide powers to determine the licence at any time without a right of appeal. A fine of £50 was imposed if any agent changed his place of conducting agency business without notifying the Treasurer within fourteen days. It had already been laid down under Section 30 of the 1758 Act that no agent could charge more than sixpence in the pound for receiving seamen's wages and prize money.

Applications to get on the Register of Licensed Agents had to be made to the Navy Pay Office, Somerset House, London. Those applicants resident in Portsmouth, Plymouth, Chatham or Sheerness applied to the Chief Clerk of the Navy Pay Office at each of these ports. They had to do this before 1 September 1809. Advertisements were placed in the local papers and *The London Gazette* informing Agents for seamen and others that in future they had to be licensed. George Rose attended personally at the ports to grant licences visiting Portsmouth on 17 August. Enquiries were made as to the applicant's fitness, but the two sureties for the bond did not have to be any clearly defined persons, except of course that they were liable for £200 on default of the Agent. In the case of Isaac Myers and Henry Hart of 60 Saint Mary Street, Portsmouth, their sureties were non-Jews Valentine Rumley an Army and Naval Clothier of 88 Broad Street, Portsmouth, and George Blake a Cabinet Maker of 24 Ordnance Row, Portsmouth.[3] The bond was executed at the Navy Pay Offices. Attested by one of the assistants or by Attorneys, where the applicants resided more than six miles from the Pay Offices.

George Rose originally turned down an application from Isaac Myers's father-in-law, Judah Jacob of 6 Ordnance Row, Portsea, who was found guilty of not paying over prize money due to a seaman in the court case of 1802. There had also been further complaints against Jacob. The opinion of the Admiralty Law Officers was sought as Jacob made representations that without a licence he was ruined. Because of the English legal tradition of enactments not being able to be enforced retrospectively, Judah Jacob obtained his licence. 'I do this with great reluctance, and I shall feel it my duty to leave a minute of the proceeding in this Office', wrote Rose on 16 September 1809[4]

Towards the end of 1809 the first list was printed of persons licensed by the Treasury of His Majesty's Navy to receive the wages and prize money of Petty Officers, Seamen and Marines.[5] Of 174 names listed about 66 were Jews with something like one half of the agency business in the naval ports carried out by them. The Navy Agents were first and foremost traders. They became licensed by Statute to improve their businesses, by continuing to accept deferred payment for their goods and loans granted to seamen. The majority of the Jewish Agents were slopsellers.

Slops, that is ready-made clothing as was worn by the seamen, did not conform to any set pattern. Over the years, the exigencies of life at sea, custom and the purser combined to mould the sailors' dress into something resembling a uniform. In Plymouth, about ten years after the setting up of the Navy Slop Office in 1756, Abraham Joseph of Barbican Quay became an accredited wholesale slop contractor. He supplied the dockyard stores from which the seamens' clothing was sent to the individual ship pursers. Not only was the clothing supplied by the purser of poor quality and ill-fitting, but the cost was deducted from a man's meagre pay unless he was obviously destitute on first joining. Here was an exceptional opportunity for small retail slopsellers. They had to be willing to defer payment and to satisfy the strong individual tastes of the seamen. Dress regulations were vague, which resulted in a uniform without uniformity. So at the time of Trafalgar, we find Jewish slopsellers supplying the seamen with their shore-going rig-outs: wide-brimmed turned-up straw, leather, or tarred canvas hats having gaudy ribbons with ships' names painted on: checked or striped shirts; black or coloured kerchief loosely tied around the neck, a short blue jacket with bright buttons and white piping; flowing blue or white striped trousers; white stockings and black shoes with square metal buckles.

*Seamen ashore about the time of the Battle of Trafalgar. From a watercolour by J. Jellicoe. As so often in these scenes the Jewish pedlar is included (at far left). The mens clothing would have been supplied by the Slopsellers "A uniform without uniformity".*

The seamen were attracted by the colourful rig-outs the slopsellers had on offer, as graphically recounted in *'Ben Brace. The Last of Nelson's Agamemnons.'* Although fiction, it is true to the period in atmosphere and typical of naval literature of the time:-

> *'So I left Betsy, who was a cloth or two in the wind and sailing a little by the head, with the rest; and away I steered to Moses. He was at home, or someone so cursedly like him, that I should not have known one from the other; but all Jews are alike. The shark knew me, for many's the time I had taken a jacket from his kit when he came on board, and knowing how sharp these fellows are to catch a seaman I thought I would let him bite at the bait well before I hooked him, so said I 'Moses, here we are; all alive, and with plenty of prizes' – To be sure that was rather more smoke than reality.*
> *'My Gosh! yes, say's Moses. "How much wosh you take for your prize money?*
> *There's a nibble! thought I, this fellow would swallow bait, hook, line, and all . . . 'How much, Moses? Why, how much do you think I ought to get?'*
> *'Five pounds' says Moses.*
> *'Five devils' says I; 'More like fifty, and that would hardly be enough for all the work we have had.'*
> *'It's a sight of money, Mr Toprail' said Moses, 'Fifty pounds: it vill be long times before it is pay, ay?'*
> *'Yes' said I, 'So long that a man might die before he got it. What's the price of his new turn out here?'*
> *'Oh, it's very sheap, Mr Toprail, very sheap, just three pounds. You can take it Mr Toprail, upon the security of your prize money. If you make me your agent, I can let you have many things: as you say, you may be dead and buried before the money is paid. I'll give you twenty pounds and this suit of clothes for your share. You are an able-seaman, I know.'*
> *'Then you are wrong, my jolly friend Moses, for I'm captain of the fore-top.'*
> *'Petty Officer's ruling' said Moses, 'Fifty pounds! quite impossible. I'll give you thirty-three now, this morning in one hour, and that's more worth to you, than fifty, four years from this time.'*
> *'Thirty, and the suit of rigging complete: white ducks, blue*

*jacket, black tie, white stocking, long-quartered shoes, new hat with Royal Sovreign marked on the ribbon. That, or go. Give us your hand upon it. I dare say you will get more than half back in traps . . .'*

The author, Captain Frederick Chamier, could well have been referring to the well-known Jewish slopsellers Abraham and Lewis Moses of Broad Street, Portsmouth, who, to give an actual example, went aboard the sloop *Bonne Citoyenne* on 9 March 1811, to take prize orders from about half her crew for the capture of *La Furieuse*:-

WILLIAMS PRINTER. 131 QUEEN STREET, PORTSEA (OPPOSITE BISHOP STREET)

*'TAKE NOTICE. That no Prize Money can be received, under this Order, except by an Agent duly licensed, in conformity to the Act of Parliament, of the Forty-Ninth year of King George the Third, or by the Wife, one of the Parents, or Children of the Granter, and that every Offence against the said Provision of the above recited Act, is punishable as a Misdemeanour'*

Spithead on board H M Ship *Bonne Citoyenne* 9 DAY OF March 1811 AT SEVEN DAYS SIGHT PAY TO Messrs A and L Moses, OR ORDER, THE AMOUNT OF MY SHARE OF PRIZE OR BOUNTY MONEY, FOR THE CAPTURE OF *La Furieuse*
WHEN SERVING ON BOARD HIS MAJESTY'S SHIP OR VESSEL THE *Bonne Citoyenne* IN QUALITY OF Carpenters Mate.

*To the Agent for the said capture; or*
*the proper Officers of Greenwich Hospital.*

*(Signed) Thomas Eastwood*

---

THESE ARE TO CERTIFY, THAT WE HAVE EXAMINED THE SAID Thomas Eastwood WHO SIGNED THE ABOVE ORDER IN OUR PRESENCE, AND FROM THE DOCUMENTS HE HAS SHEWN US, VIZ.

AND HIS ANSWERS TO OUR QUESTIONS WE HAVE REASON TO BELIEVE HE WAS SERVING ON BOARD THE SAID SHIP AT THE TIME OF MAKING THE CAPTURES ABOVE SPECIFIED; HE SAYS HE WAS BORN AT Knottingley IN THE COUNTY OF Yorkshire THAT HE IS 28 YEARS OF AGE, OF A fair COMPLEXION, blue EYES AND light HAIR.

GIVEN UNDER OUR HANDS.
Thomas Linsen. Lieut Commanding Officer.
Thomas P. Hobbs. Purser.

Almost two years previously the British Sloop *Bonne Citoyenne* of twenty guns had, after clever handling, out-fought the heavier *Le Furieuse,* forcing the Frenchman to strike her colours, the prize being brought into Halifax. On the *Bonne Citoyenne's* return to home waters, Abraham and Lewis Moses knew the *Le Furieuse* had already been advertised as condemned in the High Court of Admiralty, so could proceed in accepting the Prize Orders which were immediately lodged with the *Bonne Citoyenne's* Prize Agent George Hulbert of 42 Saint Mary Street, Portsmouth. Hulbert made the distribution five months later on 26 August 1811:-

Paid to Messrs A and L Moses for capture of *Le Furieuse* by *Bonne Citoyenne*

| | | | | |
|---|---|---|---|---|
| 6 | Senior Petty Officers at £155.17s.0d.each | £935. | 2s. | 0d. |
| 5 | Petty Officers at £103.18s.0d.each | £519. | 10s. | 0d. |
| 28 | Able Seamen at £51.19s.0d. each | £1454. | 12s. | 0d. |
| 8 | Landsmen at £34.12s.6d. each | £277. | 0s. | 0d. |
| 13 | Boys at £17.6s.0d. each | £224. | 18s. | 0d. |
| 60 | | £3411. | 2s. | 0d. |

The Moses brothers would have deducted the statutory 2½% commission of £85.5s.0d. for collecting the prize money, and in addition recouped any money lent with interest, and/or slops sold.

The Prize Order given by Carpenter's Mate Thomas Eastwood to Abraham and Lewis Moses was of a seaman still serving in the Royal Navy. However those seamen discharged before receiving their prize payments could still give Prize Orders to a third party. Before the Moses brothers transacted their prize business aboard *HMS Bonne Citoyenne,* some of the crew had already been discharged. One, able seaman John Harrison, had returned north and given a Prize Order for his share in the capture of the *Le Furieuse* to Levy Samuel of High Street, Sunderland a Jeweller and Licensed Navy Agent on 28 February, 1811. Samuel collected £51.19s.0d. deducted £1.6s.0d. commission together with any goods sold and/or money lent before accounting to John Harrison. (It is interesting to note that this statutory form was printed by Levy Alexander, the old established printers of Whitechapel Road, London. The first Hebrew prayer book printed in England was produced in 1770 by Levy's father, Alexander Alexander.)

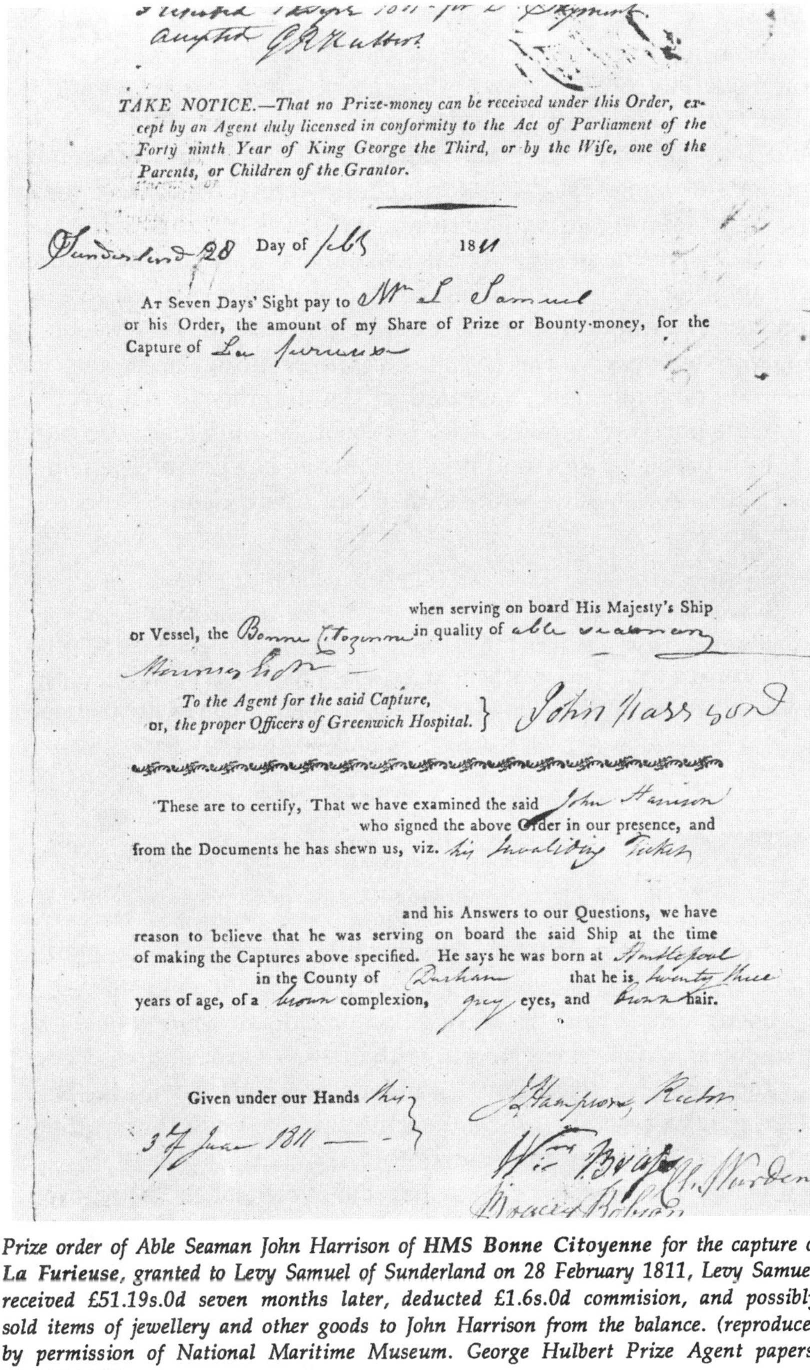

TAKE NOTICE.—*That no Prize-money can be received under this Order, except by an Agent duly licensed in conformity to the Act of Parliament of the Forty ninth Year of King George the Third, or by the Wife, one of the Parents, or Children of the Grantor.*

Sunderland 28 Day of Feb 1811

At Seven Days' Sight pay to Mr L Samuel or his Order, the amount of my Share of Prize or Bounty-money, for the Capture of La Furieuse

when serving on board His Majesty's Ship or Vessel, the Bonne Citoyenne in quality of able seaman

*To the Agent for the said Capture, or, the proper Officers of Greenwich Hospital.* } John Harrison

These are to certify, That we have examined the said John Harrison who signed the above Order in our presence, and from the Documents he has shewn us, viz. his Invaliding Ticket

and his Answers to our Questions, we have reason to believe that he was serving on board the said Ship at the time of making the Captures above specified. He says he was born at Hartlepool in the County of Durham that he is twenty three years of age, of a brown complexion, grey eyes, and brown hair.

Given under our Hands this 3 June 1811

*Prize order of Able Seaman John Harrison of HMS **Bonne Citoyenne** for the capture of **La Furieuse**, granted to Levy Samuel of Sunderland on 28 February 1811, Levy Samuel received £51.19s.0d seven months later, deducted £1.6s.0d commision, and possibly sold items of jewellery and other goods to John Harrison from the balance. (reproduced by permission of National Maritime Museum. George Hulbert Prize Agent papers Hul/41/AB).*

Living and working in the naval towns gave the traders an advantage in knowing warship movements. Some traders let their surplus residential accommodation solely to naval officers in return for permission to trade aboard the warships at the exclusion of their competitors. Captains would then generally only allow one of the larger and better known slopsellers to board their ships to trade in return for Prize Orders, so avoiding clamour and indiscipline. The hawkers and petty traders boarded on pay days only. Local newpapers were another source of information for the traders giving arrivals and sailings of those ships in harbour or at anchor off-shore. Most important for the Navy Agents were the advertisements in *The London Gazette* detailing prize payments, sales and condemnations, repeated in the monthly *Steel's Navy Lists*. Among the port communities word was soon heard of any prize captures made by a particular ship and prize payments. Lewis Moses, again of 94 Broad Street, Portsmouth, wrote to the Prize Agent George Hulbert on 27 March 1814:-

> Dear Sir,
>
> I have taken the liberty to bring the list of men belonging to the *Sophie* that have advanced in clothing they have all signed it and it is witnessed by the 1st Lieutenant and Clerk. I have also made out a list which you will find enclosed. I have been told by one of her Officers that you intend to pay her tomorrow, if so you will have the goodness to let me know.
>
> I am
> Dear Sir
> Your obedient and humble Servant
> L. MOSES.

Apparently the whole crew bought slops from Lewis Moses amounting to £1090. A typical example was a Peter Hunter who for £14 received 1 fine suit, 4 linen shirts, 2 pairs of worsted hose, 2 pairs of white shoes, 1 box of handkerchiefs, 2 Guernsey frocks, with 1 duck frock and trousers. The Moses brothers also acted for Alexander Simmonds, bosun of the same eighteen gun brig sloop *HMS Sophie* collecting £191.8s.7d. from the Prize Agent George Hulbert on Simmonds's behalf.[6]

It was for the warrant ranks that the Agents held accounts. One example concerned Robert Tinnion who in August 1810 was second master of the brig *Firm* and employed Judah Jacob as his Navy Agent. Mrs Tinnion had made an unfounded complaint against Jacob after his accounts were looked over by William Taylor of the Portsmouth Navy Pay Office. In fact, Robert Tinnion was quite satisfied with Jacob on the recommendation of Lieutenant Little Commander of the *Firm*, and had known Jacob for seven years. He had found him a satisfactory agent in every way.

*An imaginary frolic from "The English Spy of 1825" depicting, the boatswain's mate of HMS Leander on learning he has just been left a fortune by his uncle. The scene is set in Broad Street Point, Portsmouth with King James' Gate on the left. In the centre at No. 94 is the Slopshop of Abraham and Lewis Moses. Caricatures of two Jews appear in front of the shop. (National Maritime Museum)*

The account of Judah Jacob with Robert Tinnion has many similarities with that of Joseph Joseph, the Liverpool Privateer's Agent. Money was lent at an interest of 5%, the 2½% commisision barely covering Jacob's trouble for dealing with the account. But, as with Joseph, goods were sold, this time slops amounting to £2.15s.6d. So Jacob was able to increase his turnover by acting as Tinnion's agent. The logs of Tinnion were written up by Jacob, who dealt with much of the Warrant Officer's financial affairs whilst at sea. Often the Navy Agents went even further, giving friendly advice. Jacob wrote to Tinnion's commanding officer, Lieutenant John Little, on 19 May 1811:-[7]

> Dear Sir,
>
> Your polite favour under date of the 12th inst. I duly received and beg to observe, that whatever you stand in need of by your drawing *on me* shall be duly honoured – a second payment of your Prize Money is advertized and is now paid – and *your* portion is nigh £900 – have not yet received but don't know exactly – you have now acted with propriety towards your sisters and I shall take care if *you* deem it advisable to send over to you my clerk and see your money paid in your hands as soon as I receive it – and that you may use your own discretion in placing it in those hands you deem proper. Pray let me know by the return if I shall send over the person to pay into your own hands.

## ACCOUNT OF R. TINNION AND JUDAH JACOB

| | | | £ | s | d |
|---|---|---|---|---|---|
| 1808 | | | | | |
| Nov | 17 | 2 Log Books | | 7 | - |
| | 25 | Cash advanced | 2 | - | - |
| 1809 | | | - | - | - |
| Jan | 4 | Cash advanced | 2 | - | - |
| | | Black silk hand-kerchief | | 8 | 6 |
| | 15 | Blue cotton hand-kerchief | | 3 | 6 |
| | | 3 pair fine worsted hose | | 12 | - |
| | | 2 pair mitts | | 4 | 6 |
| | | Spring braces | | 5 | 6 |
| | | Cash advanced | 1 | - | - |
| | | Fine blue pantaloon trousers | 1 | 19 | - |
| | 17 | For writing 2 logs and journals | 3 | 3 | - |
| | 18 | Power of Attorney | 1 | - | 6 |
| | | Penknife | | 2 | 6 |
| | 19 | Postage of Journals | | 5 | 6 |
| | | Cash advanced | 2 | - | - |
| | | Waterage at sundry times on your business | | 9 | - |
| | | My draft on Messrs Ladbroke & Co | - | - | - |
| | | in favour of Mrs Martha Gallot | 20 | - | - |
| | | Stamp1/6: 2 Logs 7/- 2 bottles ink 3/- | | 11 | 6 |
| | 20 | Pens | | 5 | 6 |
| March | 19 | Postage | | | 8 |
| April | 25 | Cash Mrs Tinnion | 1 | - | - |
| August | 27 | Postage of Certificate for endorsement | | 2 | 4 |
| | | Paid fees and passing your account | - | - | - |
| | | from 28 Aug 1808 to 27 Aug 1809 | 1 | 5 | - |
| | | Cash to Mrs Tinnion | 2 | - | - |
| | 29 | Postage | | | 7 |
| | | Commission on £73.2.0 amount of | - | - | - |
| | | wages received | 1 | 16 | 6 |
| 1810 | | | - | - | - |
| Jan | 8 | Cash to Mrs Tinnion | 15 | - | - |
| | | Enquiry in London to find out what In goods came from Liverpool | | 7 | - |
| | | | 58 | 9 | 7 |

| | | | £ | s | d |
|---|---|---|---|---|---|
| 1810 | | FORWARD | 58 | 9 | 7 |
| | | Paid Portsmouth carrier and porter for goods from Liverpool | 2 | 6 | 9 |
| June | 18 | Rent at £12.12.0 per annum | 1 | 11 | 6 |
| | | Interest on £25 cash advanced for 3 months and upwards before any money was received for you | | 7 | - |
| | | Bill to E. Collis at Guernsey | 5 | - | - |
| Aug | 6 | Receipt stamp | | 1 | - |
| | | Paid Mr Tinnion | 5 | 7 | - |
| | | BALANCE | 73 | 2 | 10 |

| | £ | s | d |
|---|---|---|---|
| Amount of wages received as by letter of advise from Philpot and Greenland Navy Agent of 33, St Swithens Lane London: Pay 28 August 1808 to 28 August 1809 | 68 | 8 | 9 |
| Compensation | 12 | 7 | 8 |
| | 80 | 16 | 5 |
| Navy Deductions | 3 | 7 | 4 |
| | 77 | 9 | 1 |
| Property Tax | 4 | 7 | - |
| | 73 | 2 | 1 |

*Author's Note:*
*There is an item error of ninepence in the original account manuscript.*

Take your measure *round your head with a bit* of string and forward it to *me* in a letter and I will send your *hat* by *packet* or any other articles or necessories you may *want* – I was truly astonished to find by your letter you was left pennyless that out of all the money your Uncle received for you you are not sixpence the better however this shall be a good lesson for you how careful you must *act* with your next pay. Your bill for £10 shall be duly honoured the expence of sending over to you will not be very much out of such a sum of money – and there is a *likelihood* of being another payment – Your Uncle told me he would send your sister's some money but he has not done it and they have received no more than what you gave them Drafts for. I hope you will bear in mind my conduct towards you of taking a friendly part and giving you that advice for your and sister's *benefit hereafter* as I well know your *Uncle* has had all your property – what astonishes me – he gives you an *infamous character* to the Public in *General* dont imagine I exert myself so much for my interest, for the small commission is of no *great concern to me* but conceive I am justified in my giving that advice to you and your Sisters being Orphans – I hope you wont omit writing by return of Post to *me* all the particulars

I remain.

J. JACOB.

Mrs Jacob joins me in respects to you, and both our respects to Mrs Little –

It can be seen how the established Navy Agents, acting for the senior warrant officers and in this case a Lieutenant in command of a small gun-brig would employ clerks and take a personal interest in their customers. Even the Agents acting for the seamen would put themselves out. John Taylor, a Liverpool seaman serving in the Royal Navy, gave Joseph Joseph of Liverpool a Power of Attorney on 12 March 1804 to collect unpaid wages due six years previously whilst an able seaman aboard *HMS Colossus* for just a short period from 4 February to 22 May 1798. Joseph wrote to the Navy Pay Office London stating he had Taylor's certificate of service. The Pay Office tried to delay, 'You must give an account of what ship he belonged to after his discharge from the *Colossus* otherwise his wages cannot be received.' Undeterred Joseph communicated with John Hunt of Drury Lane, London, Prize Agent for George Murray then Captain of the *Colossus*, who reported back, 'John Taylor discharged from *HMS Colossus* at Lisbon through the medium of Commissioner Coffin. Put on board the *Tartar* Transport Captain Gouch at Lisbon for England.' Whether the Navy Pay Office eventually paid is unknown, but it does show how the Admiralty delayed payment, forcing the seamen to approach the Navy Agents who in turn made every effort on their behalf.[8]

To return to the procedure in the payment of prize money. As soon as the Navy Agent received Prize Orders, notification would immediately be lodged with the main Prize Agent who held the Distribution Lists. They in turn would keep separate accounts for each of the Navy Agents informing them of the monies held to their account four or five days before the prize payments for distribution were advertised, sending statements once a year or on request. The Navy Agents would then draw money at their own convenience. The co-operation of the Prize Agents was imperative to the Navy Agents. Moses Solomon, anxiously writing to George Hulbert of 42 Saint Mary Street, Portsmouth, was even prepared to give up his 2½% agency commission:-[9]

47 James Street, Plymouth Dock
26 October 1813

Sir,

Pardon the liberty of my addressing you, but having made a considerable advance to the Nova Scotia's Officers and Men, nearly the whole of them having employed me I therefore request the favour of your informing me when the money will be paid and what it is a man. As it is usual of allowing 2½ per cent on all monies received I therefore have no objections of allowing you the same if you'll be kind enough to let me have an answer as early as possible will oblige.

Sir, Your most obedient, humble servant
M. SOLOMON

Notwithstanding this letter the prize agents did not deduct a further commission on distribution before paying the Navy Agents. However where a Prize Agent was dealing with a large number of prize payments an intermediate agent was instructed to deal with Recall Disbribution Lists, that is for prize money unclaimed. One of these intermediate agents, James Poulain of Salters Hall Court, Cannon Street, London, charged the Prize Agents 2½% for the lowest qualities (Boys, Landsmen, Ordinary and Able Seamen) and 1¼% for the Petty Officers. In effect the seamen paid yet again. But with Poulain dealing with 600 Recall Distribution Lists in 1804 the system demanded this intermediate agent.[10]

The Distribution Lists drawn up by the Prize Agents would be ruled in six columns. The first contained the names of the persons entitled to shares arranged in classes according to rank; the second showed the quality (i.e. rating) of the persons entitled; the third, the amount of the respective shares; the fourth, the time of the shares being paid; the fifth was alloted to the signature of the party receiving; and the final column for the name of the witness attesting the receipt.

Up to about 1803 Agents, Attornies, and other persons representing the seamen would be allowed to look through the Prize Distribution Lists and to sign their names in the fifth column as Attornies for as many claimants as they thought proper on recall days, receiving the money a few days later. This practice obviously laid itself open to fraud with many disputes. Subsequently the main Prize Agents altered the system and insisted that their clerks or recall agents compared the claimants' authorities with the actual Distribution Lists to see they were bona fide before payment. From 1805 procedures operating the recall lists were better regularised as Prize Orders had in future to be on a statutory form under section 92 of 45 George III Chapter 72.

The Navy Agents were kept busy with accounts, correspondence, attending distribution prize payments often aboard ship, and travelling up to London from the naval ports to visit the main Prize Agents, particularly to examine previous Recall Distribution Lists. Their cheapest mode of travel was by means of vans similar to stage coaches but much larger and clumsier. They travelled from Portsmouth at £1.1s.0d. inside and 12s.6d., or sometimes as cheap as 6s.6d., outside. The journey took as long as sixteen hours and was much favoured by the seamen. In 1805 the service improved with the 'Nelson' from the 'Blue Posts Inn' completing the journey from Portsmouth in nine hours. The Navy Agents for their return journey from London caught the 'Royal Mail' from the 'Angel' by St Clements, The Strand at quarter past seven in the evening and arrived at the 'George' Portsmouth at ten minutes past six the following morning.[11]

The main complaints against the Navy Agents were of forcing slops at enhanced prices on the seamen in lieu of prize money. Then of retaining unclaimed shares for long periods, which once paid to the Navy Agents, could not be recouped by Greenwich Hospital. Finally they faced accusations of not paying prize money in full after deducting more than sixpence in the pound commission.

The reputable traders acting as Navy Agents benefited under the system of licensing as the workings of the 1809 Act gradually curtailed the malpractices of the undesirables which had given all the traders a bad name.

Withdrawal of licences was announced in *The London Gazette* and local papers. Often on the grounds of the Agent 'Changing his place of abode without giving notice in order to evade just claims of seamen', or 'For abusing the trust reposed in him'. Sometimes in the announcements would appear 'Withdrawn on the ground of his having refused to account for moneys received for seamen unless they would agree to take part in slops'; and not accounting to seamen for moneys received with details given. For instance *The London Gazette* of 29 July 1816:-

LICENCE NOT BE RENEWED

*Navy Pay Office London*

> Notice is hereby given, that by virtue of the authority vested in me by the Act of Parliament, forty-ninth of George the Third, Chap 123, I do hereby forbid the renewal of the licence granted to David Israel of No. 72 Broad Street Portsmouth, on the 14th December 1812 to act as an agent in the receipt of pay, wages, prize and bounty-money, for and in respect of the service of petty-officers, seamen, and others serving in any of His Majesty's ships; the renewal of which licence is forbidden by me, on the ground of his not having duly accounted to John De Wit or Dewett, late of His Majesty's Ship *Terpsichore* for prize-money received by him.
>
> GEORGE ROSE

Another announcement in *The London Gazette* of 20 January 1816 listed twenty-seven agents whose licences had been withdrawn, eleven being Jews.

Sir George Rose and his officers in the Prize Offices let it be known that well founded complaints against Agents were investigated and compelled them to put matters right. If justified, the Prize Office would sue the Agents and their sureties upon their bonds. Rose did not abuse his power in any way. On the contrary he was scrupulously fair in his dealings with the Agents no matter their religious beliefs.

There was the occasion in 1810 when the licences of Isaac Myers and Henry Hart of 60 St. Mary Street, Portsmouth were withdrawn and subsequently reinstated. It had been proved that these Agents had pressed slops on seamen of *HMS Elizabeth* in part payment of prize money due to them. Additionally, a local slopseller, a Mr Hoad, had shown that the seamen had been overcharged. A pair of shoes were charged at 9s.6d. instead of 8s.6d., a pair of blue trousers 15s.0d. instead of 12s.6d. and a black silk handkerchief 7s.0d. instead of a market price of 6s.0d. A commission of 5% instead of 2½% had also been charged. George Rose received a deputation from Mrs Myers and her mother at the Navy Pay Office, Somerset House, London asking him to reconsider the matter as not only their families would be financially ruined, but they would also find it impossible to meet their commitments on sums already received for a considerable number of seamen. The meeting took place on 16 August. Four days later Henry Hart wrote to Rose offering to voluntarily increase his bond from £200 to £500, with Isaac Myers making the same offer. Both agents tendered a sincere apology and promised to put matters right to the seamen of the *Elizabeth*. Yet Rose had already suggested the increased bond for legal ratification to the Admiralty solicitors the day after meeting Mrs Myers. There was no legal objection, and the licences were reinstated on the increased bonds. This was just one example of Sir George Rose acting in a considerate manner towards the Agents he desired to control.[12]

Early in 1812 Rose helped Isaac Myers again and Lewis Moses of Portsmouth by informing them he had requested the captain of *HMS Mermaid* to allow them on board to collect money due which they probably would not have otherwise known about. It transpired that one of the *Mermaid's* seamen had already been discharged so Rose took the trouble of asking Greenwich Hospital to let Isaac Myers know when the seaman's pension became payable, so he could claim on it for money owing. In September 1813 when Sir George Rose learnt that the seamen of *HMS Cornwall* had revoked powers of Attorney given to Barrow Moss of Plymouth Dock for their prize money in the capture of Java, Rose arranged for Moss to put in a claim for slops. Provided that they were fairly priced, Rose saw to it Moss would be paid.[13]

Sir George Rose co-operated with the Agents where possible because he soon realised they performed a useful function by giving small advances to the seamen. If the Navy Agents failed, or the Admiralty stopped them functioning without replacing the Agents with an easy method for the seamen to obtain their prize money, then there would have been trouble throughout the Fleet. Yet on occasions the Navy Agents were defrauded by the seamen.

Up to 1819 there was nothing to stop a seaman revoking Prize Orders as happened to Barrow Moss. Some seamen gave orders for prize money to a second Agent after having received money in advance from a former Agent. Another hazard for the Agent was where his client deserted – Elias Moss of Chatham wrote to the Principal Officers and Commissioners of HM Navy London on 1 April 1814:-[14]

> Honourable Sirs,
>
> I beg leave to acquaint you that being Agent for William Cliff late Boatswain of His Majesty's Sloop Ranger I advanced him upwards of one hundred pounds during the time of that brig being in the Baltic, since which the Ranger arrived at Sheerness, and in the month of January last the said William Cliff had leave of absence and came to

Chatham but did not afterwards join his Brig or has he ever since been heard of, I have at very great expense, and trouble in getting his accounts papers which I have accomplished and obtained a certificate for his pay between 19 March 1812 and 8 August 1813 but refused payment on account of his being marked R on the books of the Ranger.

I therefore humbly beg leave for payment to your Honours that I shall be a very considerable loser unless you will be so good to take my case into consideration and be pleased to order the R to be taken off that I may be enabled to receive the pay due to the said William Cliff.

I have the honour to be with great respect Honourable Sirs

Your most obedient and very humble servant

E MOSS – Navy Agent.

Elias Moss never recovered his £100. On a seaman deserting he forfeited his pay, and any prize money went to Greenwich Hospital.

By the end of the Napoleonic Wars in 1815 the number of Navy Agents for Petty Officers, seamen and marines had grown to nearly 400 of which about one third were Jews. The Naval towns of Portsmouth, Plymouth and Chatham had experienced an economic boom, not only with vastly increased activity in the dockyards, but in the trading activity with the Fleet and soldiers of the garrisons. Some of the Jewish traders had prospered.

*Chatham circa 1830. (from an engraving by E. Findon).*

# CHAPTER 9

## THE PORT COMMUNITIES

*Join a community, by which alone your work can be made universal and eternal in its results*

Nineteen Letters. S.R. Hirsch 1836

There is one fond Royal Navy lower deck connection with Anglo-Jewry – Rum! It was at Penzance in 1804 that a perpetual warden of the local Hebrew congregation, Lemon Hart, established his spirit merchant firm. He later entered into partnership with his brother Jacob on 11 October 1806 with a capital of £5000. The firm moved to London in 1811 to become purveyors of rum to the Royal Navy, supplying 100,000 gallons in 1849.[1] Henry Ralph was the only Navy Agent in Penzance licensed in 1809 and moved to Plymouth Dock in 1814 to become a leading member of the 'Dock Minyan'.

The Plymouth Jews took to the minor trades. In Frankfurt Place was Elizabeth Emanuel, a straw hat manufacturer, and Esther Cohen a pen and quill manufacturer and sealing wax maker at 101, James Street. Her husband Mark Cohen was a Navy Agent. Whilst in the Barbican the keeper of the Navy Tavern, Southside Street, was Benjamin Hart, 'One of the principal inns much resorted to by masters of merchant ships' where was also found the Navy Post Office. For the little time the traders had for amusement there were two theatres, one in George Street, Plymouth, the other in Cumberland Street, Plymouth Dock. However, it seemed that both; 'Have nothing to recommend them in outward appearance, nor are the accommodations within such as to attract a polished audience.' The social event of the year for the Plymouth Hebrew congregation was the annual supper of the Machinath Nefesh – a friendly benefit society – held in December with geese, turkey, beef and veal often on the menu.

Of the Jewish traders in Plymouth Dock most were silversmiths also acting as Navy Agents but there was also Israel Abel, a grocer in Queen

Street and Samuel Benjamin, an umbrella maker in Fore Street. They came together and formed their own Minyan Room in a private house (a quorum of ten males for the commencement of a service) but a breakaway congregation from Plymouth Synagogue was avoided by mutual consent, with Chief Rabbi Hirschell approving a co-ordinating agreement in 1815.

Between 1806 and 1815 just one of the main London Prize Agents, Ommaney and Druce of 22 Norfolk Street, Strand, had sent about £4250 prize money on accounts held for six Jewish Navy Agents in Plymouth.[2]

Joseph Joseph of The Barbican, Plymouth received £2258.10s.6d. over the nine year period on Prize Orders held for various seamen. He was the eldest son of Abraham Joseph, who it will be remembered, was slopman and Agent to Prince William Henry (later King William IV). Like his father, Joseph Joseph was a prominent member of the Plymouth Synagogue practising, as a qualified Mohel, the religious rite of circumcision. Licensed as a Navy Agent in 1809 with his books examined by Sir George Rose in April 1814, the licence was revoked in July 1817 on Joseph Joseph's bankruptcy.[3] He still continued as a slopseller with his eldest son Henry. On the recommendation of King William IV Henry later took up a legal post in Gibraltar to become the colony's Recorder and lay leader of the Gibraltar Hebrew congregation. A daughter of Abraham Joseph had married Nathan Joseph (not a relation) who was also a Navy Agent. Nathan Joseph had arrived in England at Gravesend in 1784 from Ranspork in Bohemia at the age of 18, first settling in Dartmouth as a jeweller and moving to Broad Street, Plymouth in 1802. He received close on £600 from Ommaney and Druce. Licensed in 1809 Nathan Joseph became one of the longest serving Navy Agents, carrying on until 1845. Then there was Samuel Hart of 33 Market Street, Plymouth Dock (becoming Devonport in 1824), who had received £826.11s.6d. on account of Prize Orders, but his licence was subsequently revoked in January 1817 for not paying prize money of £2.6s.6d. to a seaman of *HMS Jalouse*. He was a silversmith, watchmaker and miniature painter. His son Solomon Hart, the portrait painter and later Librarian to the Royal Academy, wrote in his memoirs, '*I was born at Plymouth in 1806. At the age of 7 I was sent to school in Exeter. There I only remained for a short time. I returned to Plymouth in 1814. Being an Israelite I was debarred from entering Dr Bidlake's Grammar which was restricted to Churchmen. I was placed with the Rev. Israel Worsley a Unitarian Minister for 5 years. He was an excellent man.*'

The Grammar School was in Catherine Street close to the synagogue where the Jewish community acted in their traditional religious customs much in the same way as that of Portsmouth. As the war at sea shifted from the North Sea increasingly to the Atlantic, Mediterranean and West Indies, so Plymouth became more important as a naval base with economic activity and expansion, particularly for Plymouth Dock lying about 2 miles across the Sound from Plymouth. Travellers of the period spoke of, *'The dirty town of Plymouth and the bustling streets of Plymouth Dock'* whilst an inhabitant of Dock recorded in 1804 *'In peace trade stagnates, numerous houses and shops are shut up, the streets are silent, inactivity and despondency pervade everyone. War instantly changes the scene. The frequent equipment and return of fleets occasions the expenditure of vast sums of money; and multitudes of speculators resort hither from all parts of the kingdom to participate in the spoils. Shops of every description open in endless succession: not a house is vacant: clamour and bustle pervade the streets.'* Plymouth Dock was generally clean but unlit. It was at North Corner and Mutton Cove that the tradesmen would hire the watermen to take them out to the men-of-war lying in the Hamoaze. At these quays were the *'Sailors and their lasses, drunk and sober, bearded Jews, salesmen and soldiers.'*

*Entrance to the Dockyard, Fore Street, Plymouth Dock circa 1828. (from an engraving by W. Le Petit).*

A thirty foot high dockyard wall ran between North Corner and Mutton Cove to the south, with the entrance from Fore Street. Just inside was the Chapel behind the master porter's house where the Military Guard Office stood, and over it the Navy Pay Office with a captain's guard of marines on duty. Buildings for the commissioners followed with a basin sufficient for a seventy four gun ship bounded on each side by jetty heads. Adjoining one of the jetties was a 480 feet long Rigging House with Sail Loft, and further store-houses completing a quadrangle. To the south a ship camber, boat-house, and blacksmith's shop about 210 feet square, with the Anchor-Wharf in front. Northwards of the ships the Mast-House and Pond in which a large number of masts and yards were kept in water to prevent their cracking from exposure to the sun. Here was the Bunker's Hill with its watch-house and battery of nine-pounders. Close by were futher rope-houses and the Mould Loft where the different parts of ships to be built were laid down according to plans sent by the Navy Board. Further docks completed the yard with close to North Jetty a house where pitch was kept continually boiling.

As the dockyard grew so did the population of Plymouth Dock, from 23,787 in 1801 to 30,083 in 1811, greater than Plymouth which in the latter year had 21,156 people. In the Dockyard itself 1100 were employed in 1800 rising every year. Until 1814 the 'Yardies' were paid quarterly in arrears with new workmen waiting six months for their first wages, obliging the local tradesmen to give considerable credit. With the approach of pay day a careful watch was kept for the frigate bringing the money by sea from London, so avoiding the highwaymen. As the frigate sailed up the Hamoaze the bells of Plymouth Dock rang out, with dancing in the streets. The traders collected their outstanding debts using the town's three banks of which Barrow Moss, silversmith and Navy Agent, of North Corner Street, had an account with Glencross Marshall and Company the Naval and Commercial Bank, in Fore Street.[4]

Before leaving the West Country mention must be made of the Jewish communities of Falmouth and Penzance, both established in about 1740. Falmouth was concerned mainly with merchant shipping, there being only one Navy Agent in the sea-port, Solomon Solomon who left in 1819. The local tradesmen would go out into the bay and down channel to meet the merchant vessels before making their first landfall. Here was the opportunity for the seamen to exchange their foreign currency and to make their purchases, mainly of slops. In later years the 'Outfitters Cutters' as they were known, included the 61 tons *Frances* owned by

Samuel Jacob and nicknamed 'The Synagogue'.

*Chatham Memorial Synagogue. Rebuilt by Simon Magnus (silversmith, pawnbroker and licenced Navy Agent) in 1870.*

Unlike the single Jewish Navy Agents in Falmouth and Penzance, by 1809 no less than five out of the seven licensed Chatham Navy Agents were Jews, with the same number of Jewish Agents in Sheerness. The original Chatham Synagogue was built about the year 1760 at the western extremity of the High Street with a cemetery behind. The small Jewish community traded mainly as slopsellers with the Navy, Army Garrison and workmen from the Royal Dockyard, which was then the largest industrial enterprise in south-east England. The Dockyard, protected by the fortifications of military engineers encompassing small lanes off the main High Street, was however to become far less important to the Admiralty by the time the Napoleonic Wars ended. The foremost Jews of Chatham were the Magnus family. Lazarus, a licensed Navy Agent in 1809, lived at 302, High Street, to be followed by his son Simon remaining a Navy Agent until 1852. They were also silversmiths.

Noting a slackening of trade in Chatham some Jews moved on to the important port and dockyard of Sheerness at the mouth of the River Medway and established a community there about 1790. One of the principal founders was the silversmith and Navy Agent Samuel Abrahams. It will be remembered that it was at Sheerness in 1802 that Ordinary Seaman John Levy was flogged round the fleet, with Isaac

Joseph, a local slopseller of Blue Town Sheerness, giving evidence at Levy's Court Martial. Henry Russell, who became the famous singer and composer of patriotic songs, was born at Sheerness in 1812.

*Landing place close to the dockyard of Sheerness. Slopsellers and other shops appear in the centre background. (from an engraving by J. Rogers circa 1830, when little had changed since the Napoleonic wars).*

A year earlier a new wooden synagogue was built in Blue Tavern, between Sheppey and Kent Streets. The Jewish cemetery was about a mile away behind the High Street in Hope Street. Like their co-religionists in Portsmouth it was not unknown for them to trade on Sabbath by going aboard the men-of-war lying at the Nore, resulting in the learned Dayanim of the Beth Din (an ecclesiastical tribunal) imposing suitable spiritual penalties. In 1810, during the last year of the old synagogue, a large reward of 20 guineas was offered to find the culprit who had profaned a sacred service by throwing a wild cat through one of the synagogue windows.

It was in Portsmouth that a vicious attack on a Jewish slopseller, Asher Nathan and his wife Rosa, was made at their home in White Hart Road, close to The Point. On Sabbath evening Friday 20 April 1810, they were sitting by the fire when at about 10 o'clock there was a banging on their door. One of the panels was broken. Rosa went to the door. Two Royal Navy Officers stood there calling her 'A bloody Jew bitch' and another in plain clothes struck her in the face. Others from an adjoining lodging house carried on the abuse. When Asher Nathan appeared he was first threatened with a dirk and then hit with a stick causing his mouth to bleed. The attackers then ran off. Next evening, Phineas Israel, a salesman, later to become a Navy Agent, on returning to his lodgings heard two Royal Navy Naval Officers in Rosemary Lane just off The Hard shouting 'Let's stave in the bloody Jews' windows in White Hart Road'. Phineas Israel quickly went to warn Asher Nathan and then set off for a constable. In the meantime a James Bullock and a William Martele, Masters of two local coasting sloops, were walking in White Hart Road when they were set upon by a group of five men hurling abuse. Mistaken for Jews, James Bullock was struck on the head whilst Martele ran off to fetch a constable. Two Officers named Martin and Wilson and a George Le Estrange were later charged.[5] Robberies were committed against the shopkeepers for their goods, but no other violent attacks on the Portsmouth Jewish community were reported to the Justices or mentioned in the local press.

There were other risks for the traders.

On 10th March 1808, with strong winds blowing, the log of *HMS Mars* recorded: 'At Spithead A.M. employed cleaning ship, received some powder, the ships company paid wages P.M. Joseph Jones sentinel at the fore chains to keep boats off fired, and unfortunately killed a man in a wherry near the ship'.

Joseph Jones was tried for murder at Winchester the following July. He was defended by the Portsmouth Solicitor Mr Moses Greetham who reported the case to Charles Bicknell the Admiralty Solicitor on 30th July:-

> Joseph Jones (the defendant) is a private Marine belonging to His Majesty's Ship *Mars* and at the payment of the wages of her crew at Spithead in March last, several boats with slopmen having pressed alongside the ship the sentries repeatedly ordered them off and at length the defendant fired and unhappily killed Abraham Abrahams a Jew; which was found wilful murder by the Coroners Jury, he was however afterwards bailed by the order of Mr Justice Grose to be tried at Winchester Assizes before Mr Justice Bailey.
>
> The Judge in his summing up the evidence told the Jury that if they should be of opinion that the necessity of firing was sufficient and he pointed out the difficulties that occurred in preventing liquor being brought in the ship fraudulently in slopmens hampers under the denomination of slops and the dreadful consequence of the crew getting drunk by such means they ought to acquit him if they should be of the opionion that he pointed his musquet merely to alarm the

> people in the boats in order to enforce his orders and fired without any intention of injuring any person but by such firing the deceased unhappily met with his death they ought to pronounce a verdict of manslaughter, but if they should think he deliberately took aim and intentionally shot the deceased his crime was murder. The Jury with very little consideration found it manslaughter and the Judge told him that he was perfectly satisfied that he thought he was strictly doing his duty but that it appeared he had been somewhat hasty and strongly advised him to caution in future and sentenced him to pay a fine of six shillings and eightpence which I paid and he was immediately discharged.

*The Hampshire Telegraph* reported, 'the most unfortunate occurence' in the shooting of Abraham Abrahams slopseller of The Hard, Portsea – 'The deceased was of singularly inoffensive manners and his unfortunate death is much to be lamented'.

After the trial Judge Bailey did write to the Secretary of the Admiralty suggesting:-

> . . . such orders should they be continued I cannot but think it desirable that on the extraordinary occassion in which ball cartridges are delivered out, there should be an officer on board, without whose direction no marine should be permitted to fire.[6]

Regulations were tightened. Royal Marines sentinels were given strict orders to fire only blank cartridges with their cartouch boxes being examined regularly by the Marine Armourers. However, on one occasion in September 1813, no less than fifteen wherries with their complements of slopsellers and traders surrounded the seventy four gun *Centaur* at Spithead, the crew having just been paid. Guard boats had set off from the ship to keep the wherries away from the *Centaur's* sides and to bring some order to the slopsellers', eager to get aboard. Also to make it easier for a check to be kept on those traders and slopsellers smuggling liquor on board. A marine Laurence Finnigan shouted out to one of these wherries about 100 feet from the ship *'You Jew-looking buggers if you don't keep the boat off I'll blow your brains out'*.

Finnigan opened fire, not with a blank, and the ball passed through the arm and hipbone of James Veall a slopseller of St James Street, Portsea. *'Oh! I am a dead man - my poor wife and family'*. Captain J.C. White of the *Centaur* immediately ordered the slopseller aboard where the assistant surgeon dressed the wound and sent Veall ashore where he recovered. Finnigan was committed to the Assizes though it appeared he never came to trial.[7]

In fact, about nine months before this incident, a means of controlling the traders was to bring all the slopsellers, vendors of watches and itinerant peddlers within the provisions of the Hawkers and Pedlars Act. From December 1812 no one could trade aboard any of His Majesty's vessels of war without an annual licence costing £4. An Admiralty order to prevent any person trading without a licence was hung up on board every ship in the service. It was envisaged that there were 1,000 engaged in what was known as the shipping trade in Portsmouth; 800 at Plymouth and further 700 at Chatham, Sheerness, the Downs and Irish Station producing for the Treasury £10,000 per annum.[8]

Here it would be opportune to give the strength of the Royal Navy. At the end of 1812 there were 145,000 seamen and marines manning 748 ships in commission of which 539 were at sea, 175 in port and fitting out with the remaining 34 acting as Guard, Hospital and Prison ships. In addition 212 were in reserve and under repair with 57 being built. A total of 1,037 ships of different ratings. At the probable peak of trading at the end of 1812 there were about 2,500 hawkers, pedlars and slopsellers trying to trade with these seamen and marines. This would seem to result in a ratio of one trader to every sixty potential customers. In fact, the trading opportunities were much reduced as the vast majority of the warships were at sea, under repairs, or on foreign stations. Of the 175 in port, not all could be boarded and many had incomplete crews. When James Veall was shot by a sentry on board the *Centaur*, it would have had a crew of about 650 Officers and men whilst each of the fifteen wherries carried from four to eight passengers. On this basis there would have been about one trader to every eight crew members excluding the Officers, though of course the traders were not all trying to sell the same goods. Not only were these petty traders likely to be shot at, or end up in the sea at times of inclement weather, they were sometimes in fierce competition with each other. Their individual trade was comparatively small and many were considered among the lowest stratum of traders in the naval ports, being to a great degree just travelling hawkers and pedlars.

The old established traders ashore using their recognition as Licensed Navy Agents were best able to transact a lucrative business. Lewes Moses of 94, Broad Street, Portsmouth is a good example who, it will be remembered, sold slops to the 120 complement of the eighteen gun sloop *Sophie* in 1814 for almost £1,100. Broad Street on the Point was the best trading position owing to its proximity to the sea with boats being able to land goods close or directly to the traders' premises. Some of the more successful slopsellers aspired to owning wherries to carry their goods.[9]

*Looking across Portsmouth Harbour from Block House Fort, Gosport, to the Round Tower and Semaphore Tower. Note the slipways facilitating easy access to the rear of shops in Broad Street and Bath Square for the Slopsellers taking the merchandise out in wherries to the Man-of-War lying at their moorings circa 1828. (from an engraving by J. Salmon).*

Point is on the eastern side of Portsmouth Harbour, surrounded by sea at high water, with Broad Street running down the centre of the isthmus and the Customs House off Broad Street at the Outer Camber. The famous Quebec Tavern is at the northerly end, whilst the other was where the watermen congregated.

The old Portsmouth wherries had a world-wide reputation for seaworthiness. They were particularly useful in reaching the warships lying at anchor by Spithead. They were hired not only by the seamen to return to their respective ships and used by the traders, but also for carrying out stores, naval equipment and even the fleet's washing. Some control over the watermen's fares was brought in 1809 and later, in 1812, a system of licensing. All boats had to be kept in order with proper masts, sails, oars, rudders and other gear and tackle, under penalty of forty shillings. The waterman's name and address, together with his licence number, had to be clearly indicated. At one time there must have been a thousand of these Portsmouth watermen, but with the regulations and the end of the war this number was halved by 1817. Among those generally rough and uncouth watermen can possibly be noted some from the Jewish community:-[10]

| | | |
|---|---|---|
| In 1814 | Boat Number 442 | Thomas Abraham of 1, Haslar Row, Gosport |
| | Boat Number 553 | Joseph Hart of East Street, Point |
| | Boat Number 623 | Robert Lyons of Hardings Yard, North Street, Gosport |
| | Boat Number 732 | Joseph Abraham of 5, Green Lane, Somers Town |
| In 1815 | Boat Number 393 | James Lyons of 2, Strong Buildings, Portsea |
| In 1816 | Boat Number 3 | Benjamin Phillips of 4 Sandwich Street, New Buildings |
| | Boat Number 325 | Thomas Daniel of 1, St Georges Square, Portsea |

Other than The Point, the majority of the Jewish traders lived and worked from houses partly used as shops in Portsea, bounded by The Hard facing the harbour, north to the Dockyard Gates, east along Queen Street then back to The Hard via St Georges Square and Ordnance Row.

A typical example within this area of practically one square mile was College Street, just off The Hard and therefore not in such a good trading area. Here were the middle stratum of traders in properties often comprising a shop with sitting room behind, on the ground floor, three bedrooms above, and a cellar (important to be dry for storage), kitchen and rear yard. The Jewish Navy Agents in College Street at various times during and just after the Napoleonic Wars were Nathan and Phineas Abrahams (silversmiths and jewellers); S. Simpson (elder of the Portsmouth Hebrew congregation); Moses Symonds at number 6; Moses Solomon at number 9; Abraham Moses at number 20 (silversmith and elder of the Portsmouth Hebrew congregation); whilst at number 30 was Lyon Levy followed by Mark Friedeberg and then Isaac Moses (elder of the Portsmouth Hebrew congregation).

Off College Street was Hanover Street where Phillip Barnard kept for a time the Antelope Public House, perhaps the only Jewish inn keeper in Portmouth during the Napoleonic Wars. Next to Hanover Street was Union Street where the properties were even smaller with just a cellar, two rooms and a yard, well and pump. It was here, at number 10 Union Street on the corner of Queen Street, that Benjamin Levi, one of the original founders of the Portsmouth Synagogue and his son Jacob, were engravers in seals, stamps, plate copper and pewter. They also acted as Navy Agents.

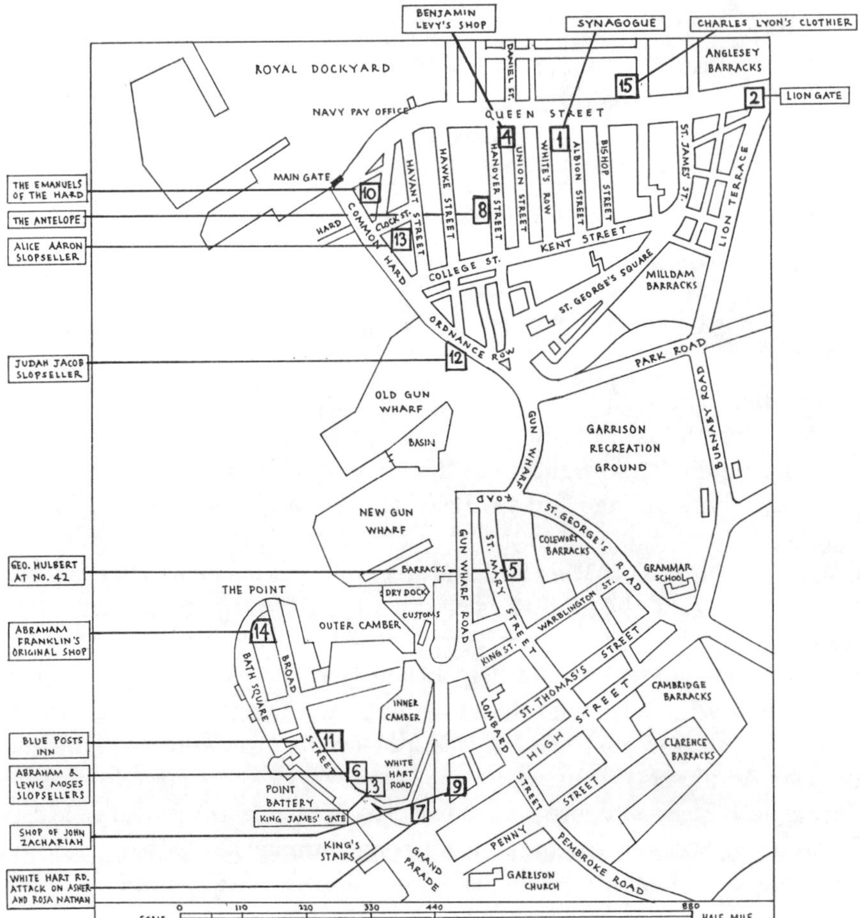


PORTSMOUTH AND PORTSEA IN THE NAPOLEONIC PERIOD

GWP

The corner shops in Queen Street were quite large with living rooms and numerous bedrooms, the other shops being much smaller. Queen Street was a busy, long thoroughfare running from the Dockyard Gates to Lion

Gate, forming the northern border of the Portsea trading area. Here were the silversmiths and pawnbrokers, some of whom were Navy Agents. At number 184 was Lewis (Lazarus) Franklin, who had first come to Portsmouth from London about the year 1798, soon to be followed by his brother Abraham. The latter took a job for a short time as a shop boy to Lemele Davids, pawnbroker and silversmith, in Havant Street, Portsea, then as a clerk to John Zachariah of 69, High Street, Portsmouth, the premier Jewish trader of the Napoleonic Wars. Abraham Franklin joined the Volunteers and in later life recounted tales of lonely patrol duties on the sea shore. Abraham worked for a Mrs Aaron in a shop on The Point at Bath Square on the understanding he was to have sole possession of the business on his marriage to Mrs Aaron's daughter Miriam which eventually took place in December 1807.[11] Both Franklin brothers were licensed Navy Agents and active in synagogue affairs, Lazarus being President for a time. They had a shop together in Broad Street, Point, where in December 1811 one of their assistants, John Levy, made off with watches and goods to the value of £150. Levy was eventually tracked down in Brighton, charged, and ended up in a prison hulk for seven years.[12] In November 1814 Lazarus moved to 26 Queen Street where he was a licensed Navy Agent and also owned a pawnbroking and silversmith shop at number 184 in the same street which he eventually sold to Levy Zachariah (Junior) in September 1818.[13] The Franklin brothers moved to Liverpool where they continued as Licensed Navy Agents, Abraham going on to Manchester where he was particularly successful.

The Zachariah family was the outstanding Jewish trading family in Portsmouth particularly the three brothers Jacob, Levy and John. The father Isaac was one of the oldest Jewish inhabitants. Levy, born in 1778, became a slopseller in Broad Street being admitted to Hirams Masonic Lodge in 1802 where he gave his occupation as Navy Agent.[14] He did not become licensed, and by 1816 was living at 10 High Street, Portsmouth, owning property in Daniel Street, Portsea.

Jacob Zachariah was for many years a silversmith at 85 Broad Street, opposite the famous Blue Posts Inn, until selling by auction in May 1813. His Naval Agency licence was revoked the following December for *abusing the trust reposed in him*. Jacob moved to a shop at 92 High Street, Portsmouth, where in February, 1814, George Rose, Treasure to the Navy, still refused to restore his licence.[15] However, Jacob prospered mainly as a jeweller to the Officers who frequented the High Street, and had his own residence nearby in Green Row, Pembroke Road, Portsmouth.

It was John Zachariah who became the best known of the brothers. He had established himself as a silversmith by the beginning of the nineteenth century at 69 High Street, Portsmouth, where he was also a licensed Navy Agent from 1809, so dealing with both the Officers and lower deck. He was known as 'London Jack' possibly because he had gone to London as a youth to learn the silversmith trade.

*View down High Street, Portsmouth towards John Zachariah's shop. (from an engraving by F. Shepherd).*

The High Street was the centre of the better class trade, its famous inns attracting many celebrated personages. The distinctive buildings included the residences of the Port Admiral and the Commanding Officer of the Royal Marines, also the Portsmouth Bank. Contemporary Portsmouth guides described the High Street as '*Spacious and handsome – very noble buildings – the principal place of trade, and many of the shops are fitted up in a neat and attractive manner*'.

John Zachariah was one of the few Jewish traders who expanded his business by advertising, announcing in *The Hampshire Courier* of 4 May 1812:-

## To the Officers of the Royal Navy

JOHN ZACHARIAH AND CO. having just received from the Manufacturers a large supply of the new UNIFORM NAVAL BUTTON warranted to be of a superior sort, and not to be equalled in this town, they can sell them at the following low price:-

| | |
|---|---|
| Coat Buttons ........................ | 4s. per dozen |
| Waistcoat ditto ................... | 2s. |

Likewise a great choice of new Uniform Epaulettes.
N.B. Z and Co. can give for Foreign Coins as under.

| | £. | s. | d. |
|---|---|---|---|
| Doubloons | 4. | 2. | 6 each |
| Ports | 2. | 3. | 0 |
| Louis | 1. | 2. | 0 |
| Napoleons | 0. | 19. | 0 |
| French Crowns | 0. | 5. | 5 |
| Rupees | 0. | 2. | 4 |
| Spanish Dollars | 0. | 5. | 2½ |

69 High Street, Portsmouth

Money changing with the Officers and seamen arriving home after long foreign cruises formed a major part of the business. John Zachariah announced in another advertisement, this time in the *Hampshire Telegraph* of 10 June 1811, *'Being authorised by one of the first Bullion Houses in London flatter themselves they will give to the very extent for all Foreign Coins, at the London price'.*

The shop was a veritable emporium selling such items as elegant assortments of plate; handsome gold dial and repeating watches; diamond rings and pins; pearl and coral ear-rings; beautiful assortments of cornelian coral and amber necklaces; handsome gold chains, seals and keys; gold and silver snuff boxes; swords, sabres, dirks and belts; pistols and guns in cases; Navy and Army epaulets; silk sashes; day and night telescopes; quadrants; musical instruments; portable desks; shaving cases; silver and tortoiseshell spectacles; pen, pocket, and table knives and forks, scissors and razors; gilt and plated spurs; German pipes and tubes; eight-day table clocks; and a great variety of plated goods of the best quality, silver edged.[16]

By March 1813 Zachariah and Company at 69, High Street,

Portsmouth were Sword Cutlers and Jewellers to His Royal Highness The Duke of Clarence, the future 'Sailor King'. Appropriately John Zachariah was the first Portsmouth Jewish trader to hold a Royal Appointment.

*HMS* ***Shannon*** *towing her prize the American frigate* ***Chesapeke*** *into Halifax 6 June 1813. John Zachariah jeweller, sword cutler and Navy Agent of 69 High Street, Portsmouth dealt with most of the prize money for the Petty Officers, Seamen and Marines of* ***HMS Shannon*** *for the capture of* ***USS Chesapeke****. (from a lithograph by L. Hague). (National Maritime Museum)*

Yet another side of John Zachariah's business was that of Naval Agency carried on with the seamen. He was fortunate to hold the Prize Orders for most of the crew of *HMS Shannon*. This was the ship which, on 1 June 1813, off Boston, fought the most celebrated evenly matched single ship action in the annals of the Royal Navy. In it *HMS Shannon* fought and captured the *USS Chesapeke*. The action between these two frigates lasted only fifteen minutes, with heavy casualties on both sides. The Prize Agent, John Hulbert of 42, Saint Mary Street, Portsmouth, acting for his brother George, of Norfolk Street, Strand, London, distributed £15,469 for the hull, stores and Head Money.[17] Captain Broke of the *Shannon* eventually received £2,449. On 13 November 1817 he wrote to his Agent George Hulbert from Broke Hall, near Ipswich:-[18]

My Dear Sir,

You will oblige me by telling me what sums of prize money, if any, remain unpaid to John Brown 1st of the Shannon for Susan and Emmeline or any other prize under your disposal – also what sums (if any) were paid on his account, and to his power, to John Zachariah, the Jew Agent at Portsmouth who is reported to have received most of the Chesapeake payment and only given the said John Brown £5 – if it is so, can I get him any redress by application to Mr Rose?

I am my Dear Sir
Yours truly
P. B. V. BROKE

George Hulbert confirmed the money had been paid, and there is no record of any complaint being made to George Rose. John Brown's prize money probably amounted to about £13.0s.0d. with the difference of £8.0s.0d. possibly arising because John Zachariah had more than likely allowed him an advance either in cash or against purchases in his shop, other than the 6s.6d. commission. Captain Sir Philip Broke had his own reservations by underlining *'if it is so'* indicating that he was aware seamen were given advances of their prize money in one form or another by their Navy Agent before distribution.

Another famous frigate Captain of this period, Sir William Hoste, complained to George Rose, Treasurer of the Navy, regarding the supposed misconduct of John Zachariah over the non-payment of prize money. Parts of George Rose's letter of 5 April 1812 in reply to Captain Sir William Hoste aboard *HMS Bacchante,* then lying at Spithead, are recorded here to show how the original licensing act of 1809 was interpreted.[19]

The Law which I obtained for the protection of Petty Officers and Seamen from the impositions of low Agents (49: Geo 3: Ch 123. Sect 37) enacts 'that if it shall appear to the Treasurer of His Majesty's Navy, for the time being, that any such Licensed Agents hath abused the trust reposed in him, by not duly accounting to any person or persons by whom he shall have been empowered to receive any Wages, Pay, Prize Money, Bounty Money, or other allowances of money as aforesaid, for the sum or sums of money by him received in their behalf, or by practising and Fraud or Imposition on any such person or persons; *then and in that case* it shall and may be lawful . . . to revoke the License . . .' You will see from this quotation that I should not be warranted in withdrawing the license on any other grounds than stated in the Act. I have endeavoured by every means in my power to repress the Insolence of these Agents as well as to prevent their Frauds and punish their Offences, but I should do more harm than good if I were to attempt to exercise an authority I could not support. My anxiety to satisfy you that I can do nothing effectual in Zachariahs case, has induced me to enter so much in detail in this matter.

I am etc.,

GEORGE ROSE.

Complaints were also made over the head of George Rose. Here, he is replying to John Barrow, second secretary of the Admiralty, 21 July 1813[20]:-

Sir,

I have attentively considered the Statements in the anonymous letter enclosed in yours of the 13th inst – It is certainly true that low Agents, often thoroughly unprincipled men, obtain from Seamen and inferior Petty Officers in His Majesty's Navy, Powers for receiving Prize Money a small part of which only is too frequently accounted to the Parties: but it must be admitted that the Seamen sometimes defraud these Agents by giving Orders for Prize Money to a second after having received Money in advance from a former Agent.

The Writer imputes to the superior Officers their standing tamely by, and suffering Impositions on the men – with what justice that is alleged the Naval Commissioner at your Board can form a more correct judgement than myself: when Powers are granted by Seamen the Officers at Greenwich Hospital are bound to pay under them, without enquiring what consideration was given to them, or whether the value shall afterwards be fully accounted for, but every complaint of Fraud or Imposition made to me, or of abuses of any sort practised by Agents of the above description is immediately enquired into, and on proof of its being well founded I do not fail to withdraw the License from the Guilty person and to direct him and his sureties to be prosecuted; recent occasions for my interposition have occured . . .

When I have heard of Bargains with Seamen for their Prize Money, for sums less than were likely to be due to them, I have compelled a full payment; and I am sure it is unnecessary for me to add to their Lordships that I have used a watchful care for the Interests of the Seamen, using at the same time the best means I could devise for making it generally known how Parties should apply for redress and protection when necessary.

. . . I have been prevented by an appreciation that such an innovation (Prize Orders only to be given to relations and not Agents)

> might occasion great disatisfaction among the Seamen by putting a stop to their getting Advances occasionally . . . It may perhaps be worthy of their Lordships consideration whether it may not be useful to instruct the Captains in the Navy to discourage as far as they may think prudent and advisable, the Seamen under their command from giving Powers to low Agents to receive their Prize Money on obtaining small sums in advance which always afford opportunities for Frauds on the one side or the other, which no vigilance can guard against . . .
>
> I am etc.,
>
> G. ROSE

The Treasurer was conscious of these complaints and felt aggrieved at the impression given of his Prize Branch not functioning to curb the activities of the unscrupulous. In fact, Thomas Boswell, Chief Clerk at the Prize Office, kept a register of all distributions and share of prizes, their amounts and by whom and where payable. Information was given to applicants, with a register kept of all Licensed Navy Agents in chronological order. This showed the date when the application was received and from whom, the date and number of the licence, the place of abode and changes of abode if any, and when the licence was cancelled, with any remarks which were thought necessary.

Before admitting an applicant to the register and granting a licence, enquiries as to his fitness were made. Boswell immediately informed the Treasurer, George Rose, and the Paymaster John Smith, of any irregularities or misconduct by the Licenced Agents. The Pay Offices at Portsmouth, Plymouth, Chatham and Shearness kept their own separate registers and investigated any local complaints. Extra staff were employed for this purpose. However, difficulties arose because of the shortage of accomodation. Henry Maule, first pay clerk at Sheerness, reported in January 1810:-

> *The few houses large enough to let into lodgings are in the hands of Tradesmen and Slopsellers who find it most in their interest to let them to Naval Officers who grant them the privilege of supply their ships with slops, a source of wealth, which soon renders them independent.*[21]

All licences withdrawn were advertised in *The London Gazette* as required by section 38 of the 1809 Act, and in addition George Rose arranged with John Murray, publisher of the *Navy List*, to insert this announcement in the issue for October 1813:-

The following information is inserted at the particular request of the Treasurer of His Majesty's Navy – In all cases where well-founded complaints have been made against agents for petty officers and seamen in His Majesty's service the Treasurer of the Navy has compelled them to do ample and immediate justice to the parties; and in cases where the misconduct of the agents appeared to be of a nature to call for it, the Treasurer has withdrawn the licences and directed the agents and their sureties to be sued upon their bonds. The following instances are stated that parties who are injured may know how to seek redress. LICENCES REVOKED – John Molyneux, Liverpool for not having accounted for moneys received for seamen. John Palfreman Liverpool, on the same ground. Matthew Rowe Portsea on the same ground. Matthew Kirk London on the same ground. Harry Adams Portsea on the same ground. Abraham Jones Sheerness on the same ground. Henry Hart Portsea on the same ground, but since renewed. Aaron Moses Sheerness on the same ground, but renewed in consequence of character and favourable circumstances. Gregory Briggs Gravesend for changing his place of abode without giving notice in order to evade just claims of seamen upon him. Asher Nathan Plymouth on the same ground. Thomas Forester London on the same ground. John Abrahams London being a minor, Samuel Davis London for charging a seaman with money under the pretence of the same having been distributed among clerks in the navy office. Michael Davis London licence expiring renewal of it withheld positively on the ground of his having refused to account for moneys received for seamen unless they would agree to take part in slops. Charles Rorke London for having practised an imposition upon a seaman.

Previously to the licences being restored in the cases alluded to, references were made to respectable naval officers on the spot where the agents resided, for their opinion of the propriety thereof, and occasionally additional security for the future good conduct of the agents were required.

There was now an awareness of the workings and success of Rose's licensings of the Navy Agents, yet he was still not satisfied in his endeavours on behalf of the seamen. A further Act was passed into law on 18 July 1814, 'An Act for regulating the Payment of Navy Prize Money and the Transmission of Accounts and Payment of Balances to Greenwich Hospital'. Some parts of the Prize Acts were repealed and most of the sections dealt with Prize Agents. As for the Licensed Navy Agents, under section 58 the security for the bond was increased from £200 to £300.

Section 89 regularised the enactments regarding the impersonating of Officers or seamen to obtain Prize Money and wages, or forging letters of attorney. On lawful conviction the offender was deemed guilty of a felony punishable by death, but under section 90 no action could be brought after three years from commiting the offence. Such offences had already been put before the public's attention in no uncertain way by the following notice issued towards the end of the eighteenth century:-[22]

## FORGERY OF PRIZE ORDERS

At the last Assizes for the County of Cumberland, held at Carlisle. *John Townsend* was convicted of Forging an Order and Certificate to obtain the Prize Money due to one Isaac Banks who has been a Seaman on board the *Nymph*. He was also found guilty of uttering Forged Orders to obtain Prize Money in the name of Henry Banks *and was sentenced to be HANGED.*

This Man has been in the practice of assuring Seamen and Marines, that he could readily get their Prize Money from Greenwich Hospital, and, after obtaining their Orders, he commonly forged a Certificate to complete his purpose. In some instances he received the Money from Greenwich Hospital, and in the case for which he was Prosecuted he had obtained more than £40 out of which he gave to the Person really entitled, only sum of £5.

*He was executed at Carlisle*

As the Directors of *GREENWICH HOSPITAL PROSECUTE* all those who are discovered *personating or assuming false names or character, or forging, or uttering forged Orders or Certificates* to obtain Prize Money, *and the punishment is Death,* it is hoped the fate of this Man will operate as a warning to prevent others from being Guilty of these Crimes.

The Right Honourable Lord Ellenborough heard another important Naval Agency case on 9 July 1814, just nine days before the new Prize Money Act. A Michael Davis of Browns Buildings, St Mary Axe, London, had his licence revoked on 14 April 1813 for refusing to pay certain seamen of *HMS Gloucester* their respective shares of Prize Money unless they agree to take the value of such shares in slops. Yet Davis still practised Naval Agency by receiving £64 after 14 April 1813 due to three seamen for the capture four years previously of St Paul in the Isle of Bourbon, close to Mauritius. Davis defended himself and proved that as the orders to receive prize money were given to him whilst the licence was running, and as there was no clause in the Acts which prevented him accepting such prize money even though by the time of distribution his licence had been revoked for another reason, he felt himself not guilty of any misdemeanour. Lord Ellenborough agreed as 'the order to receive the money was dated in December 1812 which was during the period of his licence and therefore competent to receive it'. Legal argument followed but Lord Ellenborough directed the Jury that the case before them was not within the 1809 Act and Davis was cleared. The Judge was particularly scathing of Mr Skeen, clerk to the Prize Agent, and Thomas Maude who had offered to obtain the money for Davis provided he received a private commission of sixpence in the pound – *'I hope Skeen will understand that such things are not to be endured, that must ultimately come out of the pocket of these poor sailors'.*[23]

On 25 May 1815 the legal loophole found by Michael Davis was closed as a further Act came in repealing and making new provisions affecting letters of Attorney and wills of seamen. By section 39 of 55 George III Chapter 60, it was an offence for Agents to act after expiration or revocation of their licences. Further legislation was to follow authorising, in July 1817, that executors or administrators of deceased Licensed Navy Agents may be permitted to receive prize and bounty monies upon orders given to deceased Agents, provided they took out a licence as laid down in the original Acts of 1809 and 1814. So one finds widows becoming Licensed Navy Agents.

Although the war came to an end in August 1815, prize money was still being distributed some years afterwards because of the slow legal process following capture. In fact for just one year between 1 July 1817 and 30 June 1818, no less than £344,377 was distributed to the Royal Navy from 170 prize concerns and grants.[24] This was for net proceeds, some of which dated back virtually to the commencement of the Napoleonic Wars. Prosperity had in fact been mounting in England since 1811 as Napoleon's Continental blockade broke up, with a post-war boom reaching a climax in 1818, and plunging to depths the following year.

The number of Licensed Navy Agents reached its peak in 1816 with close on 400 Agents listed, of which about 140 were Jews, representing 35% of the total. Of this total many had already decided not to renew their licences because as the war ended there was far less need of their services. All impressing and entering of seamen had been countermanded; 200 men-of-war were to be paid off, and the Royal Navy was immediately reduced by 12,000 seamen and 5,000 marines. Between 1810 and 1813 there had been 19,200 naval and marine personnel based in Portsmouth, at the end of the war this fell to 12,600. Trade declined, businesses were auctioned for the best possible price; in November 1818 Godwin and Company, one of Portsmouth's banks, failed and by March 1820 as many as 247 Navy Agents had not renewed their licences. Yet the population of Portsea continued to rise from 11,000 in 1811 to 12,622 in 1821, whilst that of Portsmouth had slightly declined from 7,839 to 7,269 during the same period. There were still 57 prominent tradesmen in the twin towns in February 1820.[25]

After John Zachariah had sold up his business and home at 69, High Street, Portsmouth, by the end of 1815 he moved to London. His place, as leading Jewish trader, was soon to be taken by another silversmith, a family to become renowned throughout Anglo-Jewry, and to remain established in Portsmouth for 100 years: the 'Emanuels of The Hard'.

It was in April 1816 that David Hart, another prominent Jewish silversmith and slopseller, sold his freehold property at 3, Common Hard, Portsea, which prior to 1809 was in the occupation of I. Levi another Licensed Navy Agent. The auction sale advertisement at The George Inn in the *Hampshire Courier* of 8 April 1816, detailed the property which over the years was to become a landmark under the ownership of the Emanuels:-

PORTSEA

*A substantial Freehold Dwelling House and capital Situation for business.*

To be SOLD by AUCTION by MR JOHN COLLINS (unless previously disposed of by Private Contract, of which the earliest notice will be given) at the George Inn, Portsmouth, on Thursday, the 2nd May next, at the hour of six in the evening: all that MESSVAGE or DWELLING-HOUSE, being No. 3 situate at Common Hard, in the Town of Portsea, near the entrance to the Dock Yard, now in the occupation of Mr David Hart, Silversmith and Slopseller.

The shop is large and well fitted up with counters, shelves, and glass cases, and has a parlour behind commanding it; there is a side passage to enter the house. A drawing room in front with a back chamber on the first floor, and the same on the second floor. A sitting room and two chambers over the kitchen, and two chambers and a dressing room in the attics; there are two kitchens very large and commodious, with grates, dressers, shelves, convenient fixtures, and servants' bed-rooms over the kitchens; there is a large wash with a copper and grate; two reservoirs lined with lead, a well and pump with excellent water and good cellars under the house.

Besides being as well adapted for Trade and Business from its contiguity to the Dock Yard as any situation in Portsea, it is also fitted as a Lodging House, for which it is equally adapted, and from the arrangement of rooms, passages, and offices two families as lodgers can at the same time have lodgings with separate and distinct offices, and it has for many years been in much request, by the officers of the navy in particular.

The whole is in the best repair with stores, grates and every convenient fixture. Possession may be had on the completion of the Purchase; a view of the Premises by applying to Mr David Hart, and further particulars by applying to Mr Joseph Hart, No. 37, Lemon Street, Goodman's Fields, London, the Auctioneer, and to

Messrs MINCHEN AND WEDDELL
Solicitors, Gosport.

Moses Emanuel was the purchaser. He had originated from Steinhardt in Bavaria, Germany, first living at 23 Hanway Street, London, and becoming a naturalized British subject in September 1801 before moving to Portsmouth. His eldest son Ezekiel, only 18 years of age in 1816, ran the shop trading as a silversmith, jeweller, and watchmaker. The Emanuels of The Hard were never Licensed Navy Agents, but Ezekiel soon got down to improving the business. One of his advertisements in the *Hampshire Telegraph* of 24 May 1819 proclaimed:-

*No. 3, Common Hard, Portsea.*

E. EMANUEL (from London) returns thanks to the Inhabitants of Portsea, Portsmouth and Vicinity, for the encouragement he has received the short space of time he has resided here, and begs to acquaint them that he continues to give the London prices for every article in the BULLION or GOLD and SILVER LINE, and all sorts of FOREIGN COIN.

N.B. – Country Shopkeepers supplied with new Plate etc. wholesale – A collection of Roman and English Coins constantly on sale. Three Doors from the Dock-Gates.

Ezekiel's brother Emanuel Emanuel at the age of 17 years was charged at the Quarter Sessions for an assault against Lewis Lazarus, a respected pawnbroker and Licensed Navy Agent of 16, Bishop Street, Portsea, an elder of the Portsmouth Hebrew congregation. *The Hampshire Telegraph* of 24 October 1825 did not report the provocation only that, '*The Jury after considerable hesitation gave a verdict of guilty and the Court immediately sentenced him to pay a fine of one penny*'. An inauspicious start in the career of Emanuel Emanuel, who was to become the first Jewish Mayor of Portsmouth 41 years later.

In the following week's issue of *The Hampshire Telegraph* Michael Emanuel of 16, Broad Street, Portsmouth, was quick to disclaim any connection with Emanuel Emanuel, it was not his son – but that of Moses Emanuel of 3, Common Hard. Not for the last time was confusion to arise between these two unrelated Emanuel families to become known as 'Emanuels of The Hard' and 'Emanuels of Ordnance Row'.

The progenitor of the 'Emanuels of Ordnance Row' was Samuel Emanuel of 20, College Street, Portsea, the sole survivor of the disastrous boat accident of February 1758 when 12 Jews lost their lives by drowning after trading aboard *HMS Lancaster*. Samuel was therefore one of the earliest congregants of the Portsmouth Hebrew community whose decendants were to be continuously connected with the naval town for over 150 years. Samuel's son Michael Emanual married Hannah Isaac in 1797. She was a daughter of Levy Isaac who by coincidence had 30 years previously performed the religious rite of circumcision on his future son-in-law. Michael Emanuel had a pawnbroking business right next door to the Blue Posts Inn, immortalized by Captain Marryat in his novel '*Peter Simple*'. Michael Emanuel's premises were quite large having a frontage of 16'6" and a depth of 62'5" for which he received £975 for the lease in March 1809.[26] Levy Isaac died on 29 January 1814 at 92 years of age, just three days after his wife Boonley, who had also reached the advanced age of 83 years. *The Hampshire Courier* reported, 'They were the oldest inhabitants on the Point having lived in one house, much respected, nearly 60 years'. It was in fact No. 16 Broad Street where Levy Isaac had a small silversmith business, the premises passing to Michael Emanuel. One of Michael's sons. Henry Emanuel, born in 1807, eventually set up at 13, Ordnance Row, Portsea, as a Pawnbroker, Jeweller and Watchmaker.

Another branch of the family, John and Joseph Emanuel, were at numbers 3 and 12 Ordnance Row as Licensed Navy Agents between 1818 and 1825.

Some of the traders took an active part in synagogue life, and with some affluence during the Napoleonic Wars the synagogue's finances were never in real difficulty. Even in 1800, when the cemetery in Fawcett Road needed to be extended, £100 was quickly found to purchase a strip of adjoining land for which a lease of 1,000 years was granted at a peppercorn rent. Joseph Levy, slopseller; David Lazarus, salesman; Michael Emanuel, watchmaker; and Abraham Emdin, salesman were the signatories to the Trust Deed.[27] The Synagogue's Minute Book of this period often referred to the Portsmouth congregation as 'The Great Synagogue', not portraying a large edifice but 'Great' in its practices and principles.

On occasions the synagogue would be mentioned in the local Portsmouth papers particularly for special prayers and services for Royalty. When, for instance, Princess Charlotte died, *The Hampshire Telegraph* of 24 November 1817 reported, 'The High Priest of the Hebrew Synagogue in London (the Rev. Solomon Hirschell) composed a solemn and effecting service for the occasion, which was repeated at the Synagogue at Portsea, by Mr Alexander Barnet, Rabbi of that congregated body here on Wednesday afternoon last – the altar-piece and communication table being covered with black'. The gentile interpretation of the Ark containing the holy scrolls and reading desk draped in black may to Jewish eyes be rather piquant but it shows above all a willingness to understand and not ostracize the Jews of Portsmouth.

As some recognition to the Portsmouth Hebrew congregation and their undoubted connection with the Royal Navy, Admiral Sir Richard Bickerton KCB, Commander-in-Chief, Portsmouth and Captain the Honourable Sir George Gray Bart., Resident Commissioner of Portsmouth Dockyard together with other notables of the Portsmouth area attended a concert at the synagogue. It was given virtually at the end of the war by the popular tenor John Braham with two other Jewish singers making up a fine trio.[28]

Within a year of the war ending many seamen were in such distress that some starved. For others temporary relief was given from a charitable fund which had raised £15,000.[29] Charles Dibdin the prolific composer of sea songs had already written:-

I sing the British seaman's praise,
A theme renowned in story;

It well deserves more polished lays,
It is your boast and glory.
When mad-brained war spreads death around
By them you are protected;
But when in peace the Nation's found,
These bulwarks are neglected.

Whilst the war was in progress the Admiralty had cared insufficiently for the seamen, and it is therefore of little surprise that when it ended they felt the seamens' hardships were none of their affair. The Admiralty could now return to entirely volunteer crews with the stigma of unpopular impressment removed. Many payments of prize money were left outstanding, the ships' companies were paid off and that more or less was that as far as it concerned the Admiralty.

During the long war is it any wonder that the seamen had approached the traders to obtain some money in return for their Powers of Attorney and Prize Orders? The traders therefore performed an important, though at times dubious, function by helping to finance and clothe the seamen through the Admiralty abandoning their full responsibilities. The Treasurer of the Navy, George Rose, before he died in January 1818 had stood out in trying his best for the seamen by regularising the system of Naval Agency. But as he himself admitted the seamen had come to rely on the traders by long usuage and to remove this accommodation could have resulted in considerable discontent throughout the Fleet. The mutinies at the Nore and Spithead in 1797, were still too fresh in everyone's memory.

The young Jewish immigrants from the Continent keen to set up in trade with their first generation of English born children, fitted ideally into this situation. They were after all pedlars, old clothesmen, dealers and, in the more specialist crafts of silversmiths and jewellers, let alone pawnbrokers, able to supply just what the sailors required – slops, watches, trinkets, and above all small advances of ready money. Where else in England but generally in the naval towns, were these originally poor Ashkenazic Jews able in any sizeable numbers to be given the opportunity of trading? The Royal Navy had, as if by default, given the Jews a chance to succeed and establish themselves where few other opportunities existed.

It is certainly the case that some Jews lacked commercial honesty and defrauded the seamen. The brothers Judah, Samuel, and Daniel Jacob of Portsea were examples, with another member of the same family, John, falling foul of the authorities in one way or another. All were essentially slopsellers, with Daniel and John losing their Naval Agency licences for practising frauds on seamen.

After the case of 1802, in which Judah Jacob was proven guilty of fraud he had been treated with great suspicion and was the subject of a number of enquiries which proved unfounded on investigation. As already described, he also seemed to have dealt fairly with Robert Tinnion. However, Judah resigned his licence as a Navy Agent in February 1812, one of the very few to do so, without a reason being found. The next month he inserted an advertisement in *The Hampshire Courier* offering to let his premises at 6, Ordnance Row, Portsea – *'Standing in the direct road from Portsmouth to the Dock Yard, and general landing place of Portsea, must be considered a truly advantageous situation for trade, particularly as a lodging house for Naval Commanders, as such it has stood unrivaled for many years past.'* No rent was quoted, but his adroit advert soon attracted a tenant and part of the contents of Judah Jacob's home was put up for auction on 11 May 1812. It gives an insight into this intelligent man with his books, paintings and comfortable home:-

PORTSEA

> To be SOLD by AUCTION by MR MARCER, on the premises on Monday 11th of May 1812 and following day.
>
> Part of the elegant HOUSEHOLD FURNITURE, about 100 ounces of useful Plate, Linen, China and Glass, valuable Paintings and glazed Prints in gilt frames, a complete Iron Chest, fitted as a bookcase etc. etc. of MR JACOB (quitting his residence) No. 6, Ordnance Row, near the Hard: among the paintings are, a view of Portsmouth Harbour (by the late celebrated marine painter, Elliott), Jepthas' Daughter bathing, and the Woodman; a set of four excellent prints of the Battle of the Nile (glazed) and various others.
>
> The Furniture comprises, an elegant lofty full-size four-post bedstead, with handsome carved mahogany feet pillars; gilt and bronze cornice; rich chintz calico furniture, with full drapery valance, fringed and lined throughout; chintz calico and moreen draw window curtains, with gilt and bronze pole cornices; bedsteads with dimity furnitures, fine seasoned goose feathers beds, hair mattresses, palinzes, counterpanes, Marseilles quilts and blankets. In mahogany are dining,

> Pembroke, library, dressing, and other tables, circular front lobby drawers, twelve neat chairs, and two arm ditto with satin hair nail-over seats, a mahogany framed sofa covered with satin hair, and two bolsters; an eight day clock in mahogany case (by *Knight* of Portsea) one ditto (by Jamison) ten japanned chairs, with cushions and covers, an 18 inch mirror, in rich gilt frame, a 15 inch ditto, pier and dressing glasses, tea caddies, a plated tea urn, ditto, bread basket, kitchen requisites, and various other articles.

The reason for Judah Jacob's resignation as a Navy Agent and moving could have been that in September 1811 enquiries were being made by the Portsmouth Pay Office into allegations by a Midshipman James Cockerell of his being defrauded of £700 by the brothers Daniel and Samuel Jacob with Judah Jacob implicated.[30] Or could it have been his wife's poor health which made him move from Ordnance Row? Judah had a number of interests, owned property in Portsea and held a Coach Office Agency for W. Horne and Company who ran the 'Rocket' from Ludgate Hill to the famous Portsmouth naval and coaching house 'The Fountain', completing the seventy-two miles journey in nine hours. W. Horne and Company discontinued using Judah Jacob as a Coach Office in February 1815. However Judah was back at 6 Ordnance Row in 1815 with his own firm, The London Coach Office. Judah's wife Rachael died in November 1815, after a long illness, but he soon re-married. Judah finally moved away to Brixton, Surrey, in June 1818 after selling up 6, Ordnance Row to another slopseller and draper, a Robert Houghton.[31] His retirement was short. When Judah Jacob died in Janury 1819 he left an estate for duty purposes of £2,000, able to produce an annuity of £200 for his widow from rents arising from property in Portsea and Portsmouth. However he had stipulated that his second wife Mary return to Portsea, to look after the properties.[32] She became a Licensed Navy Agent at 5, Ordnance Row, Portsea until 1828. Another prominent Jewish Portsmouth trader, Jacob Zachariah died about a year after Judah Jacob in March 1819 leaving an estate valued at £3,000.[33]

So we find many of the old established businesses no longer functioning, either through the death of their proprietors, or the children of the original founders moving as trade declined and opportunities were sought in other parts of the country. Auctioneers' advertisements in the local Portsmouth newspaper, *The Hampshire Courier*, give an idea of the Jewish traders' status describing stock and household contents. Solomon

Alexander was an example, moving to London in December, 1815. A business was started by his father Isaac, one of the earliest Jewish settlers in Portsmouth, whose great grandson became Sir Julius Vogel Prime Minster of New Zealand in 1873.

## TO SILVERSMITHS, SLOPSELLERS, AND OTHERS PORTSMOUTH.

To be SOLD by AUCTION by MR GARNETT, on Tuesday the 12th day of December 1815, and following days (under an Execution from the Sheriff of Hants) all the valuable and modern HOUSEHOLD FURNITURE, rich China and Cut Glass, about 60 gold, silver and metal watches, about 500 ozs. of plate, quantity seamen's slops etc of Mr S. Alexander, at his dwelling house, Broad Street, on the Point.

The furniture comprises handsome celleret sideboard, secretary and bookcase, 50 volumes of books, elegant four-post bedstead with chintz drapery furniture and window curtains, round front double and single chest of drawers richly ornamented, basin stands, tent bedsteads and furniture, prime seasoned goose feather beds and bedding, mattresses, carpets, easy and painted chairs, bed-steps, dressing glasses etc.

The drawing room furniture consists of a set of elegant drapery furniture for three windows, with pole cornice; cord and sofa tables, neat mahogany chairs, sofa, Pembroke and dining tables, Brussels carpets and hearth rugs, handsome steel fender with standards and fire-irons to match, two large pier looking glasses, chimney ornaments, large plated tea urn, paintings and glazed prints, good kitchen furniture and many other articles.

In fact this was a forced sale as Solomon Alexander had lost a legal action against his bankers Grant Barbery and Company of Portsmouth, over interest charged, the previous July, incurring damages of £841. About a year before Solomon Alexander moved, his father-in-law Moses Hart had died aged 74 years, on 15 May 1814,[34] leaving an estate with a value less than £800. Moses Hart's freehold house at 51, Broad Street, Portsmouth, was valued at only £200 reflecting the decline in trade. The will gives an insight into just one of the old Portsmouth Jewish traders:-[35]

. . . . . I give and bequeath unto my said wife Eleanor and 2 daughters Amelia and Charlotte all and singular the money and bank notes which I have now in my possession in my said dwelling house subject to the payment given to Solomon Joseph, Alexander Barnet and to the elders of the Jews Synagogue and also all and every sum of money and sums of money stock and other effects due and owing to me from Messrs Godwin and Co of Portsmouth Bankers and which I am possessed of interested in or entitled into the public funds of this Kingdom in equal parts and proportions shall share and share alike to and for their own proper use and benefit also I give and bequeath the sum of £20 to my step-brother the said Solomon Joseph of Wentworth Street Spitalfields Merchant and the sum of £5 to Alexander Barnet of College Street Portsea Clerk of the Synagogue in Whites Row to say prayers for me for a twelve month after my decease and the sum of Ten Pounds to the elders of the Jews Synagogue in Whites Row aforesaid for the use and benefit of the said Synagogue to be paid to them respectively by my executrix and executor hereinafter named within one month of my decease . . . . .

John Zachariah, the foremost Portsmouth Jewish trader, retired not long after the Napoleonic Wars ended. First came the advertisement selling the business on 30 October, 1815:-

## NO. 69, HIGH STREET, PORTSMOUTH

### *To Jewellers, Silversmiths, Watch Makers and Others*

To be SOLD by AUCTION by MR VICAT on the premises, on Monday, the 6th of November, and following days, all that valuable modern STOCK in TRADE, of Mr John Zachariah, retiring from business; comprising, an elegrant assortment of plate; handsome gold dial and repeating watches; diamond rings and pins, pearl, cornelian, and coral ear-rings; a beautiful assortment of cornelian coral and amber necklaces; handsome gold chains, seals and keys; gold and silver snuff boxes; swords, sabres, dirks and belts, a gun and case by *Nock*, pistols; Navy and Army epaulets, silk sashes; day and night telescopes, by *Dolland*, quadrants; musical instruments; portable desks, shaving cases; silver and tortoise-shell spectacles; pen, pocket and table knives and forks, scissors and razors; gilt and plated spurs; German pipes and tubes; a great variety of plated goods of the best quality, silver edged; 2 eight day table clocks; a quantity of pewter plates etc. etc.

Catalogues may be had in due time of the Auctioneer; at the place of sale, and at the principal Inns.

N.B. the whole of this stock will be sold without reserve, Mr Zachariah having engaged to give possession of his premises at a short date.

*Midshipman George Grover's dirk, sold and possibly made by John Zachariah of 69 High Street, Portsmouth in about 1814. The name "Zachariah" is inscribed at the top of the scabbard. (courtesy of Mr G. Hunt).*

Then came his household goods and furniture advertised in *The Hampshire Courier* on 4th December, 1815:-

## 69, HIGH – STREET, PORTSMOUTH

To be SOLD by AUCTION by MR VICAT, on the premises, on Wednesday the 6th of December, 1815, all the modern and neat HOUSEHOLD GOODS and FURNITURE, valuable prints etc of Mr John Zachariah, retiring from business;

> comprising elegant chimney and pier glasses, choice collection of prints in handsome gilt frames; tent bedsteads, with mahogany feet pillars and cotton furnitures, modern moreen and chintz window curtains; mahogany sofa, cord, dining, Pembroke, library, and other tables, highly finished and to match, a neat secretary and bookcase, sideboard; a set of Japon and Grecian chairs, with cushions, Brussels carpets, a pair of fine cut glass lustres; kitchen requisites, an iron chest; marquee; a good milch cow, etc. Also the remaining part of the Stock in Trade, consisting of a few highly finished gold watches; a table clock; two pair of pistols; 3 telescopes; about 30 lots of jewellery; scales and weights; counter show glasses, passage and shop lamps etc etc.

When Charles Lyons another Jewish trader moved to London, the Auctioneer's advertisement of 25th August, 1817, revealed the large stock this draper and clothier carried:-

> To the Trade and Private Families
>
> To be Peremptorily SOLD by AUCTION by MR GARNETT on Monday 25th August 1817, and following days at two o'clock until the whole is sold – The very extensive STOCK-IN-TRADE of Mr Charles Lyons, 160, Queen Street, corner of North-Street, Portsea; consisting of several hundred yards of broad cloths, kerseymeres, velveteens, cords, jeans, stocking-nets, flushings, toilenets, Marseillas, swandowns, flannels, ducks, canvas, tickings, sheeting, best town prints, callicoes, striped cottons, muslins, linen, table cloths, cotton and worsted hose, gloves, carpets, quilts, blankets, green table covers, hearth rugs, and many other articles too numerous to mention – Also, the whole of the most excellent Stock of well-manufactured Clothing, will be sold by hand the fore-part of the day till one o'clock, for the convenience of purchasers trying them on, at very reduced prices, as the whole must actually be sold C.L. having engaged in a Concern in London: the Stock of Clothing consists of 5,000 articles viz – great coats, dress coats, gig, curricles, pantaloons, Wellington and Cossack trousers, breeches, gaiters, shooting-jackets, waistcoats of all

descriptions, flannel dressing jackets, children's cloth, velvet, and instiau dresses; white shirts; Seamen's Clothing, consisting of Flushing coats, monkey Jackets, Flushing trousers, suits, red caps, flannel and stripped cotton shirts.

The whole of the above being well manufactured are worth the attention of the public early inspection is advisable.

• The whole of these extensive Premises to Let, being one of the best situations in the three Towns, commanding Town and Country Trade – For particulars apply on the Premises.

On the other hand when Abraham Franklin's mother-in-law Alice Aaron died, her home and business were sold on 6 August 1817. The auctioneer's advertisement disclosing how those trading just at slopsellers were less affluent than the Jewellers and Silversmiths:-

PORTSEA

To be SOLD by AUCTION by MR GARNETT, on the Premises on Wednesday next August 6, 1817, and following day, at eleven o'clock by order of the Executors – All the STOCK-IN-TRADE, HOUSEHOLD FURNITURE. Plate, Linen, China, etc of the late Mrs Alice Aaron, Slopseller, at her late dwelling house in Clock Street.

The Stock consists of seamen's suits, great coats, trousers, waistcoats, stockings, hats, silk and cotton handkerchiefs, cotton and other shirts, a quantity of second-hand clothes etc.

The HOUSEHOLD FURNITURE consists of dining and Pembroke tables, chest of drawers, carpet, fenders and fire irons, tent and four-post bedsteads and furniture, good seasoned feather beds and bedding, mahogany and other chairs, kitchen furniture, and many other articles – The Furniture will be sold on the first day.

The great days, when Portsmouth witnessed waggon loads of dollars from captured Spanish merchantmen being sent to the Bank of England with their military escort up to London, were over. Such a long period of trading activity was not to be witnessed again. For the Portsmouth Hebrew community a link with the original founder Benjamin Levi was broken when *The Hampshire Telegraph* of 24 April 1820 reported, *"Died on the 16 inst. aged 70, Mrs Levi widow of Jacob Levi 10 Union Street Portsea – True piety, with unbounded liberality to the poor of all denominations were the characteristics of this amiable Lady's character.'* The following June the deceased's home, that of Benjamin Levi's daughter-in-law, was put up for auction.[36]

On 21 February 1820, as the minute guns from the warships and forts echoed around the naval towns, those Jews attending special services in their synagogues held for King George III's funeral reflected on their circumstances during the King's long reign.

About eighty years previously the first Jewish immigrant craftsmen, engravers, silversmiths and jewellers had settled in the naval towns becoming the upper stratum of the mainly poor Ashkenazic settlers; followed by the roving Jewish pedlar who had discovered a more or less captive customer – the seamen of the British Fleet at Portsmouth, Plymouth, Chatham and Sheerness. From second-hand clothesmen to slopsellers was a simple process for the early Jewish settlers trading close to where the seamen came ashore. One important result, for both seamen and traders, of the 1797 mutinies was the granting of liberty for the seamen when in port. Trading aboard warships did not cease, particularly on pay days, but there was now an increased demand for those with shops ashore. Later the statutes requiring the traders to be Licensed Navy Agents enabled them to continue accepting Prize Orders as a means of deferred payment for their goods. By becoming Licensed Navy Agents, the traders advanced their status from just being common slopsellers, or second-hand clothesmen. By securing two bondsmen, usually other local tradesmen, for £200, rising to £500 by 1819, a petty trader could fairly easily become a Licensed Navy Agent, even though he may have acted for only a small number of seamen. Therefore, although there grew to be a large number of Jewish Agents it did not necessarily mean they were all carrying on lucrative trades. This understandable striving for status has manifested itself in the customary belief that up to the early part of the nineteenth century Jews trading in the ports were ships' chandlers. Within the accepted meaning, they were not, Ships' Chandlers required a knowledge of boats, seamanship, and victualling which the Jews did not have. It just sounded a more appropriate and dignified title. In fact Jews were not looked upon as being 'Used to the ways of the sea' which meant a protection from impressment. Added to which the naval town traders, whether Jewish or not, performed a useful function for the authorities and so were generally left alone by the press gangs. Yet other Jews were pressed and volunteered. Sometimes Jewish sailors used Jewish traders as their Agents. Emanuel Hart a watchmaker and Navy Agent or Fore Street,

Plymouth Dock, received £2.19s.6d. prize money on 17 June 1809, due to Ordinary Seaman Jacob Cohen of London, part of the ship's company of the 38-gun frigate *Sibylle* for his share in the capture of the French 16-gun brig *Espiegle.*[37] The four Jewish seamen aboard *HMS Britannia* at the Battle of Trafalgar all gave orders to collect their prize money of £1.17s.8½d. each to three Jewish Plymouth Navy Agents – Barrow Moss, Lewis Ralph and Manly Hart.[38]

By 1820 a tradition of Jewish service in, and trading with, the Royal Navy had been established. One important result was that a small number of relatively poor Jews had come into direct and continuous contact with the wider indigenous population. A small contribution had been made by the Jews in their connections with the Royal Navy towards the wider aspirations of the Anglo-Jewish community. The beginning of the quest for emancipation of British Jewry was not far away.

Seaman 1828.

## CHAPTER 1 – End Notes and Sources

1. Chapter 2. Pages 93 – 114. Lucien Wolf. *Essays in Jewish History* (Jewish Historical Society of England 1934). Cromwell's Jewish Intelligencers.
2. Transactions of the Jewish Historical Society of England. Volume 4 (1903). *'Some Historical Notes 1648–1680'*. Pages 194 and 196 by C.H. Firth.
3. Pages 74 and 76. A.M. Hyamson. *The Sephardim of England* (Methuen 1951).

### Other Printed Sources referred to:-

M. Adler, *Jews of Medieval England* (Goldston, 1939). Published for Jewish Historical Society of England.

H.S.Q. Henriques, *The Return of the Jews to England* (Macmillan 1905).

Dr C. Roth, *A Life of Menasseh ben Israel* (Jewish Publication Society of America 1934).

Dr C. Roth, *A History of the Jews in England*, third edition reprinted 1979 (Oxford University Press).

## CHAPTER 2 – End Notes and Sources

1. Transactions of the Jewish Historical Society of England. Volume 20 (1959-1961) *'Dr Meyer Schomberg's Attack on the Jews of London 1746'*. Pages 83 – 100 by E. Samuel.
2. Dictionary of National Biography (1897) and J. Charnock. Biographia Navalis (London 1794-1798) Volume 6. Page 272.
3. Public Record Office: ADMI-1828. Captains' Letters. Solomon Gideon and J. Charnock. *Biographia Navalis* (London 1794-1798) Volume 5. Page 21.
4. Public Record Office: ADM 107-4. Lieutenants' Certificates. Alexander Schomberg.
5. Public Record Office: ADMI-2471 and 2472. Captains' Letters. Alexander Schomberg.
6. Public Record Office: ADMI-2473. Captains' Letters. Alexander Schomberg.
7. Public Record Office: ADMI-2474. Captains' Letters. Alexander Schomberg.
8. Public Record Office: ADM51-246 and 4162. Captains' Log of *HMS Diana* and ADM 52-829 Master's Log *HMS Diana*.
9. Public Record Office: ADM 36-5440. Ship's Muster *HMS Diana* 1757-1760.
10. Public Record Office: ADMI-482. Lord Colville's Despatches 24 May 1760.
11. Public Record Office: ADM5I-1443. Captain's Log HM Yacht *Dorset*.
12. Public Record Office: ADM 107/4. Lieutenant's Certificate Maximillian Jacobs and ADM 1/1987. Captain's Letters. J. Charnock, *Biographia Navalis* (London 1798) Volume 6 page 318.
13. *The Gentleman's Magazine* 1851. Volume 35, pages 330 and 353: A. Hyamson, *Anglo-Jewish Notabilities* (Jewish Historical Society of England, 1949): W. O'Byrne, *A Naval Biographical Dictionary* (John Murray, London, 1849).

### Printed Sources Consulted for the Conquest of Canada

W.L. Clowes *The Royal Navy* 7 Volumes (London 1897-1903) Volume 3 Pages 173, 183 and 227.

*Gentleman's Magazine* Volume 30. June 1760.

A. Kitson. *The Life of Captain James Cook* (London 1911)

Commander H.S. Lecky. *The King's Ships* 3 Volumes (London 1914) Volume 2. Pages 230 and 231.

C. Lloyd. *The Capture of Quebec* (Batsford 1959).

I. Schomberg. *Naval Chronology* 5 Volumes (London 1802).

Lt. Col. W. Wood (Editor), *The Logs of the Conquest of Canada* (Toronto 1909).

**CHAPTER 3 – End Notes and Sources**

1. Public Record Office ADM 51–3878, Log *HMS Lancaster*.
2. Transactions of the Jewish Historical Society of England Volume 13 (1932/35) *'The Portsmouth Community and its Historical Background'* by Dr C. Roth, Page 164.
3. L. Wolf. *'Essays In Jewish History'*. (Jewish Historical Society of England 1934), pages 137-138.
4. The Jewish Monthly. 1950. *'The Rise of Provincial Jewry'*. Pages 94 and 95 Dr C. Roth.
5. Ibid. Source 2. Page 159.
6. W. Robinson, *Jack Nastyface, The Memoirs of a Seaman* (Wayland Publishers 1973, first published as *Nautical Economy* 1836) Page 38.
7. Captain Marryat, *Peter Simple* (London 1834) Chapter 11.
8. *The Naval and Military Sketch Book* 1844 (Anonymous). Pages 28 and 29.
9. Transactions of the Jewish Historical Society of England Volume 17 (1951/52). *'Some New Facts about the Portsmouth Jewish Community'* by Rabbi E. Newman, page 254.
10. Ibid. Source 2. Page 178.
11. D. Black. *Plymouth's Historic Synagogue* (Plymouth Hebrew Community 1961).
12. The Jewish Monthly 1950. *'The Rise of Provincial Jewry'*. Page 92, by Dr C. Roth.
13. Rev. M. Zeffert, *'The Plymouth Hebrew Congregation'*: *The Jewish Chronicle* Supplement 24 November 1922.
14. Transactions of the Jewish Historical Society of England. Miscellanies Part 6. 1962. *'Plymouth Aliens List 1798 and 1803'*, by Dr V.D. Lipman,
15. R.N. Worth. *History of Plymouth* 1871. Page 262.
16. D. Hannay. *Naval Courts Martial.* (Cambridge University Press 1914) Page 117. 'Jews' trading in wage tickets'.
17. City of Portsmouth Reference Library, Pescott Frost Collection, files of *The Hampshire Telegraph* 1887 to 1889.
18. Carreras Cigarettes. *History of Naval Uniforms.* 1937
19. *The Gentleman's Magazine*. Obituary Notice Abraham Joseph, Volume 64, Part 2. 1794. Page 1156.

**Reference has also been made to:-**

B. Emden. *'Ancestral Tapestry'*. Lecture delivered to Devon Family History Society, 1977.

C. Gill. Plymouth *A New History*. 1979 Part 2. David and Charles.

I am indebted to Dr V.D. Lipman for his notes on *'The Origins of Provincial Jewry'*.

## CHAPTER 4 – End Notes and Sources

1. Public Record Office ADM 51–1442. Log Book *HMS Magicienne* February 1802.
2. Public Record Office ADM 1–5360. Minutes of the proceedings of the Court Martial of John Cook. 3 February 1802.
3. Public Record Office ADM 36–14287. Muster Book *HMS Zealand*. January to March 1802.
4. Public Record Office ADM 51–1391. Log Book *HMS Zealand* February 1802.
5. Public Record Office ADM 51–1421. Log Book *HMS Isis* February 1802.
6. Public Record Office ADM 1–735. Secretary's Department.
7. Public Record Office ADM 102–743. Muster Book HM Hospital Ship *Spanker*. March 1802.
8. Public Record Office ADM 1–735. John Levy was discharged after his flogging suffering from *rheumatism* which was a contemporary medical term used for a person afflicted by various kinds of inflammation caused mostly from changes in temperature. Many seamen suffered from this complaint.
9. Public Record Office ADM 36–15428. Muster Book *HMS Enterprise* May 1796.
10. Public Record Office ADM 36–14464. Muster Book *HMS Merlin* 1796-1801.
11. W.L. Clowes. *The Royal Navy* 7 Volumes (London 1897-1903) Volume 4 Page 379.
12. Public Record Office ADM 36–14273. Muster Book *HMS Dolphin* 1801.
13. Public Record Office ADM 1–5338. Minutes of the proceedings of the Court Martial of John Jacobs. 27 March 1797.
14. Transactions of the Jewish Historical Society of England Volume 9 (1922) Page 126. *A Form of Prayer and Supplication for the Success of British Arms held at Bevis Marks Synagogue, Friday 19 April 1793.*
15. National Maritime Museum, Marine Society Records MSY/K/1 to 6. Boys received and discharged from Society's Ships and Landsmen Volunteers. MSY/S/1 to 5.
16. H.S. Lecky. *The King's Ships*, 3 Volumes. (London 1914) Volume 2 Page 356.
17. Public Record Office ADM 7-361. Account of Men Raised for service in HM Navy for the Port of London, 23 October 1795.
18. Public Record Office ADM 1-2631. Secretary's Department.
19. Public Record Office ADM 1-4842. Piece 492 Secretary's Department and Muster Book *HMS Mermaid* ADM 37 4341.
20. J.R. Hutchinson. *The Press Gang Afloat and Ashore* (Eveleigh Nash, London 1913). Page 244. The author has assumed the contemporary scene of Jewish tailors in 1913 applied to the early nineteenth century. This is not correct. The Jews during the Napoleonic Wars were mainly pedlars, second-hand clothes dealers and slopsellers, not tailors. Lionel Yexley, in his review of the book in *'The Fleet'* for December 1913, wrote, 'Mr. Hutchinson knowing nothing about sailors, has drawn on his imagination and written a lot of twaddle – he should have stuck to the doings of the Press Gang instead of venturing into what the sailor was and was not.'
21. Public Record Office ADM 1-3695. Secretary's Department.
22. Public Record Office ADM 36-15900. Muster Book *HMS Victory* for 1805.
23. Public Record Office ADM 6-67 (2 and 3) Discharges at Plymouth 1812-1815.
24. *The Jewish Chronicle*. 18 September 1868. Obituary of Isaac Vallentine.
25. G. Sanger. *Seventy Years a Showman* (J. Dent and Sons, London 1927) Page 35. The episode is supposed to have taken place aboard *HMS Pompey*, but there was no such ship in the Royal Navy. It could possibly have been *HMS Pompee*.

26. C.S. Forester (Editor) *The Adventures of John Wetherell* (Michael Joseph, London 1954), page 169. The Muster Book of *HMS Hussar* in the Public Record Office ADM36-16028 gives the age of John Smith as 24 when joining the ship on 9 March 1803 as a volunteer receiving a bounty of £2.0s.0d. He was born in London.

27. *Shetland Journal*. 1 September 1837.

28. The original journal is now possibly in the hands of one of Richard Barnett's descendants in New York. It was on display in the Anglo-Jewish Tercentenary Exhibition at the Victoria and Albert Museum in 1956, item number 440. I am indebted to the late Doctor Richard D. Barnett, C.B.E., former Keeper of Department of Western Asiatic Antiquities at the British Museum, for guidance concerning his namesake. I have relied on the articles 'A Jewish Link with Nelson' page 10 of *The Jewish Chronicle* 15 April 1955 and a similar article in *The Jewish World* page 72 of 20 October 1905. At the Public Record Office are *HMS Vanguard's* Captain's Log Books in ADM 51-1288 and ADM 51-1293 with the Muster Books in ADM 36-15357. Subsequently see "Richard Barnett: An Anglo-Jewish Sailor at the Battle of the Nile" by Richard D. Barnett. *The Mariner's Mirror* Volume 71 Number 2, May 1985. Pages 185-200. The Journal is here recorded. Photographs of the actual Journal have been deposited in Anglo-Jewish Archives, University College, London.

29. Public Record Office ADM 36-13638. Muster Book *HMS Royal William*.

30. Public Record Office ADM 36-15305. Muster Book *HMS Ceres*.

**Other Printed Sources Consulted**


J.J. Colledge, *Ships of the Royal Navy: An Historical Index*. 2 Volumes (David and Charles 1969).

C. Gill, *The Naval Mutinies of 1797* (Manchester University Press 1913).

Lt. Commander P.K. Kemp, *Nine Vanguards* (Hutchison 1951).

M. Lewis, *A Social History of the Navy 1793-1813* (George Allen and Unwin 1960).

C. Lloyd and J. Coulter, *Medicine and the Navy*, 4 Volumes (Livingstone 1961).

Captain A.T. Mahan, *The Influence of Sea Power upon the French Revolution and Empire* (Sampson Low Marston 1892), 2 Volumes.

J. Masefield, *Sea Life in Nelson's Time* (Sphere Books 1972).

Sir H. Nicholas, *The Dispatches and Letters of Vice-Admiral Lord Viscount Nelson* (Colburn 1844-6), 7 Volumes.

W. Robinson, *Jack Nastyface, The Memoirs of a Seaman* (Wayland Publishers Reprint 1973).

Dr C. Roth, *A History of the Jews in England* (Oxford University Press, Second Edition 1948).

Dr C. Roth, *History of the Great Synagogue* (Edward Goldston and Son 1950).


**CHAPTER 5 – End Notes and Sources**

1. Saunders W.H. *Annals of Portsmouth* (Hamilton Adams, London 1880). Pages 116 and 117.
2. Public Record Office HO.50/43. Military Correspondence and Papers.
3. Public Record Office HO.50/45. Military Correspondence and Papers.
4. Public Record Office ADM106/1560. Navy Board Records.
5. Public Record Office ADM1/580. Secretary's Department Letters.
6. Public Record Office ADM1/3698. Admiralty Solicitor Papers.
7. Public Record Office ADM7/308. Law Officers' Opinions.

8. Public Record Office ADM1/1113 and ADM1/3697. Secretary's Department Letters and Admiralty Solicitor Papers.
9. Public Record Office ADM1/3699. Admiralty Solicitor Papers.
10. Public Record Office ADM51/1797. Log of *HMS Pompee* and ADM36/17357 Muster Book of *HMS Pompee*.
11. Public Record Office ADM1/3917. Secretary's Department Letters.
12. Public Record Office ADM1/678. Secretary's Department Letters, Seamens' testimonies on which the 'Run ashore' is based, John Stubbs and the crew of the *Sir Francis Burdett*, together with letters written by Henry Nathan to his wife and William Phipps, list of crimps and correspondence of Vice-Admiral Rowley.
13. Public Record Office ADM1/1542. Secretary's Department Letters.
14. Public Record Office ADM1/3695 and 3696. Admiralty Solicitor Papers.
14. Public Record Office ADM37/7. Muster Book *HMS Princess of Orange*.
16. Public Record Office ADM37/753 Muster Book *HMS Enterprise*.
17. *The Kentish Chronicle* 16 August 1808.
18. *The London Chronicle* 27 November 1810.

**Reference was also made to the following:-**

*The Jewish Chronicle* 28 December 1900. A Hundred Years Ago: Anglo-Jewry at the commencement of the 19th Century.

*The Jewish Chronicle* Supplement April 1936 'The Anglo-Jewish Community: Some aspects of its social and economic development' by J. Rumney, Chapter 4. The lower orders: demoralisation: an attempt at reform.

**CHAPTER 6 – End Notes and Sources**

1. Public Record Office ADM1/3195. Secretary's Department Letters.
2. Public Record Office ADM1/527. Secretary's Department Letters.
3. Transactions of the Jewish Historical Society of England, Volume 17 (1953) *'Anglo-Jewish Notaries and Scriveners'* by E Samuel, pages 140-141.
4. Public Record Office ADM51/1271. Captain's Log. *HMS Arrow*.
5. H. Roden, *Treasure Seekers* (Harrap 1966), page 114. S.J. Van der Molen, *The Lutine Treasure* (Adlard Coles 1970). F. Martin, *The History of Lloyds and of Marine Insurance in Great Britain*. (Macmillan 1876) pages 183-209.
6. *The Jewish Chronicle*. 3 November 1905.
7. *Jewish Guardian*, 23 December 1921.
8. Public Record Office ADM67-278. Minutes of the Naval Asylum.
9. Ibid source 8.
10. Ibid source 8.
11. National Maritime Museum. Marine Society Records MSY/U/21 Subscription Lists. MSY/G/1. Register of Donations and Legacies. MSY/A/4 Letter books of the Marine Society.
12. Public Record Office ADM73/89. Register of children in the Naval Asylum. It was highly probable that William Hart, nominated by Benjamin Goldsmid to the Naval Asylum in February 1802 was a Jew. Benjamin must have been approached to do something for the boy. Was that approach made by the Jewish community? In all events, Benjamin responded in getting the boy nominated by going to the trouble to ask Lord Nelson for help. William Hart of London left the Naval Asylum in

November 1802 for the *Victory* and then the sloop *Bonetta*. He joined the frigate *Ambuscade* on 3 May 1804 when seventeen years of age among a list of six boys borne as part of the complement in lieu of Marines by order of Lord Nelson. William Hart was discharged from the *Ambuscade* the following September as a Boy Second Class (Public Record Office ADM37-750). He is not to be confused with the other William Hart who was one of the principal witnesses in the case of the conviction of Henry Nathan in August 1808 for crimping. His first ship was the sloop *Swan* (ADM36-13686) in January 1800, then on to *The Vanguard* (ADM36- 16035) where his place of birth was given as Wooten in Dorset. It is very doubtful therefore that he was Jewish. However in the register of children in the Naval Asylum (ADM73-89) as at December 1800, under number 26 is a Joseph Hart aged seven, with no comment after his name, as distinct from the rest of the register wherein all the children had some comment, such as what ship their late father belonged to, or some detail about the mother being for instance, a servant. It is with some caution one could perhaps consider that this particular orphan was of Jewish birth.

13. *The Naval Chronicle* Volume 7, page 516.
14. J Picciotto, *Sketches of Anglo-Jewish History*. Edited by Israel Finestein (The Soncino Press, London 1956), pages 267-274.
15. Public Record Office HO50/78. Military Correspondence and Papers.
16. Ibid source 14.
17. Transactions of the Jewish Historical Society of England Volume 21 (1968) *'First Lady of Anglo-Jewry'* by S. Lipman, pages 287-288 and L. Loewe (Editor), *'The Diaries of Sir Moses and Lady Montefiore'*. A facsimile of the 1890 edition (The Jewish Historical Society of England and The Jewish Museum 1983) Volume 1, page 3. In the defence of Acre between March and May 1799, Sir Sidney Smith sought the co-operation of the Pasha, Achmet Djezzar, to strengthen the defences of the Town. Considerable assistance in the organisation of the city's defences was given by the Pasha's Jewish chief minister, Hayim Farhi.
18. *The Naval Chronicle* Volume 11, page 478.
19. Commissioners of Naval Enquiry Tenth Report 1805. The Office of Treasurer of the Navy, and subsequent Act Anno 47, George III, Chapter 56. Page 473.
20. The Jewish Monthly. January 1948. *'Nelson and some Jews'* Pages 25-33, by Dr Cecil Roth.
21. Transactions of the Jewish Historical Society of England. Volume 20 (1964), *'John Braham, singer'*, by M. Sands, pages 203-214.
22. J.J. Abraham, *Lettsom, his Life and Times, friends and descendants*, (Heinemann 1933), page 444.
23. Ibid. Source 8.
24. Transactions of the Jewish Historical Society of England. Volume 14 (1940) *'The Brothers Goldsmid and the Financing of the Napoleonic Wars'* by Paul Emden, page 236, and Volume 18 (1958) 'Eighteenth Century Anglo-Jewry in and around Richmond, Surrey– Roehampton and the Goldsmids' by Rachel Daiches-Rubens, pages 160-163. It is interesting to note regarding Benjamin Goldsmid's house in Roehampton that the roadway now known as Roehampton Lane ran through the grounds. Benjamin tried to have this road diverted but met opposition from the local authority, so he built a tunnel in order to reach the other side of his estate, without having to cross the highway. The house and lands came into the possession of the Convent of the Sacred Heart who still own the land, having done so for about 130 years. Unfortunately the house was destroyed by enemy action during the Second World War. The tunnel is still in existence. As for Lord Nelson's home, Merton Place, Asher Goldsmid sold it in 1815, before final demolition in 1823. The whole estate is now built upon but still known as Nelson's Fields, close to South Wimbledon Underground

Station. See *Paradise Merton* by P. Rathbone, 1973, published by the author, and *A History of Merton and Morden* by E.M. Jowett, 1951, published by the Merton and Morden Festival of Britain Local Committee.

*Lord Nelson's purported stay at Benjamin Goldsmid's home on Thursday 12 September 1805, the night before leaving for Portsmouth and the Battle of Trafalgar.*

It must be remembered Lionel Goldsmid was only eight years of age when Lord Nelson stayed at his father's home. Added to which he wrote up the diary in later years so doubt will therefore arise. On the Thursday in question, Lord Minto wrote, on Friday 13 September 1805, 'I went yesterday to Merton in a great hurry as he, Lord Nelson, said he was to be home all day, and he dines at half-past three. But I found he had been sent for to Carlton House, and heard Lady Hamilton did not return till half-past five. I stayed till ten at night and took a final leave of him'. (*Life and Letters of Sir Gilbert Elliot, First Earl of Minto 1751-1806.* The Countess of Minto, 3 Volumes, Longman Green 1874, Volume 3, page 370). It is possible, but unlikely that Lord Nelson then left Merton and made the short journey to Goldsmid's home at Roehampton. He may, however, have called in to say good-bye to Goldsmid on his way back to Merton from Carlton House, which would account for the delay. One can only assume the diarist was confused with another occasion when Lord Nelson undoubtedly stayed overnight at Roehampton.

Lionel Goldsmid did not go to sea but entered the army as an officer in the 19th Light Dragoons. One of his brothers, Albert, seved with the 12th Royal Lancers in the Peninsular War and at Waterloo. All Benjamin's family adopted Christianity after his death.

25. See Appendix 8 Page –
26. Ibid. Source 20.
27. *Annual Register.* Volume 47 page 433.
28. *The Jewish Chronicle.* 27 October 1905.
29. Sermon preached at the Great Synagogue, Duke's Place, on the 14 Kislav (A.M.) 5565, answering to Thursday, 5 December 1805; being the day appointed for a General Thanksgiving for the success of His Majesty's Fleet under Lord Nelson, off Trafalgar; by the Reverend Soloman Hirschel presiding Rabbi of the German Jews in London. Printed for W.J. and J. Richardson 1805. Quarto. 16 pages. (I am indebted to Mr Phineas May, Honorary Custodian of The Jewish Museum, London, for letting me have a copy of the sermon).
30. Reverend W.C. Tucker. *The Royal Navy Song Book.* (Routledge & Sons, circa 1860).
31. Ibid. Source 20.
32. Alfred Morrison. *The Hamilton and Nelson Papers.* 2 Volumes 1893-94. Page 278. Letter number 872.
33. Public Record Office ADMI/4624. Secretary's Papers, ADM51/1556 Captain's Log *HMS Captain* and Muster Book ADM37/59.
34. Public Record Office ADM15/1 Solicitor's Papers.
35. W. James. *Naval History of Great Britain* (1878). Volume 6, pages 124-128. W. Lecky, *The King's Ships* (1913/14). Volume 1, page 133. Public Record Office ADM37/4214. Muster *HMS Astrea.*
36. Public Record Office ADM37/3616. Muster *HMS Macedonia.*
37. *The Naval Chronicle* 1811, Volume 25, page 164 and Public Record Office ADM37/23788. Muster *HMS Ceylon.*
38. Public Record Office ADM171/1. Roll, Naval General Service Medal.
39. V.D. Lipman, *Greenwich: Palace, Park and Town.* (Anniversary Address, Ancient Monuments Society, 15 June 1973).

40. Public Record Office. Register of Greenwich Pensioners 1801 to 1809 ADM73/55 and 1809 to 1815 ADM73/56.

Joseph Manuel who fought at the Battle of Trafalgar aboard *HMS Britannia* entered Greenwich Hospital 15 October 1845 at the age of sixty two. He had served twelve years in the Royal Navy. *HMS Britannia* from 1 September 1804 to 21 April 1806; *HMS Royal George* until 20 May 1809 then *HMS San Josef* for the remainder of his service. His Jewish shipmates aboard *HMS Britannia*, Nathan Manuel, Henry Levi and Benjamin Solomon, had similar careers except that they did not enter Greenwich Hospital. Early in May 1809 they were all sent to *HMS Phoebe* for a short period (Muster Books ADM36-15997, ADM37-562 and ADM37-1815).

41. National Maritime Museum. *A Description of the Royal Hospital for Seamen at Greenwich. 1855.*

42. *The Jewish Chronicle.* 2 April 1869.

43. Public Record Office ADM37/456. *HMS Resolution.* Muster and Log ADM51/1603.

**Reference was also made to the following, with particular respect to the Goldsmid Brothers:-**

C. Bermant, *The Cousinhood. The Anglo-Jewish Gentry* (Eyre and Spottiswoode, 1971), pages 17-24.

A. Levy, *Memoirs of the Life and Commercial Connections of the late Benjamin Goldsmid,* (London 1808).

J. Picciotto, *Sketches of Anglo-Jewish History,* Edited by Israel Finestein, (The Soncino Press, London 1956), pages 240-247. The Goldsmid Family.

Transactions of the Jewish Historical Society of England. Volume 14 (1940). *'The Brothers Goldsmid and the Financing of the Napoleonic Wars',* Pages 225-246. by Paul Emden.

Transactions of the Jewish Historical Society of England. Volume 17 (1953) *'An Anglo-Jewish Family',* Pages 1-10. by Albert Hyamson.

## CHAPTER 7 – End Notes and Sources

1. National Westminster Bank Archives Head Office. Paper number 242. Stillwell and Sons a monograph.

2. Public Record Office: ADM51-2396. Log of *HMS Fury.*

3. Public Record Office: HCA 30-51 and HCA 30-74.

4. Williams and Glyn Bank Archives – Royal Bank of Scotland Head Office. Woodhead and Company Papers – Instructions for Prizes Procedure Manual 1801.

5. The main source for the mode of business of the Prize Agents and Navy Agents is found in the Fourth Report of the Commissioners enquiring into irregularities, frauds and abuses practised in the naval departments and in the business of Prize Agency, 1803. The Chairman was Admiral Sir Charles Pole MP whose papers are in the National Maritime Museum WYN/109/4 and ADM/J/3952.

6. National Maritime Museum. Hulbert Papers – Petty Agency Accounts HUL 26.

7. Public Record Office. HCA 2-334 and HCA 2-383.

8. N.M. Rothschild Archives. Lucien Woolfe Papers TWA 7 and 49.

9. Pages 273-285. A. Broadley and R. Bartelot. *The Three Dorset Captains at Trafalgar* (John Murray) 1906 and Public Records Office ADM 238-10. Prize Payments Battle of Trafalgar.

10. Pages 325, 328 and 329. *The Illustrated History of Portsmouth.* W. G. Gates. 1900. Charpentier. The 'Payne' pamphlet of 1748.

11. Public Record Office ADM 49/72. Piece 44. Inspectors' Branch. Navy Pay Office.

12. Public Record Office ADM 49/72. Piece 127. Inspectors' Branch. Navy Pay Office.

13. *Portsmouth Gazette.* 23 February and 9 March 1795. Gershon Woolfe would have been one of the earliest Jewish Navy Agents. Mentioned in the Portsmouth Rate Book of 1775, at 3 Drake's Passage, Portsmouth Common (Portsmouth City Record Office) subsequently at The Hard in 1784, as a silversmith (Sadlers Hampshire Directory 1784). In the Registers of Seamen's Wills at the Public Record Office (ADM142/8) Gershon Woolfe had the wills of John Lynop and Alexander Lennox made over in his favour on 21 July 1790.

14. *Naval Chronicle* Volume 9 (1803), Pages 153 and 154. *The Times* and *Portsmouth Telegraph* for 13 December 1802. It will be remembered Lord Chief Justice (as he was to become) Ellenborough also heard the case against Henry Nathan, found guilty of crimping in August 1808. He was also to rule, in 1811, in Lindo v Unsworth, that a Jew be excused from giving notice of dishonour of a bill of exchange to the defendant on a Jewish holiday, Unsworth claiming the notice was bad. 'I think the plaintiff was excused from giving notice upon the score of his religion . . . he sent the letter off as soon as he could after the termination of the festival during which he was absolutely forbidden to attend to secular affairs. The law respects the religion of different people'. He was to give practical proof in his belief that Jews might hold land by purchasing without hesitation Benjamin Goldsmid's valuable freehold estate at Roehampton. (*The Jews and the English Law.* 1908. H.S.Q. Henriques Oxford University Press Pages 185 and 193). Judah Jacob had probably lived in Portsmouth for some time before 1795 as it was in that year he put up for auction his house in Bath Square, Point which consisted of '4 good sleeping rooms 2 cellars and yard' (*Portsmouth Gazette 3 August 1795).*

15. *Naval Chronicle* 1812 Volume 28 Page 371.

16. Portsmouth Hebrew Congregation Minute Book. Page 425. September 1811.

17. Whilst Marryat wrote of the Officers, Mathew Henry Barker, under the pseudonym 'The Old Sailor', depicted the seamen in a breezy rollicking style. Born in 1790 he went to sea in an 'Indiaman' at the age of 16 afterwards serving in the Royal Navy aboard the cutter *Swan* and surveying vessel *Investigator,* then acting master of the gun brig *Flamer.* It was whilst serving in these ships on custom and police service that he learnt of Henry Nathan the Jewish Crimp which could account for his exaggerated prejudices. In *Jem Bunt* Barker devotes two chapters (pages 232-266) to 'Nathan a Jew crimp – going down to look after "bishness" amongst the Indiamen that were waiting for convoy at the Mother Bank'. After 1815 he turned to writing and had published a number of short stories and about a dozen titles including editing a 'Life of Nelson'. He died in 1846. (The Navy and Army Illustrated. 8 October 1898. Volume 7 pages 68 and 69).

18. *Naval Sketch Book: or The Service Afloat and Ashore.* 2 volumes. Second Series 1834. London. Anonymous. Pages 37-38. Volume 2. The Author was Captain William Glascock, a contemporary of Marryat.

## Printed Sources

### PRIZE MONEY AND SEAMEN'S WAGES.


Captain Frederick Chamier. *Ben Brace. The Last of Nelson's Agamemnons.* 1836. Richard Bentley London.

Lt-Cdr. P. Kemp. *Prize Money 1946.* Gale and Polden.

M. Lewis. *A Social History of the Navy 1793-1815.* George Allen and Unwin 1960. Pages 316 to 340 (inducements).

J. Maxwell. *The Navy Pocket Paymaster and Prize Agent, 1806.*

*Naval Chronicle 1799*. Volume 2. Pages 146 to 151 and 1801. Volume 6. Pages 301 to 306. Statutes relative to Seamens' Wages.

*Regulations and Instructions relating to His Majesty's Service at Sea*. Established by His Majesty in Counsel. *1808*.

E.S. Roscoe. A revision of H.C. Rotery's. *A report to H. M. Treasury on Doits of the Crown and of Admiralty in Time of War*. HMSO. 1915.

**Naval Literature of the Eighteenth and Early Nineteenth Centuries with an Anti-Jewish Bias.**

*Greenwich Hospital*. A series of Naval Sketches by 'The Old Sailor' (Mathew Barker). London. 1826. Pages 102-107. 'The Jew'.

*Jem Bunt*. A Tale of the Land and Ocean by 'The Old Sailor' (Mathew Barker) Willoughby & Co. 1846.

The Sailors Garland or The Ticket Buyers Lamentation. Pages 33 and 34 of *Naval Ballads and Sea Songs*. 1933. Peter Davis.

**CHAPTER 8 – End Notes and Sources**

1. *Sailors and Saints* Volume 2. By the author of a *Naval Sketch Book* (Captain William Glascock). By 'mustering rigging' is meant a suit of good clothes and "a thundering old turnip", a large timepiece.
2. The Privateering Papers of Joseph Joseph. City of Liverpool Record Office. Miscellaneous Business Records 380MD/Number 44 bound in one volume 1802-1807. (KF 161).
3. Public Record Office: ADM49/72. Piece 273. Inspectors Branch.
4. Public Record Office: ADM15/1. Solicitors' Papers.
5. Navy List for December 1809. Page 65.
6. National Maritime Museum HUL 41 and Portsmouth City Record Office 626A/1/1/2 and 3. Papers of George Hulbert Prize Agent. Correspondence and Prize Orders of Abraham and Lewis Moses.
7. Public Record Office ADM 49/72 Inspectors Branch Navy Pay Office. Pieces 248-253 and 305. For the career of Lieutenant John Little see J. Marshall Royal Naval Biography. 1835. Vol 4 – Part 2. Pages 68 to 76.
8. Ibid. The Privateering Papers of Joseph Joseph, Liverpool source 2.
9. Portsmouth City Record Office. Papers of George Hulbert. 626A/1/1/2 and 3.
10. Fourth Report of 1803 enquiring into the business of Prize Agency. The examination of James Poulain. *The Naval Chronicle Volume II*. Pages 217 to 222.
11. R. Harper. *The Portsmouth Road 1895*. Page 30.
12. Public Record Office ADM 49/72. Inspectors' Branch Navy Pay Office. Pieces 265-283 and ADM 15/1 Solicitors' Papers.
13. Public Record Office. ADM 15/2 Solicitors' Papers.
14. Public Record Office. ADM 1/4440 piece 243. Secretariat Papers.

**Printed Sources for Local History of the Liverpool Hebrew Congregation and Liverpool Privateers.**

B.L. Benas. *The Records of the Jews in Liverpool*. Pages 45 to 84. *Transactions of the Historic Society of Lancashire and Cheshire*. Volume 51. (1901).

P. Ettinger. *'Hope Place' in Liverpool Jewry*. 1930. Hope Place Hebrew Congregation.

J. Picton. *Memorials of Liverpool Historical and Topographical*. 2 volumes. Second

Revised edition 1875. Longmans Green.

G. Williams. *History of the Liverpool Privateers and Letters of Marque with an account of the Liverpool Slave Trade.* 1897. Heinemann.

**CHAPTER 9 – End Notes and Sources**

1. *Jewish Chronicle.* Page 4 of May 1933 supplement and *Jewish Chronicle* 31 August 1849: Guildhall Library. City of London Archives reference 10-622. Plymouth Hebrew Congregation Records has a letter dated 27 May 1958, from the present distributors of Lemon Hart Rum – United Rum Merchants to Dr Cecil Roth. '. . . As far as we know the former owners of United Rum, Messrs Portal Dingwall and Norris, acquired the business of Mr Lemon Hart about 1860. We have always been given to understand that his Penzance business consisted largely of imports of rum from the West Indies, and that this trade went into a decline following the development of the Port of Bristol!'
2. National Maritime Museum. Prize Payments of Ommaney and Druce. PRZ/2/5.
3. Public Record Office ADM 15/2 Solicitors' Papers.
4. Archives of Barclays Bank Lombard Street, City of London. Papers of the Glencross Hodge and Norman Bank otherwise known as the Plymouth Dock Naval and Commerical Bank.
5. Portsmouth City Record Office. Justice of the Peace Records 6A(1 and 2).
6. Public Record Office. ADM 51-183 Log Book *HMS Mars*: ADM 1-3695 and 3696. Secretariat Papers: ADM 7-307. Law Officers' Opinions. *Hampshire Telegraph* 14 March 1808.
7. *Hampshire Chronicle.* 27 September 1813.
8. *Hampshire Courier.* 7 December 1812.
9. *Hampshire Chronicle and Courier.* 23 December 1816. Samuel Joseph of 69 High Street, Gosport, offered a handsome reward for any information as to the whereabouts of his large wherry lost from her moorings near the *Laurel* convict ship in Portsmouth Harbour.
10. Portsmouth City Record Office. Register of Licensed Portsmouth Wherrymen PVH7/80-82.
11. Arthur Ellis Franklin. Records of the Franklin Family and Collaterals. Second Edition 1935. George Routledge and Sons Ltd., Pages 17 to 22. Also at page 94 Lewis Franklin's grand-daughter Minnie Franklin married in 1873 Sir Alfred Yarrow, torpedo-boat builder of Glasgow, son of the founder whose mother was a Jewess, Esther Lindo.
12. Portsmouth City Reference Library. Pescott Frost Collection. Files of the *Hampshire Telegraph.*
13. *Hampshire Telegraph.* 21 and 28 September 1818.
14. Transactions Jewish Historical Society of England. Volume 25 (1975) *Jews in English Regular Freemasonry.* Page 189. John Shaftesley.
15. Public Record Office ADM 15/2. Solicitors' Papers.
16. *Hampshire Courier.* 30 October 1815.
17. Public Record Office HCA 2-335. *The Shannon and Chesapeake* by H.F. Pullen 1970. McCelland and Stewart Toronto. *Broke and the Shannon.* P. Padfield 1968 Hodder and Stoughton.
18. National Maritime Museum – Hulbert Papers – Petty Agency Accounts HUL 26
19. Public Record Office ADM 15/2. Solicitors' Paper.
20. Public Record Office ADM 15/2. Solicitors' Papers.

21. Public Record Office ADM 49/73. Inspectors' Branch Navy Pay Office. King V. Davis and ADM1/3657 Secretariat Papers.
22. *Portsmouth Evening News*. 5 April 1939.
23. Public Record Office ADM 49-73. Inspectors Branch Navy Pay Office. King V. Michael Davis. 9 July 1814. It could have been that Michael Davis was of the Jewish faith.
24. Public Record Office ADM 49-73. Piece 16. Statement of Prize Money distributed between 1 July 1817 and 30 June 1818.
25. *Hampshire Telegraph*. 7 February 1820.
26. Portsmouth City Record Office. CD 6/24/7A-b.
27. Portsmouth Synagogue Archives.
28. *Hampshire Courier*. 27 February 1815.
29. Brenton Capt. E.P. *The Naval History of Great Britain 1823-25*. (5 Volumes) London. Vol. 3. Pages 159-160.
30. Public Record Office ADM 49-72. Inspectors' Branch Navy Pay Office.
31. *Hampshire Chronicle*. 27 February and 13 March 1815. *Hampshire Telegraph*. 22 June 1818.
32. Public Record Office PROB.11/1612 and IR 26/783. Folio 35.
33. Public Record Office IR 26/806.
34. *Hampshire Courier*. 17 July 1815 and 16 May 1814.
35. Public Record Office IR 26/612. Folio 431 and PROB 11/1557 Bridport 356.
36. *Hampshire Telegraph*. 5 June 1820. Mrs Levi's maiden name was Elizabeth Waley and her son Solomon adopted her surname. A descendant Sir Bernard Waley Cohen was Lord Mayor of London in 1960.
37. Ibid. Source number 2.
38. Public Record Office ADM 238-10. Distribution of Trafalgar Prize Money.

**Printed Sources for Local History of the Portsmouth Hebrew Congregation.**

W.G. Gates, *The Illustrated History of Portsmouth*. Charpentier and Co., Portsmouth 1900. Acknowledgment by the author was given to Emanuel Emanuel for a number of prints and drawings, whilst asssitance also came among others from Alderman A.L. Emanuel JP. See particularly Pages 364-368. The Jews at Portsmouth and Pages 213-217 The Story of Point.

*Hampshire Courier*. advertisment 11 September 1815. Details of College Street Properties.

*Hampshire Courier*. advertisment 31 August 1812. Details of Union Street Properties.

*History of Portsmouth* – Mottley 1801.

R Mudie. *Hampshire*. 1838. Volume 2.

*Pinks Pictorial*. April 1909. Pages 12-15. *The History of the Jews in Portsmouth*.

Portsmouth City Record Office. *Index of Twelfth Rate 1775*, compiled by F. Edwards 1982.

*Portsmouth Guide* – Hollingworth 1823.

The Portsmouth Papers. Published by Portsmouth City Council. Number 20. November 1973. Portsmouth – *As Others Have Seen It*. Part 2 (1790-1900).

Portsmouth Reference Library. Pescott Frost Collection. Drawn from the files of the *Hampshire Telegraph*. 1887-1889.

*Slight's* Pamphlets – *History of Portsea* about 1846.

*Portsmouth: A History* by A Temple Patterson. Moonraker Press 1976.

Transactions of the Jewish Historical Society of England:- Volume 6 (1912). *The Jewish Congregation of Portsmouth 1766-1842* Pages 111-127, by The Rev. I.S. Meisels.

Volume 13 (1936) *The Portsmouth Community and its Historical Background* Pages 157-187, by Dr Cecil Roth.

Volume 17 (1953) *Some new facts about the Portsmouth Jewish Community* Pages 251-268 (The Circumcision Register 1762-1807), by Rabbi Eugene Newman.

**Printed Sources for Local History of the Plymouth Hebrew Congregation.**

D. Black. *The Plymouth Synagogue* (Plymouth Hebrew Community) 1961.

A. Brodie (Editor). *The Reminiscences of Solomon Alex Hart BA.* 1882.

W. Burt. *Review of the Port of Plymouth* 1816.

G. Dicker. *A Short History of Devonport Royal Dockyard* 1971. Published privately.

B. Emden. *'Ancestral Tapestry'.* Lecture delivered in Devon Family History Society 1977. (Unpublished).

C. Gill. *Plymouth a New History* 1979. David and Charles. Volume 2.

Transactions of the Jewish Historical Society of England. Miscellanies Part 6 (1962) *'Plymouth Aliens List 1798 and 1803'* by Dr V.D. Lipman.

*The Picture of Plymouth* 1812. Printed for Rees and Curtis.

The Jewish Monthly 1950. Pages 91 to 93. *The Rise of Provincial Jewry,* by C. Roth.

H.F. Whitfield. *Plymouth and Devonport: In Times of War and Peace* 1900. Horns and Miller, Devonport, and E. Chapple, Plymouth.

R.N. Worth. *History of the Town and Borough of Devonport* 1870. Brendon, Plymouth, and Pyke, Devonport.

*Holders Directory* 1805, 1809-1811.

*Pigot's Directory* 1798. 1823/4.

**Printed Sources for Local History of Falmouth Hebrew Congregation.**

Mariners Mirror. Vol. 64 Number 1 February 1978 Page 11. *The Cutters of Falmouth.*

The Jewish Monthly 1950. Pages 61 to 63. *The Rise of Provincial Jewry,* by Dr C. Roth.

Transactions of the Jewish Historical Society of England Vol. 17 (1953). *The Jews of Falmouth 1740-1860,* by A.M. Jacob.

**Printed Sources for Local History of Penzance Hebrew Congregation.**

The Jewish Monthly 1950. Pages 90 and 91. *The Rise of Provincial Jewry,* by Dr C. Roth.

**Printed Sources for Local History of the Chatham Hebrew Congregation.**

*Jewish Chronicle.* 21 January 1842.

J. Presnail. *Chatham. The Story of a Dockyard Town.* 1952. Corporation of Chatham.

The Jewish Monthly 1950. Pages 49 to 51. *The Rise of Provincial Jewry,* by Dr C. Roth.

*Holders' Directory.* 1809-1811.

*Pigot's Directory.* 1823.

*Universal British Directory.* 1793.

**Printed Sources for Local History of the Sheerness Hebrew Congregation.**

*Jewish Chronicle*. 28 January 1842.

*Jewish Chronicle*. 14 December 1900.

The Jewish Monthly 1950. Pages 96 to 98. *The Rise of Provincial Jewry*, by Dr C. Roth.

*Pigot's Directory*. 1824.

**Manuscript Sources**

George Redmand Hulbert, Prize Agent. 1982. A. C. Gutridge. Dissertation for Diploma in English Local History. Portsmouth Polytechnic Library.

Occupations in Portsmouth 1550-1851. Thesis of P. S. Christie 1976. Portsmouth City Record Office.

The Social Acclimatization of the Jews in Devon and Cornwall in the Eighteenth and Nineteenth Centuries. Thesis of Rabbi Bernard Susser. University of Exeter. 1975

# APPENDIX 1

## REGISTERS OF JEWISH NAVY AGENTS

The primary sources for these registers, divided according to location, are the Navy Lists. The first published list of Licensed Navy Agents for inferior petty officers, seamen and marines appeared in December 1809 and the last in June 1865. As the licences ran for three years, the agent may have ceased trading at a different date than the one given. Corrections, where possible, have been taken from directories, contemporary newspapers and manuscript sources, particularly where a tradesman was known as a Navy Agent before licensing commenced in September 1809. It was not until the 1820 Navy List that the date was given on which a licence was granted.

While every care has been taken to extract Jewish agents from the Navy Lists, there may be errors of inclusion and omission.

An attempt has been made to correct errors in the Navy Lists where legitimate confusion has occurred, particularly in the case of similar Jewish surnames and first names. Examples include Joseph Joseph, Moses Abrahams or Abraham Moses. The forename is given first, but the lists are in alphabetical order according to surname.

In many instances traders continued at the addresses given, but not as Licensed Navy Agents.

Many of the agents were related to each other, particularly those with similar addresses.

The Navy Lists do not give the Licensed Navy Agent's trade, which, where known, has been taken from directories, contemporary newspapers and manuscript sources. In the majority of instances where the trade is unknown, the agent was in all probability a slopseller.

### CHATHAM AND SHEERNESS

| | *Name* | *Address* | *Dates* | *Trade* | *Remarks* |
|---|---|---|---|---|---|
| 1 | Abraham Aaron | High Street, Chatham | Dec 1815–Sept 1820 | | Moved from Deal |
| 2 | Isaac Aaron | Globe Lane, Chatham | Dec 1815–Dec 1818 | Umbrella maker | Licence revoked 14 Dec 1818 for not accounting to John Briggs late of *HMS Caledonian* for prize money. Licence restored 14 Jan 1819 at an address in Maidstone |
| 3 | Joseph Aaron | Chatham | July 1803–Dec 1806 | | |
| | | Sheerness | Dec 1806–Dec 1817 | | Moved to London |
| 4 | Lyon Aaron | High Street, Chatham | Nov 1814–July 1819 | | |
| | | 5 Grove Lane, Chatham | July 1819–Sept 1820 | | Moved to London |
| 5 | Jonas Abraham | Sheerness | Not mentioned in lists | | Licence revoked 23 July 1813 for abusing the trust reposed in him |
| 6 | Abraham Abrahams | 331 High Street, Chatham | Sept 1822–Sept 1827 | Slopseller and tobacconist | Moved from Poole |
| | | Military Road, Chatham | Sept 1827–Sept 1828 | | Moved to London |
| 7 | Henry Abrahams | Sheerness | Dec 1815–Sept 1817 | | |
| 8 | Hyam Abrahams | Sheerness | Nov 1814–Sept 1821 | | |
| 9 | Moses Abrahams | Sheerness | Dec 1809–Dec 1816 | | Moved to Bridgewater |
| 10 | Samuel Abrahams | Chapel Street, Sheerness | Dec 1809–April 1820 | Silversmith | One of the principal founders of the Sheerness Synagogue. Licence revoked 11 April 1820 for not accounting to Emanuel Stevens of *HMS La Hogue* for prize money received |

| | | | | | |
|---|---|---|---|---|---|
| 11 | Levy Alexander | Chapel Street, Sheerness | Dec 1809–Oct 1825 | | Died in Exeter |
| 12 | Joel Barnett | Chatham | Dec 1809–? | | Mentioned in first list of Licensed Agents only |
| 13 | Asher Cohen | 73 High Street, Chatham | Nov 1814–Sept 1820 | Pawnbroker | Moved to Liverpool |
| 14 | Lewis Cohen | Globe Lane, Chatham | Dec 1815–Sept 1838 | Slopseller, furniture broker | |
| 15 | Mark Cohen | Chatham | Dec 1809–? | | Mentioned in first list of Licensed Agents only |
| 16 | David and Lazarus Davis | 68 High Street, Chatham | Nov 1842–Oct 1847 | Pawnbrokers | Moved to Northfleet. Related to no. 17. |
| 17 | Samuel Samuels Davis | 68 High Street, Chatham | Dec 1816–Sept 1832 | Slopseller | Related to no. 16 |
| | Matha Davis | 68 High Street, Chatham | Sept 1832–Oct 1847 | Silversmith | Widow carried on the business at the same address |
| 18 | Benjamin Foreman | High Street, Sheerness | Nov 1814–Sept 1820 | Tailors and drapers | |
| 19 | Isaac Isaacs | 11 Hammond Place, Chatham | Aug 1828–Sept 1831 | Slopseller | Army clothier and fancy repository in 1838 |
| 20 | John Isaacs | 92 High Street, Chatham<br>68 High Street, Chatham | April 1838–Sept 1844<br>Sept 1844–Sept 1854 | Watchmaker, clock-maker and silversmith | Traded at same address as no. 17 for 3 years |
| 21 | Lazarus Jacob | Sheerness | Nov 1814–July 1819 | | |
| 22 | Solomon Lucas | 309 High Street, Chatham | Dec 1815–July 1819 | Slopseller | Outfitter at same address in 1849 |
| 23 | Lazarus Magnus | 302 High Street, Chatham | Dec 1809–Sept 1828 | | Father of no. 24, Simon Magnus |
| 24 | Simon Magnus | 302 High Street, Chatham | Nov 1842–Sept 1852 | Silversmith and pawnbroker | Rebuilt and endowed Chatham Synagogue, dedicated in 1870 as a memorial to his son |
| 25 | Aaron Moss | Sheerness | Dec 1809–March 1813 | | Licence revoked 20 March 1813 for with-holding wages and prize money from John Huddert |
| 26 | Abraham Moss | Sheerness | Dec 1817–July 1819 | | Moved from London |
| 27 | Elias Moss | Chatham | Dec 1809–Dec 1815 | | Moved to Plymouth |
| 28 | Joseph Sloman | 91 High Street, Chatham | Dec 1817–Sept 1821 | Pawnbroker | |
| 29 | Lewis Solomon | 89 High Street, Chatham<br>3 Hammond Place, Chatham | Oct 1833–Sept 1842<br>Sept 1842–Oct 1861 | Slopseller | |
| 30 | Samuel Solomon | New Road, Sheerness<br>40 High Street, Chatham | Nov 1814–July 1819<br>July 1819–Sept 1838 | Slopseller | Also in partnership with Lewis Solomon, no. 29, at 3 Hammond Place, Chatham, as clothiers, and in 1838 as watchmakers and toymen at 2 Military Road, Chatham |

PORTSMOUTH, PORTSEA AND GOSPORT

| | | | | | |
|---|---|---|---|---|---|
| 1 | Nathan Abrahams | Dean Street, Portsea<br>College Street, Portsea | Nov 1814–Dec 1816<br>Dec 1816–July 1819 | | Moved to Farnham, Surrey |
| 2 | Phineas Abrahams | College Street, Portsea | Nov 1814–July 1819 | Silversmith and jeweller | Moved to Hull. Watchmaker 1823–1836. |
| 3 | Solomon Alexander | 62 Broad Street, Portsmouth | March 1795–Sept 1815 | Watchmaker, silver-smith and slopseller | Freehold premises auctioned 23 August 1821. |
| 4 | David Barnard | 67 Hanover Street, Portsea | Dec 1809–Sept 1832 | Pawnbroker and silversmith | Elder of Portsmouth Hebrew Congregation. His widow Rebecca moved to Southampton. Also pawnbroker 36 Havant Street, Portsea, 1785–1813. |

| | | | | | |
|---|---|---|---|---|---|
| 5 | George Barnard | 67 Hanover Street, Portsea | Oct 1827–Sept 1834 | Coal office | |
| 6 | Philip Barnard | 39 Hanover Street, Portsea | Nov 1814–Sept 1825 | Publican | Kept the 'Antelope' tavern, 39 Hanover Street, Portsea |
| 7 | Gillum Daniels | Havant Street, Gosport | June 1813–March 1814 | | Licence revoked 15 March 1814, for having failed to account to the relation of a deceased seaman |
| 8 | Daniel de Souza | 10 Ordnance Row, Portsea | Dec 1815–July 1819 | Grocer | |
| | | 15 Common Hard, Portsea | July 1819–Sept 1820 | | |
| | | 99 Queen Street, Portsea | Sept 1820–Sept 1823 | | |
| | | 4 Lion Place, Portsea | Sept 1823–Sept 1824 | | Moved to London |
| 9 | John Edwards | 34 Union Street, Portsea | Aug 1837–Dec 1840 | Money lender and slopseller | Warden and Secretary of Portsmouth and Hebrew Congregation. Lived 1793–1893. Ferry Commissioner. |
| | | 20 Common Hard, Portsea | Dec 1840–1865 | | |
| 10 | John Emanuel | 3 Ordnance Row, Portsea | July 1819–Sept 1822 | | Moved from London |
| 11 | Joseph Emanuel | 12 Ordnance Row, Portsea | June 1818–Oct 1825 | | Same address as Joseph Simon, no. 59, from July 1819 to Sept 1822, and same address as Barnett Solomon, no. 61, from Sept 1823 to Oct 1825 |
| 12 | Abraham Franklin | 13 Bath Square, Point, Portsmouth | Dec 1809–Dec 1815 | Silversmith | Moved to Liverpool in December 1825 |
| | | Broad Street, Portsmouth | Dec 1815–July 1819 | | |
| 13 | Lazarus Franklin | Broad Street, Portsmouth | Dec 1809–Nov 1814 | Silversmith | |
| | | 26 Queen Street, Portsea | Nov 1814–July 1819 | | Moved to Liverpool |
| 14 | Mark Freideberg | 30 College Street, Portsea | Nov 1814–July 1818 | | Licence revoked July 1818 for not accounting to a seaman for prize money |
| 15 | Morris Freideberg | Mitre-Alley, Portsea | Dec 1816–July 1819 | | Moved from Plymouth |
| 16 | Abraham Hart | Ranvills Court, Portsea | Dec 1809–Nov 1814 | | |
| | | 9 Broad Street, Portsmouth | Nov 1814–July 1818 | | Moved to London |
| 17 | Henry Hart | 60 St Mary Street, Portsmouth | Dec 1809–Dec 1812 | Slopseller | Licence revoked on grounds of bankruptcy December 1812. In partnership with no. 54. |
| 18 | Isaac Hart | 20 Broad Street, Portsmouth | Nov 1814–July 1819 | | |
| 19 | Joseph Hart | Common Hard, Portsea | Dec 1809–Dec 1818 | | Vice-President, Portsmouth Hebrew Congregation, 1811 |
| 20 | Abraham Isaac | Broad Street, Portsmouth | Nov 1814–Dec 1815 | | |
| 21 | Henry Isaacs | St Mary Street, Portsmouth | July 1814–July 1819 | | Licence revoked 3 Aug 1814 on grounds of fraud having taken on board *HMS Rinaldo*: blank powers, with the men's marks for the signatures of Officers (but withdrawn, as continued as an Agent until Sept 1821) |
| | | 10 Ordnance Row, Portsea | July 1819–Sept 1821 | | |
| 22 | Samuel Isaacs | Portsea | Nov 1814–Dec 1815 | Jeweller | Died in 1817 |
| 23 | Samuel Isaacs | 37 and 54 Havant Street and 20 College Street, Portsea | April 1836–Sept 1838 | | Originally had 3 addresses in Portsea |

| | | | | | |
|---|---|---|---|---|---|
| | | 11 Hawke Street and 20 College Street, Portsea | Sept 1838–Sept 1839 | | |
| | | 20 College Street (only) | Sept 1839–Sept 1842 | | |
| | | 40 Havant Street, Portsea | Sept 1842–Oct 1845 | | |
| | | 11 Common Hard, Portsea | Oct 1845–Sept 1851 | Outfitter | |
| | | 32 Queen Street, Portsea | Sept 1851–Sept 1854 | | |
| 24 | David Israel | 72 Broad Street, Portsmouth<br>5 Ordnance Row, Portsea | Dec 1815–Dec 1817<br>Dec 1817–Sept 1820 | | Moved from Plymouth. Licence revoked 29 July 1816 on grounds of not accounting to John de Wit of *HMS Terpsichore* for prize money received (but withdrawn, as continued as an Agent until Sept 1820) |
| 25 | Phineas Israel | Portsmouth | Dec 1815–July 1819 | | |
| 26 | Abraham Jacob | Broad Street, Portsmouth | Dec 1809–July 1819 (Nov 1814–Dec 1815 at Gosport) | | |
| 27 | Daniel Jacob | 15 Bath Square, Point, Portsmouth | Dec 1809–March 1814 | Slopseller | Licence revoked march 1814 for having practised a fraud upon a seaman. Brother of nos. 29 and 31 |
| 28 | John Jacob | 47 Broad Street, Portsmouth | Dec 1809–June 1819 | Salesman | Licence revoked for practising a fraud on John Hall late of HM Ships *Mercury* and *Severn* |
| 29 | Judah Jacob | 6 Ordnance Row, Portsea | Prior to 1795–Feb 1812 | Slopseller and coach booking office | Prior to 1795 lived in Bath Square, Point. Guilty of fraud in 1802. Resigned as a Navy Agent in February 1812. |
| 30 | Mary Elizabeth Jacob | 5 Ordnance Row, Portsea | Dec 1824–Sept 1828 | | Widow and executrix of no. 29 |
| 31 | Samuel Jacob | Union Street, Portsea | Dec 1815–July 1819 | | Brother of nos. 27 and 29 |
| 32 | Henry Jacobs | Prince George Street, Portsea | Dec 1816–Sept 1818 | | Licence revoked on grounds of bankruptcy Sept 1818 |
| 33 | Samuel Joseph | Middle Street, Gosport (later 69 High Street, Gosport) | April 1804–Sept 1828 | Silversmith and tobacconist | |
| 34 | Lewis Lazarus | 86 Broad Street, Portsmouth<br>12 Bishop Street, Portsea<br>16 Bishop Street, Portsea | June 1814–July 1817<br>July 1817–June 1819<br>June 1819–Sept 1828 | Pawnbroker | President and Elder of Portsmouth Hebrew Congregation. In 1828 Executor of Barnard Barnard and Moses Symons both of Hull. Moved to Bath |
| 35 | Mark Lazarus | 10 Queen Street, Portsea | June 1817–July 1819 | | Moved to Cowes, Isle of Wight |
| 36 | I. Levi | 3 Hard, Portsea | Prior to 1809 —noted April 1802 | | |
| 37 | J. and W. Levi | 10 Union Street, Portsea | Dec 1809–? | Engravers | Mentioned in first list of Navy Agents only. Jacob died 8 Jan 1816 aged 74 |
| 38 | David Levy | 3 Broad Street, Portsmouth<br>65 High Street, Portsmouth | Sept 1838–Sept 1843<br>Oct 1843–Sept 1854 | | |
| 39 | George Levy | 115 Queen Street, Portsea<br>46 Saint Georges Square, Portsea | Sept 1822–Sept 1826<br>Sept 1826–Sept 1835 | Grocer and agent for Albion Fire office | Elder of the Portsmouth Hebrew Congregation |

| | | | | | |
|---|---|---|---|---|---|
| 40 | John Levy | Clock Street, Portsea | Nov 1814–July 1819 | | Moved to Southampton |
| 41 | Joseph Levy | Point, Portsmouth | Nov 1814–July 1819 | | |
| 42 | Lyon Levy | 30 College Street, Portsea | Dec 1809–? | | |
| | | St Mary Street, Portsmouth | Nov 1814–July 1819 | | |
| 43 | Michael Levy | St Mary Street, Portsmouth | Nov 1814–1819 | | |
| 44 | Abraham Moses | 20 College Street, Portsea | Dec 1809–March 1819 | Silversmith and slopseller | Elder of Portsmouth Hebrew Congregation |
| | | 94 Broad Street, Portsmouth | March 1819–Sept 1823 | | |
| | | 36 St James Street, Portsea | Sept 1823–Sept 1839 | | |
| 45 | Benjamin Phineas Moses | High Street, Gosport | June 1817–July 1817 | | Licence immediately revoked for irregular procedures. Moved from Plymouth |
| 46 | Benjamin Moses otherwise Moss | 1 and 14 Clock Street, Portsea | Nov 1840–Sept 1844 | Slopseller and outfitter | |
| | | 1 Clock Street, Portsea | Sept 1844–1865 | | |
| 47 | Isaac Moses | 2 Wickham Street, Portsea | Nov 1814–July 1819 | | Elder of the Portsmouth Hebrew Congregation |
| | | 30 College Street, Portsea | July 1819–Sept 1821 | | |
| | | 2 Ordnance Row, Portsea | Sept 1821–Sept 1826 | | |
| 48 | Joseph Moses | Daniel Street, Portsea | Nov 1814–July 1819 | | Moved to London |
| 49 | J. Moses | 1 Ordnance Row, Portsea | Dec 1816–July 1819 | | |
| 50 | John (Junior) Moses | 48 Havant Street, Portsea | Dec 1841–Oct 1845 | Outfitters and sword cutlers | Died May 1857. Business continued by his son Alexander |
| | | 25 The Hard, Portsea | Oct 1845–Sept 1854 | | |
| | | 26 The Hard, Portsea | Sept 1854–1865 | | |
| 51 | Lewis Moses | 94 Broad Street, Portsmouth | Dec 1791-Dec 1815 | Slopseller, clock and watchmaker | In partnership with no. 44 |
| 52 | Moses (Junior) Moses | South Street, Gosport | Dec 1815–July 1819 | | Moved from Cawsand, Plymouth |
| | | 126 High Street, Gosport | July 1819–Sept 1820 | | |
| 53 | Samuel Moses | 2 Ordnance Row, Portsea | Dec 1809–Nov 1814 | | Related to no. 47 |
| | | Wickham Street, Portsea | Nov 1814–July 1819 | | |
| 54 | Isaac Myers | 60 St Mary Street, Portsmouth | Dec 1809–Nov 1814 | Slopseller | In partnership with Henry Har, no. 17, until Dec 1812. Moved temporarily to Bristol, until his licence was restored on 5 March 1818 after correcting his error and accounting satisfactorily |
| | | 75 St Georges Street, Portsea | Nov 1814–Dec 1817 | | |
| | | 40 Bishop Street, Portsea | July 1819–Sept 1824 | | |
| 55 | Jacob Nathan | 73 Broad Street, Portsmouth | Dec 1809–July 1819 | Slopseller | |
| 56 | Moses Nathan | 50 Broad Street, Portsmouth | Nov 1814–July 1819 | | |
| 57 | Samuel Phillips | 5 Common Hard, Portsea | Dec 1809–March 1818 | Coach booking office | |
| 58 | Hyam Raphael | 31 Unicorn Street, Portsea | Dec 1815–July 1819 | | |
| 59 | Moss Sailman | 6 Old Rope Walk, Portsea | Nov 1814–Dec 1815 | Bookbinder | |
| 60 | Joseph Simon | Union Street, Portsea | Nov 1814–July 1819 | | While at 12 Ordnance Row, Portsea, same address as Joseph Emanuel, no. 11 |
| | | 12 Ordnance Row, Portsea | July 1819–Sept 1822 | | |
| | | 8 Clock Street, Portsea | Sept 1822–Oct 1825 | | |
| 61 | S. Simpson | College Street, Portsea | July 1814–June 1818 | | Elder of the Portsmouth Hebrew Congregation |

| | | | | | |
|---|---|---|---|---|---|
| 62 | Barnett Solomon | 13 Ordnance Row, Portsea | Nov 1814–Sept 1820 | | While at 12 Ordnance Row, Portsea, same address Joseph Emanuel, no. 11 |
| | | 31 St Mary Street, Portsmouth | Sept 1820–Sept 1823 | | |
| | | 12 Ordnance Row, Portsea | Sept 1823–Sept 1828 | | |
| 63 | Betsey Solomon | 38 College Street, Portsea | Dec 1828–Oct 1830 | | As widow and administrator of Barnett Solomon, no. 61. Moved to London |
| 64 | Moses Solomon | 9 College Street, Portsea | July 1819–Sept 1820 | | Moved from Exeter |
| | | 33 Butcher Street, Portsea | Sept 1820–Sept 1835 | | |
| | | 8 Ordnance Row, Portsea | Sept 1835–1865 | Curiosity shop | |
| 65 | Solomon Solomon | Butcher Street, Portsea | Nov 1814–July 1819 | | |
| | | 5 Ordnance Row, Portsea | July 1819–Sept 1821 | | |
| | | 67 St Mary Street, Portsmouth | Sept 1821–Sept 1822 | | |
| | | 8 Butcher Street, Portsea | Sept 1822–Oct 1825 | | |
| 66 | Samuel Solomons | Dean Street, Portsea | Nov 1814–Dec 1815 | | Moved to London |
| 67 | Isaac Spiers | Middle Street, Gosport | Nov 1814–Dec 1815 | | |
| 68 | Moses Symonds | 6 College Street, Portsea | Nov 1814–July 1819 | | |
| 69 | Leah Wineman | 39 Hanover Street, Portsea | Sept 1825–Sept 1828 | | As widow and administrator of Michael Levy, no. 43. 39 Hanover Street was the 'Antelope' tavern no. 6 |
| 70 | Gershon Woolf | The Hard, Portsea | 1784–1798? | Silversmith and sword cutler | |
| 71 | Abraham Yoell | Broad Street, Portsmouth | Nov 1814–Dec 1816 | Pawnbroker and silversmith | |
| | | 176 Queen Street, Portsea | Dec 1816–Oct 1825 | | |
| | | 184 Queen Street, Portsea | Oct 1825–Sept 1828 | | |
| 72 | Henry Yoell | Broad Street, Portsmouth | Dec 1816–July 1819 | Watchmaker | Moved to Cowes, Isle of Wight |
| | | 1 Clock Street, Portsea | July 1819–Sept 1821 | | |
| 73 | Jacob Zachariah | 85 Broad Street, Portsmouth | Dec 1809–Dec 1813 | Silversmith | Licence revoked 23 Dec 1813 for abusing the trust reposed in him. Died in 1819. His executors were Lewis Lazarus, no. 34, and Levy Zachariah, no. 75 |
| 74 | John Zachariah | 69 High Street, Portsmouth | Dec 1809–July 1819 | Silversmith | Moved to London |
| 75 | Levy Zachariah (Junior) | 184 Queen Street, Portsea | Nov 1814–Sept 1822 | Pawnbroker | Moved to London |
| | | 13 Union Street, Portsea | Sept 1822–Oct 1825 | | |

## PLYMOUTH AND PLYMOUTH DOCK (DEVONPORT FROM 1824)

| | *Name* | *Address* | *Dates* | *Trade* | *Remarks* |
|---|---|---|---|---|---|
| 1 | Abraham Aaron | Southside Street, Plymouth | Dec 1809–July 1819 | Slopseller and watchmaker | Plymouth Aliens List. Born 1767, from Litzelstadt, Germany. Arrived Gravesend 1783. Moved to London |
| 2 | Saul Charles Aaron | Plymouth Dock | Dec 1815–July 1819 | | Moved to Salisbury |

| | | | | | |
|---|---|---|---|---|---|
| 3 | Lemon Abraham | Old Town Without, Plymouth | Nov 1814–Dec 1815 | | |
| | | 23 Notte Street, Plymouth | July 1819–Sept 1823 | | |
| 4 | Reuben Abrahams and | Barbican, Plymouth | Nov 1814–Dec 1815 | | |
| 5 | Samuel Alexander | | | | |
| 6 | Abrahams | Fore Street, Plymouth Dock | July 1813–Jan 1816 | | Licence revoked for not giving notice of abode |
| 7 | Mark Cohen | 101 James Street, Plymouth Dock | Nov 1814–Dec 1815 | | Esther Cohen was a pen-and-quill manufacturer and sealing-wax maker at 101 James Street, Plymouth Dock, from about 1809 to 1824 |
| | | Fore Street, Plymouth Dock | Dec 1815–July 1819 | | |
| 8 | Abraham Emanuel | 71 James Street, Plymouth Dock | Dec 1809–Sept 1821 | Jeweller and silversmith | Plymouth Aliens List. Born 1764, from Mertz in Mannheim. Arrived Harwich 1777. Moved to London |
| 9 | Ezekiel Emanuel | 11 Frankfort Place, Plymouth | Dec 1809–July 1819 | | Moved to London |
| | | 9 Park Street, Plymouth | July 1819–Sept 1820 | | |
| 10 | Manly Emanuel | Frankfort Place, Plymouth | Nov 1814–March 1821 | | Moved to London |
| 11 | Philip Ezekiel | 6 Duke Street, Plymouth Dock | Dec 1815–July 1819 | Silversmith, watch and clockmaker | |
| 12 | Morris Freideberg | James Street, Plymouth | Nov 1814–Dec 1816 | | Moved to Portsea |
| 13 | Emanuel Hart | Fore Street, Plymouth Dock | 1795-July 1819 | Watchmaker | |
| 14 | Samuel Hart | 33 Market Street, Plymouth | 1795-July 1819 | Watchmaker and miniature painter | Licence revoked 20 Jan 1817 for not paying prize money of £2.6.6., but reinstated as name appears in Navy Lists up to July 1819 |
| 15 | Hyman Hyman | 44 Bedford Street, Plymouth | Sept 1842–Nov 1845 | Silversmith and goldsmith | |
| | | 26 George Street, Plymouth | Nov 1845–Sept 1853 | | |
| | | 3 Sussex Place, Union Street, Plymouth | Sept 1853–Sept 1858 | | |
| 16 | Isaac Isaac | Southside Street, Plymouth | July 1814–July 1819 | Slopseller | |
| 17 | David Israel | Queen Street, Plymouth Dock | Dec 1812–Dec 1815 | | Moved to Portsmouth |
| 18 | Jacob Jacobs | Plymouth | | | Mentioned in original list of Licensed Agents of Dec 1809 only |
| 19 | Morris Jacobs | North Corner Street, Plymouth Dock | Dec 1816–Sept 1820 | | Moved to Exeter |
| 20 | Baruch Jonas | 63 James Street, Plymouth Dock | Dec 1814–Nov 1816 | Silversmith | Licence revoked 15 Nov 1816 for not informing Navy Pay Office of change of address. Subsequently reinstated |
| | | North Corner Street, Plymouth Dock | Dec 1816–July 1819 | | |
| 21 | Jonas Jonas | James Street, Plymouth Dock | Dec 1815–July 1816 | | Licence revoked on grounds of having been committed to Exeter Gaol on suspicion of forging an order in the name of Thomas Warren of *HMS Lightening*, thereby receiving £31.15.2. from Greenwich Hospital. On 19 Aug 1816 George Rose wrote to Jonas Jonas refusing to take off restriction |

(PRO ADM15-2)

| | | | | | |
|---|---|---|---|---|---|
| 22 | Abraham Joseph | Barbican, Plymouth | about 1770–1794 | Mercer and wholesale slopseller | Slopman to HRH Prince William Henry |
| 23 | Joseph Joseph | Barbican, Plymouth | Dec 1809–July 1817 | Silversmith and slop merchant | Licence revoked on grounds of bankruptcy |
| 24 | Nathan Joseph | Broad Street, Plymouth<br>15 Queen Street, Plymouth Dock | Dec 1809–Sept 1828<br>Sept 1839–Sept 1845 | Jeweller and silversmith | Went to London between 1828 and 1839. Plymouth Aliens List. Born 1766, from Ranspark, Bohemia. Arrived Gravesend 1784 |
| 25 | Samuel Joseph | Plymouth | Dec 1809–July 1819 | | |
| 26 | Elijah Levey | Plymouth | Dec 1815–July 1819 | | |
| 27 | Phineas Levi | 15 Catherine Street, Devonport | Oct 1843–Sept 1855 | Slopseller | Born Portsea. A Commissioner for Devonport in 1829. President of the Plymouth Hebrew Congregation in 1834, 1850 and 1851. Moved to London |
| 28 | Aaron and B. Levy | 45 Bedford Street, Plymouth | Aug 1835–Sept 1855 | Gold and silversmiths | Held the Royal Warrant from 1838 |
| 29 | Abraham Levy | 41 Southside Street, Plymouth | Dec 1815–Sept 1820 | Pawnbroker, slopseller and watchmaker | |
| 30 | Joel Levy | Near The Parade, Plymouth | Nov 1814–July 1819 | Silversmith | Buried in Old Jewish Cemetery on Plymouth Hoe |
| 31 | Henry Joseph Levy | Plymouth | Nov 1814–Dec 1815 | | |
| 32 | Marks Levy | 50 Bedford Street, Plymouth<br>40 Union Street, Plymouth<br>132 Union Street, Plymouth | Aug 1842–Sept 1851<br>Sept 1851–Sept 1857<br>Sept 1857–1865 | Pawnbroker, silversmith, watch and clockmaker | |
| 33 | Sampson Levy | Foxhole Street, Plymouth<br>21 George Street, Plymouth | Nov 1814–Dec 1816<br>Dec 1816–Jan 1819 | | Licence revoked 15 Jan 1819 for not accounting to widow of Joseph Hodgman, late of *HMS Triton*, for prize money, and for moving to Liverpool without informing the Navy Pay Office |
| 34 | Joseph Lyons | 4 North Corner Street, Plymouth Dock | Dec 1815–July 1819 | Slopseller | Moved to Exeter |
| 35 | Charles Marks | 17 Treville Street, Plymouth<br>24 Treville Street, Plymouth<br>22 Whimple Street, Plymouth<br>43 Union Street, Plymouth | Dec 1834–Sept 1838<br>Sept 1838–Sept 1841<br>Sept 1841–Oct 1847<br>Oct 1847–Oct 1859 | Silversmith | Born Portsmouth 1801. His son Simeon married Rose, daughter of Phineas Levi, no. 27 |
| 36 | A. Mordecai | Fore Street, Plymouth Dock | Nov 1814–Dec 1816 | | |
| 37 | Mark Mordecai | Barbican, Plymouth<br>48 Queen Street, Plymouth Dock<br>71 Fore Street, Devonport<br>68 St Aubyn Street, Devonport | Dec 1809–Nov 1814<br>Nov 1814–Sept 1828<br>Sept 1828–Sept 1840<br>Sept 1840–Oct 1846 | | President of the Plymouth Synagogue in 1823 and 1830 |
| 38 | Moses Jacob | Queen Street, Plymouth Dock<br>15 Duke Street, Plymouth Dock | Dec 1815–July 1818<br>July 1818–Sept 1821 | | |
| 39 | Moses Moses | Pembroke Street, Plymouth Dock | Dec 1809–Dec 1815 | Broker | |

| | | | | | |
|---|---|---|---|---|---|
| 40 | Moses Moses (Junior) | Cawsand, Plymouth | Nov 1814–Dec 1815 | | Moved to Gosport |
| 41 | Benjamin Phineas Moses | Plymouth Dock | Dec 1815–Dec 1817 | | Moved to Gosport |
| 42 | Barrow Moss | Pembroke Street, Plymouth Dock | Dec 1809–Dec 1811 | Silversmith | From Dec 1817 to July 1819, Elias Moss, no. 43, and Nathan Joseph, no. 24, acted as his executors. Elias Moss, no. 43, continued from July 1819 to Sept 1832 |
| | | North Corner Street, Plymouth Dock | Dec 1811–Dec 1817 | | |
| 43 | Elias Moss | 38 George Street, Plymouth Dock | Dec 1815–Sept 1822 | | Moved from Chatham |
| | | 52 St Aubyn Street, Plymouth Dock | Sept 1822–Oct 1826 | | Moved to Liverpool |
| 44 | Aaron Nathan | 6 King Street, Plymouth Dock | Dec 1815–July 1818 | | |
| | | Millbrook, Near Torpoint | July 1818–Sept 1820 | | |
| | | 37 George Street, Plymouth | Sept 1820–Sept 1821 | | |
| 45 | Asher Nathan | 30 George Street, Plymouth | Jan 1810–March 1812 | | Licence revoked for not giving notice of change of abode in order to evade just claims of seamen |
| 46 | Henry Nathan | James Street, Plymouth Dock | Nov 1814–Dec 1816 | New and secondhand clothes seller | |
| | | 2 Durnford Street (Stonehouse), Plymouth | Dec 1816–Sept 1822 | | |
| 47 | Lyone Nathan | 21 Clowance Street, Plymouth Dock | Dec 1809–Sept 1822 | | Licence revoked July 1819 for not accounting to John Johnson, late of *HMS Spider*, but restored the following month as committed more from unintentional neglect than a dereliction of his duty |
| | | 108 Union Street, Plymouth | Sept 1822–Sept 1826 | | |
| | | 21 Union Street, Plymouth | Sept 1826–Sept 1832 | | |
| 48 | Michael Nathan | James Street, Plymouth Dock | Dec 1809–July 1819 | Silversmith | |
| 49 | Abraham Ralph | 2 Union Terrace, Union Street, Plymouth | Oct 1855–Oct 1859 | | |
| 50 | Henry Ralph | George Street, Plymouth Dock | Nov 1814–July 1818 | | Moved from Penzance. Leader of the Dock 'Minyan' |
| 51 | Lewis Ralph | George Street, Plymouth Dock | Dec 1809–Sept 1820 | | Secretary to a Masonic Lodge |
| 52 | Joseph Sloman | Fore Street, Plymouth Dock | July 1814–July 1819 | Silversmith | |
| 53 | Moses Solomon | 47 James Street, Plymouth Dock | Oct 1813–Dec 1816 | | |

NOTE: There was one George Street in Plymouth Dock and another in Stonehouse, Plymouth. For convenience, Stonehouse has been linked with Plymouth as distinct from Plymouth Dock.

LONDON

| | *Name* | *Address* | *Dates* | *Trade* | *Remarks* |
|---|---|---|---|---|---|
| 1 | Abraham Aaron | 53 Great Prescott Street, Goodmans Fields | July 1819–Sept 1821 | Slopseller | Moved from Plymouth |
| | | 1 Somerset Place, Commercial Road | Sept 1821–Sept 1822 | | |

| | | | | | |
|---|---|---|---|---|---|
| 2 | Joseph Aaron | Lancaster Court, Strand | Dec 1817–July 1819 | | Moved from Sheerness |
| | | 11 Clements Inn | July 1819–Sept 1831 | | |
| 3 | Lyon Aaron | 35 St Swithens Lane | Sept 1820–Sept 1823 | | Moved from Chatham |
| 4 | Samuel Abraham | 34 Somerset Street, Aldgate | Jan 1819–Sept 1820 | | |
| 5 | Abraham Abrahams | 5 Grace's Alley, Well Close Square | Sept 1828–Sept 1829 | Slopseller and tobacconist | Moved from Chatham |
| | | 1 Morgan Street, Commercial Road East | Sept 1829–Oct 1830 | | |
| 6 | Benjamin Abrahams | 59 St Mary Axe, Leadenhall Street | Dec 1809–? | Merchant | Mentioned in first list of Navy Agents only |
| 7 | John Abrahams | 59 St Mary Axe, Leadenhall Street | Jan 1810–May 1812 | | Licence withdrawn 11 May 1812 on grounds of being a minor |
| 8 | Mary Abrahams | Great Prescott Street, Goodmans Fields | Nov 1814–Dec 1816 | | |
| | | Bridge Street, Covent Garden | Dec 1816–July 1819 | | |
| 9 | Samuel Abrahams | 56 Wood Street, Cheapside | July 1820–Sept 1822 | | |
| 10 | Aaron and Mary Cohen | St Mary Axe | Nov 1814–Dec 1815 | | |
| 11 | Joseph Cohen | 9 Fishmonger Alley, Southwark | Dec 1815–Sept 1820 | | |
| 12 | Lyon Cohen | 20 and 21 Upper East Smithfield | March 1820–Sept 1823 | Slopseller | See Abraham Hart and Lyon Cohen, no. 29 |
| 13 | Mark Cohen | 114 Upper East Smithfield | Dec 1816–July 1819 | Quill merchant | |
| 14 | Noah Davis and Michael Lyon | 6 Fishmonger Alley, Fenchurch Street | Nov 1814–Dec 1816 | Tailor and slopseller | |
| | | 4 Smiths Buildings, Leadenhall Street | Dec 1816–July 1819 | | |
| | | 6 Nightinghall Lane, London Docks | July 1819–Sept 1820 | | |
| | | 3 Manor Row, Tower Hill | Sept 1820–Sept 1821 | | |
| | | 13 Ratcliffe Highway | Sept 1821–Nov 1835 | | |
| 15 | Noah Davis | 131 Ratcliffe Highway | Nov 1835–Sept 1842 | | Also at 55 High Street, Gravesend, 1835–Sept 1842 |
| | | 3 Dowgate Hill, Walbrook | Sept 1842–Oct 1845 | | |
| | | 5 Lyon's Inn, Strand | Oct 1845–1845 | | |
| 16 | Marcus Davis | 5 Lyon's Inn, Strand | Jan 1854–Oct 1862 | | Patentee of silent wheels for carriages |
| | | 2 Newcastle Street, Strand | Oct 1862–1865 | | |
| 17 | Phineas Davis | 23 Great Prescott Street, Goodmans Fields | March 1819–Sept 1821 | | As executor of Samuel Isaacs, deceased, Dec 1821–Oct 1825 |
| | | 4 Fetter Lane | Dec 1821–Oct 1825 | | |
| 18 | Daniel de Souza | 49 Leaman Street, Goodmans Fields | Sept 1824–Sept 1827 | | Moved from Portsmouth |
| | | 30 Great Prescott Street, Goodmans Fields | Sept 1827–Oct 1830 | | |
| 19 | Abraham Emanuel | 29 Minories | Sept 1821–Sept 1823 | Jeweller and silversmith | Moved from Plymouth Dock |
| | | Union Place, Upper Holloway | Sept 1823–March 1824 | | |
| 20 | Eve Emanuel | 29 Minories | March 1824–March 1827 | | As executrix of no. 19 |

| | | | | | |
|---|---|---|---|---|---|
| 21 | Ezekiel Emanuel | 24 South Audley Street, Grosvenor Square | Sept 1820–Sept 1822 | | Moved from Plymouth |
| 22 | John Emanuel | 18 Bevis Marks, St Mary Axe | Dec 1816–July 1819 | Watchmaker | Moved to Portsea |
| 23 | Manly Emanuel | 34 North Audley Street | March 1821–Sept 1821 | | Moved from Plymouth |
| | | 32 York Street, Commercial Road | Sept 1821–Sept 1822 | | |
| 24 | Lazarus Franklin | 53 Charlotte Street, Portland Place | Sept 1828–Sept 1829 | Silversmith | Moved from Edinburgh |
| 25 | Abraham Harris | 4 Sharps Buildings, Rosemary Lane | Aug 1816–Sept 1824 | Jewellery salesman | |
| | | 46 High Street, Shadwell | Feb 1831–Sept 1833 | Slopseller | |
| | | 4 Sharps Buildings, Rosemary Lane | July 1842–Sept 1848 | | |
| 26 | Emanuel Harris | 321 Strand | Nov 1814–Dec 1815 | | |
| | | 22 Newcastle Street, Strand | Dec 1815–Sept 1822 | | |
| 27 | Abigail Rachael Harris | 9 Gun Square, Houndsditch | Oct 1822–Sept 1826 | | As executrix of Emanuel Harris, no. 26 |
| | | 7 New Square, Minories | Sept 1826–Sept 1829 | | |
| 28 | Abraham Hart | Northumberland Street, Strand | July 1818–July 1819 | | Moved from Portsmouth |
| | | 20 Little Alie Street, Goodmans Fields | July 1819–Sept 1820 | | |
| | | 45 Duke Street, Aldgate | Sept 1820–Sept 1821 | | |
| 29 | Abraham Hart and Lyon Cohen | 21 Upper East Smithfield | Nov 1814–March 1820 | Slopseller and wool draper | See Lyon Cohen, no. 12 |
| 30 | John Hart | 20 Little Alie Street, Goodmans Fields | April 1817–June 1819 | | Licence revoked 18 June 1819 for not accounting to William West, late of *HMS Alemere*, for prize money received on his account |
| 31 | Alexander Isaac | Little Alie Street | Nov 1814–Dec 1815 | | |
| | | Somerset Street, Aldgate | Dec 1815–July 1818 | | |
| 32 | Alexander Isaac and Leon Joseph | Great Alie Street, Goodmans Fields | July 1818–Sept 1821 | | See Alexander Isaac, no. 31 |
| 33 | Philip Isaac | 6 Northumberland Street, Strand | Dec 1816–July 1819 | Merchant | |
| | | 8 Great Prescott Street, Goodmans Fields | July 1819–Sept 1835 | | |
| | | 56 Great Prescott Street, Goodmans Fields | Sept 1835–Oct 1846 | | |
| | | 9 King Street, Finsbury Square | Oct 1846–Oct 1850 | | |
| 34 | Abraham Isaacs | 6 Northumberland Street, Strand | Dec 1817–July 1819 | | Same address as no. 33 |
| | | 16 London Road, Southwark | July 1819–Sept 1820 | | |
| | | 45 Little Minories | Sept 1820–Sept 1821 | | |
| | | 17 White Lion Street, Goodmans Fields | Sept 1821–Sept 1824 | Tobacconist | |
| 35 | Isaac Isaacs | 34 Somerset Street, Aldgate | Dec 1816–July 1819 | | |

| No. | Name | Address | Dates | Occupation | Notes |
|---|---|---|---|---|---|
| 36 | John Isaacs | Albion Buildings, Aldersgate Street | Nov 1816–Dec 1817 | | Licence revoked on grounds of having moved from his place of abode without notification |
| 37 | Samuel Isaacs | St Mary Axe, Leadenhall Street | Dec 1815–July 1819 | | |
| | | 40 Mansell Street, Goodmans Fields | July 1819–Sept 1821 | | |
| 38 | Abraham Israel | Leman Street, Goodmans Fields | Dec 1815–July 1819 | | |
| 39 | John Jacob | 11 Clements Inn | Sept 1821–Sept 1822 | | Moved from Nottingham. Same address as no. 2 |
| 40 | S. Jacob | Smiths Buildings, Leadenhall Street | Dec 1809–? | | Mentioned in first list of Navy Agents only |
| 41 | Moses Joel | Robin Hood Lane, Poplar | Nov 1814–Dec 1815 | | |
| | | 38 Ratcliffe Highway | Dec 1815–July 1819 | Slopseller | |
| 42 | Jacob Jonas | 9 York Street, Commercial Road | May 1815–Dec 1818 | | Licence revoked for not accounting to John Henderson of *HMS Tremendous* for prize money |
| 43 | Simon Jonas | 39 Albion Street, Commercial Road | Dec 1809–Dec 1816 | | From Sept 1820 to Sept 1822 had the same address as Ann Levy, no. 53 |
| | | 8 York Street, Commercial Road | Dec 1816–Sept 1820 | | |
| | | 77 Ratcliffe Highway | Sept 1820–Sept 1821 | Army Agent | |
| | | 27 King Street, Commercial Road | Sept 1821–Sept 1822 | | |
| 44 | Aaron Joseph | 19 John Street, Sidney Square, Commercial Road | Feb 1846–Sept 1849 | | |
| | | 6 Watney Street, Commercial Road East | Sept 1849–Sept 1858 | | |
| 45 | Nathan Joseph | 28 Minories | Sept 1828–Sept 1831 | Jeweller and silversmith | Was at Plymouth Dec 1809–Sept 1828. Returned to Plymouth Dock Sept 1839–Sept 1845 |
| | | 46 Great Prescott Street, Goodmans Fields | Sept 1831–Sept 1833 | | |
| | | 52 Great Prescott Street, Goodmans Fields | Sept 1833–Sept 1839 | | |
| 46 | Lewis Lazarus | 131 Fleet Street | Sept 1832–Sept 1835 | | Also at Bath. In partnership with Zachariah Levy |
| 47 | Samuel Lazarus | Adams Court, Aldgate | June 1810–Dec 1815 | | Licence revoked 22 April 1819 for not accounting to George Smith of *HMS Furieuse* for prize money received |
| | | 15 Castle Place, Castle Street, Whitechapel | Dec 1815–April 1819 | | |
| 48 | George Isaac Leon | 7 St Michael's Alley, Cornhill | Aug 1850–Sept 1853 | Watchmaker | |
| 49 | Lewis Leon | 23 New Broad Street | July 1853–Oct 1859 | Merchant | |
| 50 | Isaac Levi | Duke Street, Aldgate | Dec 1809–? | Grocer | Mentioned in first List of Navy Agents only |
| 51 | Phineas Levi | 95 Fenchurch Street | Sept 1855–Sept 1858 | | Moved from Devonport |
| 52 | Abraham Levy | Mount Street, Whitechapel Road | Dec 1809–? | | Mentioned in first List of Navy Agents only |
| 53 | Ann Levy | 77 Ratcliffe Highway | March 1819–Sept 1821 | | From Sept 1820 to Sept 1822 had the same address as Simon Jonas, no. 43 |
| | | 27 King Street, Commercial Road | Sept 1821–Sept 1823 | | |
| | | 10 King Street, Commercial Road | Sept 1823–Sept 1827 | | |
| | | 3 Friar Street, Blackfriars | Sept 1827–Oct 1830 | | |

| | | | | | |
|---|---|---|---|---|---|
| | | 3 Tomlins Buildings, Suffolk Street, Southwark | Oct 1830–Sept 1834 | | |
| 54 | Isaac Levy | 81 Whitechapel Road | 1795-Jan 1808 | | The only Jewish Prize Agent |
| | | 14 Mount Place, Whitechapel Road | Jan 1808–Nov 1814 | | |
| | | 4 Commercial Chambers, Minories | Nov 1814–March 1828 | | |
| 55 | John Levy | Mount Place, Whitechapel | Nov 1814–July 1819 | | |
| 56 | Jonas Levy | 135 Whitechapel | Dec 1809–Dec 1816 | Watchmaker and jeweller | |
| 57 | Lyon Levy | York Street, Covent Garden | Dec 1809–Nov 1814 | | |
| | | Holywell Street, Strand | Nov 1814–July 1819 | | |
| 58 | Mark Levy | 2 Catherine Street, Commercial Road | Dec 1816–July 1819 | Watchmaker before 1796 | |
| | | 7 Weston Street, Nr Grafton Street, Soho | July 1819–Sept 1820 | | |
| 59 | Samuel Mordecai Levy | 21 Mansell Street, Goodmans Fields | July 1839–Sept 1840 | | |
| | | 3 Jewry Street, Aldgate | Sept 1840–Sept 1841 | | |
| | | 27 Jewry Street, Aldgate | Sept 1841–Sept 1842 | | |
| | | 149 Leadenhall Street | Sept 1842–Oct 1845 | | |
| 60 | E. and M. Lindo | 30 Leadenhall Street | Nov 1814–Dec 1815 | Merchants | |
| 61 | Samuel Moses Manson | Lime Street | Nov 1814–Dec 1817 | | |
| | | Seine Street | Dec 1817–July 1819 | | Moved to Edinburgh |
| 62 | Moses Marks | Rosemary Lane | Nov 1814–Dec 1815 | | |
| 63 | Jacob Moses | 53 Lime Street | Nov 1814–Dec 1816 | Haberdasher | |
| | | 1 Beech Street, Barbican | Dec 1816–July 1819 | | |
| | | 35 St Swithens Lane | July 1819–Sept 1821 | | Moved to Edinburgh |
| 64 | Lewis Moses | 5 Milton Terrace, Borough Road | Sept 1822–Oct 1825 | | |
| | | 5 Racket Court, Fleet Street | Oct 1825–Sept 1826 | | |
| 65 | Aaron Moss | 11 Craven Buildings, Drury Lane | Dec 1815–July 1819 | | Moved to Lewisham, Kent |
| 66 | Abraham Moss | Cock Hill, Shadwell | Nov 1814–Dec 1817 | Slopseller | Moved to Southend |
| 67 | H. Nathan | 13 Swallow Gardens, Rosemary Lane | Nov 1814–July 1819 | | |
| 68 | Moses Nathan | Wapping Street | Dec 1816–July 1819 | | |
| 69 | Henry Ralph | 40 Duke Street | May 1821–Sept 1822 | | |
| | | 5 Browns Buildings, St Mary Axe | Sept 1822–Sept 1823 | | |
| | | 5 Cock and Hoop Yard, Houndsditch | Sept 1823–Oct 1825 | | |
| | | 3 Love Court, Goulstone Square, Whitechapel | Oct 1825–Sept 1826 | | |
| | | 8 Angel Court, Strand | Sept 1827–Sept 1831 | | Between 1826 and 1827 was in Liverpool |

| | | | | | |
|---|---|---|---|---|---|
| 70 | Samuel Solomon | Crown Street, Finsbury Square | Dec 1809–? | Merchant | Mentioned in first List of Navy Agents only |
| 71 | Betsey Solomon | 33 Duke Street, Aldgate | Oct 1830–Sept 1831 | | As widow and administrator of Barnett Solomon. Moved from Portsea |
| | | 10 Angel Place, Blackfriars Road | Sept 1831–Sept 1832 | | |
| | | Haydon Square, Minories | Sept 1832–Sept 1835 | | |
| 72 | A. Solomons | 71 Rosemary Lane | Dec 1816–July 1819 | | |
| 73 | Joseph Solomons | Billiter Lane | Nov 1814–Dec 1815 | | |
| 74 | Samuel Solomons | 4 Butler Buildings, East Smithfield | Dec 1815–July 1819 | | Moved from Portsea |
| | | 49 Cable Street, St Georges East | July 1819–Sept 1822 | | |
| | | 51 Cable Street, St Georges East | Sept 1822–Oct 1828 | Jewellery salesman | |
| | | 4 New Road, St Georges East | Oct 1828–Sept 1832 | | |
| 75 | John Zachariah | 4 Skinners Place, Somerstown | July 1819–Sept 1821 | | Moved from Portsmouth then moved to Bath |
| 76 | Levy Zachariah | 13 George Street, Minories | Oct 1825–Sept 1828 | Pawnbroker | Moved from Portsmouth. Was executor to Jacob Zachariah of Portsmouth with Lewis Lazarus, no. 46 |
| | | 2 Hanway Street, Oxford Street | Sept 1828–Oct 1830 | | |
| | | 191 High Holborn | Oct 1830–Sept 1831 | | |

OTHER LOCATIONS

| | *Name* | *Address* | *Date* | *Trade* | *Remarks* |
|---|---|---|---|---|---|
| 1 | Abraham Aaron | Deal | Nov 1814–Dec 1815 | | Moved to Chatham |
| 2 | Saul Charles Aaron | Castle Street, Salisbury | July 1819–March 1821 | Auctioneer | Moved from Plymouth Dock |
| 3 | Isaac Aaron | 36 Weak Street, Maidstone | Jan 1819–July 1819 | Umbrella-maker | Moved from Chatham |
| | | 131 New Road, Brighton | July 1819–Sept 1822 | | |
| 4 | Abraham Abraham | 147 High Street, Southampton | April 1828–Sept 1831 | Silversmith and jeweller | |
| 5 | Abraham Abrahams | New Street, Poole | July 1819–Sept 1820 | | Moved to Chatham |
| | | Market Street, Poole | Sept 1820–Sept 1822 | | |
| 6 | Gabriel Abrahams | Church Street, Falmouth | April 1827–Sept 1834 | Broker (Bullion Office) | |
| 7 | Moses Abrahams | Bridgewater | Dec 1816–Sept 1820 | Silversmith and jeweller. Moses Abrahams was in partnership with a Mr Levy under style of Abrahams and Levy, 19 Milsom Street. Jewellers to His Majesty. Commenced business in Bath in December 1819 | Moved from Sheerness. Licence revoked 3 Nov 1819 for inserting an order payable to him, for prizes which were not captured until after their execution. But reinstated as he continued in the Lists. |
| | | 19 Milsom Street, Bath | March 1821–Sept 1822 | | |
| 8 | Nathan Abrahams | Farnham, Surrey | July 1819–Sept 1821 | | Moved from Portsea |
| 9 | Phineas Abrahams | 24 St John Street, Hull | July 1819–Sept 1820 | Silversmith and jeweller | Moved from Portsea |
| | | King Street, Burlington Quay, Yorkshire | Sept 1820–Sept 1821 | | |

| | | | | | |
|---|---|---|---|---|---|
| | | Waterworks Street, Hull | Sept 1821–Sept 1822 | | |
| | | 22 Paradise Place, Hull | Sept 1822–Sept 1823 | | |
| | | 28 Briggate, Leeds | Sept 1823–Sept 1832 | Watchmaker until 1836 | |
| 10 | Aaron Barnard | King Street, Deptford | Nov 1814–July 1819 | | |
| 11 | Barnard Barnard | 7 Queen Street, Kingston-on-Hull | June 1816–Sept 1822 | Corn dealer | Lewis Lazarus of Portsea was his executor |
| 12 | Rebecca Barnard | 17 High Street, Southampton | March 1835–Sept 1838 | | Widow of David Barnard of Portsea |
| 13 | Asher Cohen | 26 Pool Lane, Liverpool | Sept 1820–Sept 1822 | Pawnbroker | Moved from Chatham |
| 14 | David and Lazarus Davis | 2 Victoria Place, Perry Street, Northfleet | Oct 1847–Sept 1849 | Pawnbrokers | Moved from Chatham |
| | | 9 Dudley Street, Wolverhampton | Sept 1849–Oct 1850 | | |
| 15 | Emanuel Emanuel | Deal | 1797–1826 | Watchmaker | |
| 16 | George Emdin | High Street, Guernsey | Nov 1814–July 1819 | | |
| 17 | Abraham Franklin | Pool Lane, Liverpool | July 1819–Sept 1823 | Silversmith and watchmaker | Moved from Portsmouth |
| | | 64 Bridge Street, Manchester | Sept 1823–1834 | | |
| 18 | Lazarus Franklin | 17 George Street, Liverpool | July 1819–Sept 1822 | Silversmith and watchmaker | Moved from Portsea |
| | | 53 North Bridge, Edinburgh | Sept 1822–Sept 1828 | | Moved to London |
| 19 | Jacob Hart | Canterbury | Dec 1809–? | | Mentioned in first List of Licensed Agents only |
| 20 | John Jacob | St Peter's Gate, Nottingham | Sept 1820–Sept 1821 | | Moved to London |
| 21 | Morris Jacobs | Butcher Row, Exeter | Sept 1820–Sept 1824 | Tailor and Clothesman | Moved from Plymouth Dock |
| | | 125 Fore Street, Exeter | Sept 1824–Sept 1831 | | |
| | | 169 Fore Street, Exeter | Sept 1831–Sept 1832 | | |
| 22 | Joseph and Zephon Job | Truro | | | |
| 23 | Samuel Joseph | 12 Old Dock, Liverpool | Dec 1809–July 1819 | Army Agent, pawnbroker and silversmith | |
| | | 98 St James Street, Liverpool | July 1819–Sept 1821 | | |
| | | 110 St James Street, Liverpool | Sept 1821–Oct 1825 | | |
| | | 53 Pool Lane, Liverpool | Oct 1825–Sept 1832 | | |
| 24 | Lewis Lazarus | 14 Market Place, Bath | Sept 1828–Sept 1835 | Pawnbroker | Also in London. Warden of Bath Synagogue |
| 25 | Mark Lazarus | High Street, Cowes, Isle of Wight | July 1819–Sept 1822 | | Moved from Portsea |
| | | Post Office, Bath | Sept 1822–Sept 1823 | | |
| | | 3 Horse Street, Bath | Sept 1823–Sept 1824 | | |
| 26 | Benjamin Woolfe Levi | Gibraltar | July 1814–Sept 1818 | | |
| 27 | Emanuel Levy | Dover | Dec 1809–? | | Mentioned in first List of Licensed Agents only |
| 28 | John Levy | 28 Above Bar, Southampton | July 1819–Sept 1820 | | Moved from Portsea |
| 29 | Joseph Lyons | 85 North Street, Exeter | July 1819–Sept 1821 | | Moved from Plymouth Dock |
| | | Arlington Street, Exeter | Sept 1821–Oct 1825 | | |
| 30 | Louisa Marks | 35 St Pauls Square, Birmingham | Dec 1859–Oct 1863 | Gilt jeweller | |
| | | 145 Hockey Hill, Birmingham | Oct 1863–1865 | | |
| 31 | Isaac Moses | Deal | Nov 1814–Dec 1815 | | |
| 32 | Jacob Moses | 12 Hill Place, Edinburgh | Sept 1821–Sept 1823 | Haberdasher | Moved from London |
| | | 30 Lothian Road, Edinburgh | Sept 1823–Sept 1827 | | |

| | | | | | |
|---|---|---|---|---|---|
| 33 | Moses Moses | Dover | Nov 1814–Sept 1820 | | |
| 34 | Aaron Moss | Lewisham, Kent | July 1819–Oct 1825 | | Moved from London |
| 35 | Elias Moss | 32 Great Crosshall Street, Liverpool | Oct 1826–Sept 1832 | | Moved from Plymouth Dock |
| 36 | Isaac Myers | 57 Broad Quay, Bristol | Dec 1817–July 1819 | Slopseller | Moved from Portsmouth and back to Portsea |
| 37 | Henry Ralph | 80 Gerrard Street, Liverpool | Sept 1826–Sept 1827 | | Moved from and back to London |
| 38 | John Ralph | Falmouth | May 1821–Sept 1824 | | |
| 39 | Levy Samuel | High Street, Sunderland | Dec 1809–July 1819 | Jeweller | |
| 40 | Lyon Samuel | North Shields | Dec 1809–? | | Mentioned in first List of Licensed Agents only |
| 41 | Nathan Samuel | 7 North Side, Old Dock, Liverpool<br>65 Cable Street, Liverpool | Nov 1814–Oct 1825<br>Oct 1825–Sept 1832 | Watchmaker, jeweller, slopseller and pawnbroker | President of the Liverpool Congregation in 1820 |
| 42 | Isaac John Saulman | 144 Long Hill Gate, Manchester | July 1819–Sept 1821 | | |
| 43 | Alexander and David Solomon | Guernsey | Nov 1814–Dec 1815 | | |
| 44 | Emanuel Solomon | St Dunstan's Street, Canterbury | 1785–Sept 1823 | Silversmith and watchmaker (1752–1835) | |
| 45 | J. Solomon | Harbour Street, Ramsgate | Nov 1814–Dec 1815 | | |
| 46 | Moses Solomon | 13 Southgate Street, Exeter | Dec 1815–July 1819 | | Moved to Portsea |
| 47 | Samuel Solomon | Camden Street, North Shields | Nov 1814–July 1819 | | |
| 48 | Solomon Solomon | Falmouth | Dec 1809–July 1819 | Broker (Bullion Office) | |
| 49 | Moses Symons | 6 Queen Street, Kingston-upon-Hull | July 1819–Oct 1825 | Watchmaker | |
| 50 | Lemon Woolf | Penzance | Nov 1814–Dec 1815 | | |
| 51 | John Zachariah | 45 New King Street, Bath<br>24 Great Stanhope Street, Bath<br>1088 Montague de la Cour, Brussels<br>32 Rue de la Ferme, Maturin, Paris | Sept 1821–Sept 1822<br>Sept 1822–Oct 1825<br>Oct 1825–Sept 1826<br>Sept 1826–Sept 1829 | | |

TABLE OF LICENSED NAVY AGENTS

| | *Total Navy Agents 1809* * | *Total Jewish Navy Agents 1809* | *Percentage Jewish Navy Agents to Total 1809* | *Total Navy Agents 1816* ** | *Total Jewish Navy Agents 1816* | *Percentage Jewish Navy Agents to Total 1816* | *Total Navy Agents 1820* *** | *Total Jewish Navy Agents 1820* | *Percentage Jewish Navy Agents to Total 1820* |
|---|---|---|---|---|---|---|---|---|---|
| Portsmouth, Portsea & Gosport | 40 | 23 | 57.5 | 73 | 44 | 60.2 | 27 | 20 | 74.0 |
| Plymouth & Plymouth Dock | 29 | 14 | 48.2 | 51 | 31 | 60.7 | 21 | 15 | 71.4 |
| Sheerness | 11 | 5 | 45.5 | 17 | 9 | 53.0 | 6 | 5 | 83.3 |
| Chatham | 7 | 5 | 71.5 | 10 | 6 | 60.0 | 9 | 7 | 77.7 |
| London | 40 | 10 | 25.0 | 141 | 25 | 17.7 | 47 | 21 | 44.5 |
| Elsewhere in the British Isles | 47 | 9 | 19.0 | 105 | 26 | 24.7 | 40 | 19 | 47.5 |
| Totals | 174 | 66 | 38.0 | 397 | 141 | 35.5 | 150 | 87 | 58.0 |

Notes:

* First available list of Licensed Navy Agents. Source: *Navy List*, Sept 1809

** Peak in growth of Navy Agents. Napoleonic Wars ending in 1815. Source: *Navy List*, March 1816 (Figures for 1814 may appear larger, but the lists include Prize Agents)

*** Decline in numbers of Navy Agents, taking account of licences expiring after 1815. Source: *Navy List*, March 1820

# APPENDIX II

## BATTLE OF TRAFALGAR PRIZE MONEY

Register of Jewish Navy Agents extracted from the account of the Distribution of Proceeds arising from the capture of the French and Spanish ships *Swiftsure, Bahama, San Juan de Nepamuceno* and *San Ildefonso* under the command of Lord Viscount Nelson at the Battle of Trafalgar 21 October 1805. Showing 1,815 seamen of the British Fleet giving Prize Payment Orders to 52 Jewish Navy Agents.

Source: Public Record Office ADM238-10 (Pages 109, 110 and 111 of the manuscript are missing).

| Name | Location | Number of Seamen acted for | Amount Collected | | | Commission Received | | |
|---|---|---|---|---|---|---|---|---|
| | | | £ | s | d | £ | s | d |
| Abraham Aarons | Plymouth | 42 | 94 | 19 | 0½ | 2 | 7 | 5½ |
| Samuel Abrams | Sheerness? | 29 | 63 | 10 | 0½ | 1 | 11 | 9 |
| I. Abrams | ? | 2 | 3 | 15 | 5 | | 1 | 10½ |
| A. Abrum | ? | 1 | 1 | 17 | 8½ | | | 11¼ |
| Joel Barnet | Chatham | 2 | 3 | 15 | 5 | | 1 | 10½ |
| Asher Cohen | Chatham | 3 | 5 | 13 | 1½ | | 2 | 9¾ |
| B. Cohen | ? | 1 | 1 | 17 | 8½ | | | 11¼ |
| Abraham and Ezekile Emanuel | Plymouth | 106 | 399 | 6 | 0 | 9 | 19 | 7½ |
| Abraham Franklin | Portsea | 2 | 3 | 15 | 5 | | 1 | 10½ |
| Joseph Hart | Portsea | 2 | 12 | 11 | 11 | | 6 | 3½ |
| Emanuel Hart | Plymouth Dock | 71 | 229 | 3 | 1½ | 5 | 14 | 6½ |
| Samuel Hart | Plymouth Dock | 19 | 97 | 13 | 11 | 2 | 8 | 10½ |
| Alexander Isaac | Portsea | 8 | 15 | 1 | 8 | | 7 | 6½ |
| Solomon Isaac | Plymouth | 7 | 13 | 3 | 11½ | | 6 | 7½ |
| Michael Isaacs | ? | 1 | 1 | 17 | 8½ | | | 11¼ |
| Abel Israel | Plymouth Dock | 32 | 60 | 6 | 8 | 1 | 10 | 2 |
| Judah Jacob | Portsea | 131 | 326 | 16 | 6¼ | 8 | 3 | 4½ |
| I. and D. Jacobs | ? | 11 | 20 | 14 | 9½ | | 10 | 4½ |
| Jacob Jacobs | Plymouth | 36 | 69 | 15 | 2½ | 1 | 14 | 10½ |
| Simon Jonas | London | 1 | 1 | 17 | 8½ | | | 11¼ |
| Joseph Joseph | Plymouth | 517 | 1270 | 6 | 0½ | 31 | 15 | 1½ |
| Samuel Joseph | Plymouth | 6 | 20 | 4 | 9 | | 10 | 1½ |
| Nathan Joseph | Plymouth | 161 | 553 | 13 | 4 | 13 | 16 | 10 |

| | | | | | | | | |
|---|---|---|---|---|---|---|---|---|
| Lewis Lazarus | Portsmouth | 2 | 3 | 15 | 5 | | 1 | 10½ |
| Jacob Levi | Portsea | 11 | 63 | 1 | 7½ | 1 | 11 | 6½ |
| Moses Levi | Portsea | 1 | 1 | 17 | 8½ | | | 11¼ |
| A. Levy | ? | 3 | 14 | 19 | 7½ | | 7 | 5½ |
| Isaac Levy | London ? | 3 | 5 | 13 | 1½ | | 2 | 9¾ |
| Michael Levy | Portsmouth | 64 | 120 | 13 | 4 | 3 | 1 | 11½ |
| P. Levy | ? | 1 | 1 | 17 | 8½ | | | 11¼ |
| Samuel Levy | ? | 3 | 5 | 13 | 1½ | | 2 | 9¾ |
| Levi Lyon | ? | 1 | 1 | 17 | 8½ | | | 11¼ |
| Lazarus Magnus | Chatham | 16 | 48 | 6 | 4 | 1 | 4 | 1½ |
| Abraham Moses | Chatham | 1 | 1 | 17 | 8½ | | | 11¼ |
| Samuel Moses | Portsea | 26 | 68 | 11 | 1½ | 1 | 14 | 3½ |
| A. and Isaac Moses | ? | 3 | 5 | 13 | 1½ | | 2 | 9¾ |
| Moses Moses | Plymouth Dock | 105 | 250 | 13 | 9½ | 6 | 5 | 4½ |
| A. Moss | ? | 1 | 1 | 17 | 8½ | | | 11¼ |
| Barrow Moss | Plymouth Dock | 59 | 146 | 10 | 9½ | 3 | 13 | 3½ |
| Elias Moss | Chatham | 63 | 103 | 15 | 7 | 2 | 11 | 10½ |
| Isaac Myers | Portsmouth | 4 | 16 | 7 | 4 | | 8 | 2½ |
| | | | £ | s | d | £ | s | d |
| Isaac Nathan | Plymouth | 7 | 13 | 3 | 11½ | | 6 | 7½ |
| Jacob Nathan | Portsmouth | 12 | 31 | 9 | 0 | | 15 | 8½ |
| Michael Nathan | Plymouth Dock | 31 | 58 | 9 | 11½ | 1 | 9 | 3 |
| Lewis Ralph | Plymouth | 39 | 108 | 16 | 7½ | 2 | 14 | 5 |
| L. Samuel | ? | 1 | 1 | 17 | 8½ | | | 11¼ |
| Isaac Solomon | Plymouth | 10 | 18 | 17 | 1 | | 9 | 5½ |
| I. Wolfe | Portsea? | 1 | 1 | 17 | 8½ | | | 11¼ |
| M. Woolf | ? | 2 | 3 | 15 | 5 | | 1 | 10½ |
| Aaron Youell | Portsmouth | 2 | 3 | 15 | 5 | | 1 | 10½ |
| Jacob, John and Levy Zachariah | Portsmouth | 151 | 363 | 10 | 11¼ | 9 | 1 | 9 |
| M. Zachariah | ? | 1 | 10 | 14 | 2½ | | 5 | 4 |
| TOTALS: 52 AGENTS | | 1815 | £4751 | 8 | 1¼ | £118 | 16 | 8¾ |

## NOTES

1. Surname of Agent listed last in alphabetical order. The manuscript (ADM238-10) does not give the Agent's address; reference can therefore be made to the main register of Jewish Navy Agents (appendix number 1). Where some doubt exists a question mark is inserted as reference can only be made to other sources which are inconclusive.

2. The account of Distribution of Proceeds relates to the net sum of the total prize money of £108,690 taking into account that £14,963 remained unclaimed. Distributed 10 April 1807. The Navy Agents acted for the Midshipmen, Inferior Warrant Officers, Principal Warrant Officers Mates, Marine Sergeants (Fourth Class) each receiving £10.14s.2½d. and mainly the Seamen and Marines (Fifth Class) receiving £1.17s.8½d. each. The Government Grant of £300,000 was distributed earlier on the 6 August 1806 with the Fourth Class each receiving £26.6s.0d. and the Fifth Class £4.12s.6d. It is possible that the same Navy Agent acted for both prize money and grant distributions, selling goods to the value of the prize orders less 2½% commission. The Officers received the far greater proportion of the total distributions. For instance, Captain T.M. Hardy of *HMS Victory* obtained £973 prize money and £2,389.7s.6d. of the government grant.

## APPENDIX III

# ANNOUNCEMENTS OF PRIZE PAYMENTS IN WHICH ISAAC LEVY, PRIZE AGENT, WAS CONCERNED.

(Source: *Steel's Prize Pay Lists* 1802, *Navy Lists* and *London Gazette.*)

For *HMS WEAZLE* (12) Lieut H. Gunter. Bounty for the detention of the neutral ships *Christiana, Elizabeth, Wasa Orden* and *Grassina* in June 1795, in company with the *Ranger;* paid on board the *Nautilus* on her arrival at Sheerness after 5 June 1798. Recall, first Thursdays at 81 Whitechapel Road, London. I. Levy for G. Mends.

For *HMS NAUTILUS* (16) Lieut H Gunter and *HMS NARCISSUS* (cutter) Lieut. Wright. Prize money of *La Legere,* French privateer, taken 4 April 1798; paid to the *Nautilus* on arrival in port after 14 August 1798 and to the *Narcissus* 21 August 1798 at 81 Whitechapel Road, London. Recall, first Thursdays, at the latter place. I. Levy for G. Mends.

For *HMS NAUTILUS* (16) Lieut H. Gunter. Proceeds of *Le Capitaine Thurot,* French privateer, taken in company with the *Sea Gull* and *King George* cutters, 23 July 1797. Paid on board, on arrival in port. Recall, first Thursdays at I. Levy, acting agent, 81 Whitechapel Road, London.

For *HMS NAUTILUS* (16) Lieut H. Gunter. Head money of *L'Argus,* French Privateer, taken 4 April 1799. Paid 16 January 1800 at 81 Whitechapel Road, London. Recall every Thursday at same place. I. Levy, Acting Agent.

For *HMS NAUTILUS* (16) Lieut H. Gunter. Head money of *La Legere,* French Privateer taken 1 April 1798 in company with the *Narcissus;* paid every Thursday from 11 March 1800 by I. Levy, acting agent, at 81 Whitechapel Road, London.

For *HMS FURY* (8) Lieut J Gibson. The Officers and company who were on board at the capture of the brig *Vigilantia* on 26 November 1808 will be paid the proceeds of the hull and cargo on the 20 July 1809 at 8 Fenchurch Buildings. Recall every Tuesday and Thursday between 11 and 3 for three months. Petty Officers 1st Class £54.1s.6d., 2nd Class £18.4s.6d., Landsmen £12.3s.0d., Boys £6.1s.6d. Isaac Levy, Agent.

For *HMS FURY* (8) Lieut J. Gibson. Proportions of proceeds for the *Speculation* and *Cupido (Crocodile* and *Alexander* in company) taken 21 December 1808. Paid 20 March 1810 at 4 Commercial Chambers, Minories, London. Recall at same place Tuesdays and Thursdays. Isaac Levy, Agent.

For *HMS FURY* (8) Lieut J. Gibson. The Officers and company who were on board at the capture of *Fier Broeders,* in company with the *Cruizer* on the 23 November 1808, that they will be paid their respective proportions on the net proceeds on Tuesday, 17 April 1810 between the hours of eleven and three at 4 Commercial Chambers, Minories, London, and all shares not then claimed will be recalled at the same place every Tuesday and Thursday. Isasac Levy, Agent.

For *HMS FURY*(8) Lieut J. Gibson. The Officers and company who were on board at the capture of the *Vrow Sophia* and *Yonga Neffa* in company with the *Alexandria Cruizer* and *Starling* on the 23 November 1808, that they will be paid their respective shares of the net proceeds thereof on Thursday, 3rd May 1810 between the hours of eleven and three at 4 Commercial Chambers, Minories, London, and all shares not then claimed will be recalled at the same place every Tuesday and Thursday. Isaac Levy, Agent.

For *HMS FURY* (8) Lieut J. Gibson. The Officers and company who were on board at the capture of the *Kairn Rosine* and *Actif* by the *Daphne* (*Fury* sharing by agreement) on the 4 and 8 August 1808 that they will be paid their respective shares of the net proceeds thereof on 5 June 1810 at 4 Commercial Chambers, Minories, London. Recalls same place Tuesday and Thursday. Isaac Levy, Agent.

For *HMS FURY* (8) Lieut J. Gibson. The Officers and company who were on board at the capture of sundry *Danish Boats numbers 17, 23, 24, 25 and Heppel number 18* in the months of May and June 1808 that they will be paid their respective shares thereof on Thursday, 23 August 1810 at the Commercial Chambers, Minories, London, recalled every Tuesday and Thursday for three months. Isaac Levy, Agent.

For *HMS FURY* (8) Lieut J. Gibson. The Officers and company who were on board at the capture of sundry *Danish Boats numbers, 26, 27, 28, 29 Hope 31 and a Danish Privateer, name unknown* in the months of July and October 1808 that they will be paid their respective shares of said captures on Thursday, 23 August 1810 at the Commercial Chambers, Minories, London, recalled every Tuesday and Thursday for three months. Isaac Levy, Agent.

For *HMS FURY* (8) Lieut J. Gibson. The Officers and company who were on board at the capture of the *St Jargen* and *Jax Kabett* taken by *Starling* (*Fury* in company) 25 November 1808 that they will be paid their respective shares thereof on Thursday 23 August 1810 at the Commercial Chambers, Minories, London, and will be recalled at the same place every Tuesday and Thursday for three months. Isaac Levy, Agents.

For *HMS FURY* (8) Lieut J. Gibson. The Officers and company who were on board at the capture of the *Corroborata* taken 31 December 1808 will be paid their respective shares on Thursday 23 August 1810 at the Commercial Chambers, Minories, London, and will be recalled at the same place every Tuesday and Thursday for three months. Isaac Levy, Agent.

For *HMS NAUTILUS* (16) Lieut H. Gunter. Shares of prize money *Vreedon Ordt* taken 14 July 1798 paid 21 December 1810 at 4 Commercial Chambers, Minories, recall same place Tuesday and Thursday. I. Levy, Agent.

For *HMS FURY* (8) Lieut J. Gibson. Shares of the *Aurora* (by the *Alexandria*) 25 November 1808 and *Samen, Rolano* and *Twen Broeders* by the *Daphne* 23 June 1808. Paid 3 December 1811 at 10 Commercial Chambers, Minories; recalls Tuesday and Wednesday. For the *Aurora* Captain £19.10s.8d., Commissioned Officers £5.9s.10d., Warrant Officers £2.3s.9d., Petty Officers £1.1s.2d., Second Class 14s.1d., Able Seamen 7s.0d., Landsmen 4s.8d., Boys 2s.4d. For the *Twen Broeders* and *Samen* etc., Captain £10.13s.4d., Warrant Officers 15s.10d., Petty Officers 12s.9d., Second Class 8s.6d., Able Seamen 4s.3d., Landsmen 2s.10d., Boys 1s 5d. I. Levy, Agent.

# APPENDIX IV

## PRIZE PAYMENTS IN WHICH JOSEPH JOSEPH OF BARBICAN, PLYMOUTH, DEALT WITH RE-CALLS OF PRIZE MONEY UNCLAIMED.

(Source: *Steel's Prize Pay-Lists* 1802).

*HMS QUEBEC* (32) Captain J Rogers . . . Prize Money of *L'Adelle,* taken (in company with the *Terpischore 32)* 12 August 1794; paid on board September 28, 1795. Recall, first Mondays at Mr Joseph's Barbican, Plymouth. Samuel Hemmans, agent.

*HMS MAGNANIME* (44) Captain Hon. M. de Courcy . . . Proceeds of *La Posta,* Spanish ship taken 23 February 1798; paid on board, on arrival at Plymouth. Recall, first Tuesdays at Mr J. Joseph's, Plymouth, E. Vidal of Cove, and W. V. Johnson of the *Magnanime,* agents.

*HMS MAGNANIME* (44) Captain Hon. M. de Courcy . . . Proceeds of the hulls and stores of *L'Eugenie* and *L'Audacieux,* French privateers, taken 16 March and 2 April 1798; paid on board at Plymouth 24 November 1798. Recall every Tuesday, at Mr J. Joseph's, Plymouth, E. Vidal of Cove, and W. V. Johnson, purser of the *Magnanime,* agents.

*HMS MAGNANIME* (44) Captain Hon. M. de Courcy . . . Head-money for *L'Eugenie* and *L'Audacieux,* French privateers, taken 16 March and 2 April 1798; paid on board 12 January 1799. Recall at Mr J. Joseph's, Plymouth, E. Vidal of Cove, and W. V. Johnson, agents.

*HMS MAGNANIME* (44) Captain Hon. M. de Courcy . . . Hull and head-money of *La Colombe,* French privateer, taken 21 August 1798; paid on board at Plymouth 5 March 1799. Recall by Mr J. Joseph, Plymouth, W. V. Johnson, Agents.

*HMS MAGNANIME* (44) Captain Hon. M. de Courcy . . . The return of duties paid on the cargo of the *Aposta,* Spanish ship, paid on board 30 April 1800. Recall by Mr J. Joseph, Plymouth, W. V. Johnson, Agents.

## APPENDIX V

## MEN RAISED BY THE QUOTA FOR SERVICE IN THE ROYAL NAVY FROM THE PORT OF LONDON FOR THE SIX MONTHS 26 MARCH TO 25 SEPTEMBER 1795 FROM WHICH THESE DISTINCTIVE JEWISH NAMES HAVE BEEN EXTRACTED

(Public Record Office ADM7-361) Listed surname first in chronological order of joining the Royal Navy.

| | | |
|---|---|---|
| 22 May 1795 | HART, RICHARD | Age 21 a servant of Manglesfield Street. |
| 22 May 1795 | HART, JOSEPH | Age 28 a shoemaker of St. James' West. |
| 27 May 1795 | SOLOMON, WILLIAM | Age 21 a sweep of Bermondsey. |
| 1 June 1795 | DANIEL, JOSEPH | Age 23 a baker of Osborn Street, Whitechapel. |
| 30 June 1795 | BARNARD, WILLIAM | Age 21 a bricklayer of Aldgate. |
| 6 July 1795 | SAMUEL, MOSES | Age 20 an old clothesman of Hounsditch. |

## APPENDIX VI

## LANDSMEN VOLUNTEERS SENT INTO THE ROYAL NAVY FROM THE MARINE SOCIETY 1757 - 1814.

This roll was taken from the Marine Society papers in the National Maritime Museum MSY/S. These papers do not include religion, place of birth, or ship sent to. This list of generally distinctive Jewish Names should not, therefore, be treated as conclusive. With some names it has been considered that those sent to the Royal Navy on the same or next day would in all probability have known each other. They have in these cases been listed where otherwise doubt would have excluded them. Listed surname first in chronological order of joining the Royal Navy. The figure after the name is the age.

Period 24 July 1756 to 6 June 1760 (MSY/S/1)

| | | |
|---|---|---|
| 21 April 1757 | LEVY, NATHAN | 28 |
| 3 June 1757 | ABRAM, JAMES | 22 |
| 17 July 1757 | ABRAM, PHILIP | 24 |
| 2 January 1758 | ISAAC, JACOB | 28 |
| 15 May 1759 | SOLOMON, BARTHOLOMEW | 19 |
| 6 June 1760 | LEVI, DAVID | Age not recorded |

Their heights ranged between 5' and 5' 6". Isaac Adolphus, Secretary of the Marine Society, was one of the signatories to the certificate stating 5451 men were examined and fitted out. Possible Jewish representation 0.11%.

Period 18 April 1778 to 29 November 1780 (MSY/S/2)

| | | |
|---|---|---|
| 30May1778 | MOSS, BENJAMIN | 22 |
| 25 July 1778 | MOSES, JOSIAH | 22 |
| 14 October 1778 | ISAACS, DAVID | 25 |
| 25 November 1778 | BARNARD, BENJAMIN | 19 |
| 23 Decemberr 1778 | WOLFE, WILLIAM | 23 |
| 6 January 1779 | WOLFE, JOHN | 30 |
| 14 April 1779 | ROTH, JOHN | 22 |
| 14 April 1779 | BARNETT, JOSEPH | 18 |
| 19 May 1779 | ISAACS, MICHAEL | 19 |
| 19 July 1779 | BARNETT, MARK | 23 |
| 19 July 1779 | HART, JOHN | 28 |
| 21 July 1779 | DANIELS, DANIEL | 24 |
| 21 July 1779 | MARKS, HENRY | 21 |
| 23 July 1779 | BARNARD, JAMES | 23 |
| 10 August 1779 | ISAAC, JOSEPH | 19 |
| 22 December 1779 | MARKS, HENRY | 21 |

| | | |
|---|---|---|
| 27 March 1780 | LEVY, WILLIAM | 19 |

During the period 6754 men were examined and fitted out. Possible Jewish representation of 0.25%.

Period 26 December 1780 to 27 June 1794 (MSY/S/3)

| | | |
|---|---|---|
| 30 January 1782 | ALEXANDER, JOSIAH | 22 |
| 27 December 1782 | ABRAHAMS, BARNET | 19 |
| 9 August 1790 | BARNETT, JOSEPH | 25 |
| 21 October 1790 | JACOBS, JOHN | 23 |
| 28 October 1790 | DANIEL, MORRIS | 21 |
| 14 March 1793 | SOLLIMAN, JOSEPH | 24 |
| 25 June 1793 | MYERS, JOSEPH | 20 |
| 28 June 1793 | JOSEPH, WILLIAM | 32 |
| 10 December 1793 | ISAAC, SAMUEL | 19 |
| 9 January 1794 | MOSES, WILLIAM | 19 |

During the period 3101 men were examined and fitted out. Possible Jewish representation of 0.32%.

Period 3 October 1797 to 28 September 1805 (MSY/S/4)

| | | |
|---|---|---|
| 3 October 1797 | HART, JOHN | 20 |
| 5 October 1797 | SAMUEL, JACOB | 22 |
| 6 October 1798 | BARNETT, DANIEL | 21 |
| 3 January 1799 | JACOBS, JOHN | 26 |
| 26 January 1799 | ABRAHAMS, JOHN | 20 |
| 13 August 1799 | BARNARD, JACOB | 24 |
| 8 March 1800 | JACOBS, JOSEPH | 20 |
| 31 May 1800 | LYONS, JEREMIAH | 20 |
| 8 July 1800 | MYERS, JAMES | 22 |
| 8 July 1800 | HART, JOHN | 23 |
| 18 November 1800 | HART, SAMUEL | 28 |
| 22 November 1800 | LEAVY, JOHN | 23 |
| 16 December 1800 | HART, WILLIAM | 33 |
| 16 December 1800 | LYONS, WILLIAM | 20 |
| 7 January 1801 | SAMUEL, HENRY | 22 |
| 7 January 1801 | DANIEL, THOMAS | 21 |
| 21 April 1801 | ABRAMS, JOSEPH | 24 |
| 4 August 1801 | SAMUEL, SAMUEL | 20 |
| 14 January 1803 | ISAACS, JOHN | 24 |
| 3 April 1804 | BRAHAM, JOHN | 21 |

| | | |
|---|---|---|
| 22 September 1804 | ABRAHAMS, BENJAMIN | 22 |
| 2 July 1805 | JACOBS, JOHN | 20 |

During the period 7185 men were examined and fitted out. Possible Jewish representation of 0.30%.

Period 3 October 1805 to 20 May 1814 (MSY/S/5)

| | | |
|---|---|---|
| 9 May 1806 | JACOBS, THOMAS | 30 |
| 5 August 1806 | MEYER, HENRY | 25 |
| 15 November 1806 | HYAMS, MORDECAI | 18 |
| 11 April 1807 | ISAACS, WILLIAM | 31 |
| 5 August 1807 | ISAAC, JOHN | 18 |
| 21 August 1807 | DANIELS, JOSEPH | 29 |
| 21 August 1807 | LEVY, LAZARUS | 19 |
| 12 February 1808 | COHEN, ABRAHAM | 20 |
| 22 July 1809 | EMMANUEL, JOHN | 23 |
| 3 November 1809 | COHEN, JACOB | 22 |
| 24 July 1810 | LEVY, SAUNDERS | 18 |
| 3 August 1810 | ISAACS, EMANUEL | 20 |
| 27 September 1810 | HART, THOMAS | 29 |
| 27 September 1810 | JOSEPH, MICHAEL | 19 |
| 28 May 1811 | MOSES, JESSE | 19 |
| 2 July 1811 | BENJAMIN, ABRAHAM | 22 |
| 7 October 1811 | JACOBS, JOSEPH | 22 |
| 15 October 1811 | HART, JOHN | 24 |
| 8 November 1811 | HART, PHILIP | 26 |
| 17 March 1812 | GOULD, SAMUEL | 25 |
| 25 August 1812 | WOOLFE, JOHN | 19 |
| 22 September 1812 | JACOBS, THOMAS | 21 |
| 13 January 1813 | WOLFE, GEORGE | 23 |
| 22 July 1813 | LEVY, DAVID | 19 |
| 22 July 1813 | SOLOMON, NATHAN | 19 |
| 16 August 1813 | MOSES, JONAS | 22 |

During the period 7054 men were examined and fitted out. Possible Jewish representation of 0.37%.

The possible Jewish representation gradually increased from 0.01% in 1756 to 0.036% in 1814, giving an average for the whole period of 0.25%.

# APPENDIX VII

## BOYS SENT INTO THE ROYAL NAVY FROM THE MARINE SOCIETY 1787 to 1815.

This roll was taken from the Marine Society Papers in the National Maritime Museum MSY/K the reference being quoted at the end of each name, with the Muster Book reference number of the ship to which the boy was discharged found in the Public Record Office prefix ADM. The place of birth is sometimes unknown. Religion unstated, therefore this list of generally distinctive Jewish names should not be treated as conclusive. Listed surname first in chronological order of joining the Royal Navy.

5 October 1787 JACOBS, DAVID Age 17, Height 5'0". Dark brown hair, sallow complexion pitted with smallpox. Smart boy, reads well. Discharged as a servant to Lieutenant Hewit *HMS Sandwich* on 20 October 1787 at Chatham. (MSY/K/1 and ADM36-10526).

7 January 1791 HART, GEORGE Age 16, Height 4'6". Dark hair, dark eyes, fresh complexion. Jolly. A very humorous good boy, reads well. Discharged as a servant to Captain I. S .Yorke *HMS Rattlesnake* on 22 March 1791 at Portsmouth. Left at own request 20 February 1793. (MSY/K/1 and ADM36-11481).

23 December 1791 MYERS, NEHEMIAH Age 15, Height 4'11". Black hair, amber eyes, jolly, fresh complexion, rather brown. Discharged as a servant to Captain R. Keats (later Admiral Sir Richard Keats) *HMS Niger*. A lively good boy and reads remarkably well. Discharged with Captain Keats on 10 April 1793 from *HMS Niger*. (MSY/K/1 and ADM36-13350).

11th August 1795 DANIELS, WILLIAM Age 15, Height 4'4". Brown hair, dark eyes, much pitted with smallpox, mole on right eye. A dull boy, very unlearned. Discharged as a servant to Captain Bedford *HMS Queen* on 29 September 1795. (MSY/K/2 and ADM36-11368).

27 August 1795 JACOBS, WILLIAM Age 14, Height 4'6". Brown hair, brown eyes, much freckled, some smallpox, hardy looking. Lively boy but unlearned. Discharged as a servant to Captain Berkley *HMS Emerald* on 5 September 1795. Born Oxford. Boy Third Class (MSY/K/2 and ADM36-14842).

27 August 1795 JACOBS, JAMES Age 13, Height 4'3". Light hair, grey eyes, fresh and fair. Lively boy. Discharged as a servant to Captain Berkley *HMS Emerald* on 5 September 1795. Born Oxford. Boy Third Class (MSY/K/2 and ADM36-14842).

20 February 1798 MOSES, WILLIAM Age 14, Height 4'7". Brown hair, grey eyes, fresh complexion, freckley, lively, cannot read. Discharged on 14 March 1798 as a servant to Captain Elsington of *HMS Triumph*. Born London. Boy Third Class. (MSY/K/2 and ADM36-13064).

20 February 1798 MOSES, JAMES Age 15, Height 4'8". Brown hair, grey eyes, fresh, fair and lively, cannot read. Discharged as a servant to Captain Elsington *HMS Triumph* on 14 March 1798. Born London. Boy Third Class. (MSY/K/2 and ADM36-13064).

11 October 1799 BARNETT, JOSEPH Age 13, Height 4'4". Dark amber eyes, dark hair, fresh, fair and lively. Good boy, cannot read. Discharged as a servant to Captain Apshorp of *HMS Druid* on 26 November 1799 (MSY/K/2 and ADM36-15247). Sent to *HMS Champion* on 3 November 1801 as Boy Third Class until ship paid off 3 September 1802 (ADM36-14712).

8 November 1799 LINDO, THOMAS Age 15, Height 4'9". Grey eyes, brown hair, fresh, fair and lively. Very good boy, reads well. Discharged as a servant to Captain Wells *Glory* on 19 November 1799. Born Norwich. Boy 2nd Class. (MSY/K/2 and ADM36-14045).

30 May 1800 HART, JACOB Age 13, Height 4'4". Light hair, blue eyes, fresh, fair and freckled. Discharged as a servant to Lord St Vincent *HMS Ville de Paris* on 23 July 1800. A very good boy, reads well, Borne on books as a supernumerary volunteer class for orders. Discharged to *HMS Doris* on 11 January 1801. Born Bethnal Green. Third Class Boy. (MSY/K/2; ADM36-13851; ADM36-14694. Still aboard *HMS Doris* in June 1802).

9 April 1803 MOSS, JOSEPH Age 15, Height 4'9". Flaxen hair, very light grey eyes, very fair. Cannot read. Discharged as a servant to Captain Melhuish*HMS Perseus* on 12 April 1803. Born London. Boy 3rd Class. Discharged to *HMS Ceres* on 5 September 1803. (MSY/K/2; ADM36-15629).

29 March 1805 DANIELS, ABRAHAM Age 13, Height 4'6". Brown hair, light grey eyes, fresh, fair. Discharged as a servant to Captain Bland *HMS Flora* on 31 May 1805. Born London. Boy Third Class. (MSY/K/3 and ADM36-17468).

9 May 1805 ABRAHAMS, CHARLES Age 16, Height 4'8". Brown curly hair, grey eyes, fresh fair, tolerable but dull. Discharged as a servant to Captain Macnamara *HMS Dictator* (NOTE: Name 'Adams"'crossed out in register). Born Bristol. Boy Second Class joined *HMS Dictator* 26 June 1805. (MSY/K/3 and ADM37-109).

23 April 1807 HART, SAMUEL Age 14, Height 4'8". Brown hair, grey eyes, fresh complexion. Given bible. Good reader. Discharged to Captain Marsfield *HMS Superb*. Very good boy. Joined *Superb* 31 May 1807. Boy Second Class. Born Greenwich (MSY/K/4 and ADM37-160 still aboard April 1808).

8 October 1812 HART, JOSEPH Age 13, Height 4'2". Brown hair, dark eyes, fair and freckled. Middling boy, improved. Discharged as a servant to *HMS Royal William* on 11 December 1812. Sent to *HMS Vengeur* 4th January 1813. (MSY/K/6 and ADM37-3702).

## APPENDIX VIII

## JEWS WHO SERVED IN THE ROYAL NAVY AT THE BATTLE OF TRAFALGAR 21 OCTOBER 1805

*HMS VICTORY (100 guns)*

| | |
|---|---|
| BENJAMIN, MOSES | **Landsman. Born London. Age 21. Joined ship 1 March 1805. Went from main to supernumerary list because he received his discharge whilst the ship was in commission, dated 20 August 1805 'Discharged from the service per order of Lord Nelson agreeable to orders from the Lords Commissioners of the Admiralty (being a Jew)' Public Record Office ADM36-15900 and 15901.** |
| MOSS, JOSEPH | **Boy. Born Newington, Middlesex. Age 14. Joined ship 1 March 1805. Discharged to *HMS Resolution* 6 January 1806 on orders of Vice-Admiral Rowley. ADM36-15800 and 15901. Gave his Prize Order to Judah Jacob of Portsea ADM238-10.** |

*HMS BRITANNIA (100 guns)*

| | |
|---|---|
| LEVI, HENRY | **Landsman. Born London. Age 21. Volunteered joined ship 1 September 1804. ADM36 15994 and 15996. Gave his Prize Order to Emanuel Hart of Plymouth Dock ADM238-10.** |
| MANUEL, JOSEPH | **Ordinary Seaman. Born London. Age 20. Volunteered joined ship 1 September 1804. ADM36-15994 and 15996. Gave his Prize Order to Barrow Moss of Plymouth Dock ADM238-10.** |
| MANUEL, NATHAN | **Landsman. Born London. Age 21. Volunteered joined ship 1 September 1804. ADM36-15994 and 15996. Gave his Prize Order to Lewis Ralph of Plymouth ADM238-10.** |
| SOLOMON, BENJAMIN | **Landsman. Born London. Age 21. Volunteered joined ship 1 September 1804. ADM36-15994 and 15996. Gave his Prize Order to Emanuel Hart of Plymouth Dock ADM238-10.** |

*HMS ROYAL SOVEREIGN (100 guns)*

| | |
|---|---|
| BENJAMIN, JOHN | **Substitute. Born London. Age 34. Joined ship 3 September 1805. Discharged to *HMS Formidable* 20 December 1805 by order of Admiral Young. ADM36-15754 and 15755. Gave his Prize Order to I. Trout. ADM238-10.** |

*HMS COLOSSUS (74 guns)*

| | |
|---|---|
| EMANUEL. PHILIP | **Landsman. Born London. Age 21. Joined ship 1 November 1804. ADM36-15825.** |

*HMS TEMERAIRE (98 guns)*

| | |
|---|---|
| DA COSTA, BENJAMIN | Midshipman. Born London. Age 23. Joined ship 16 June 1805 as an Able Seaman. Made Midshipman 14 July 1805. Discharged 14 January 1806. ADM36-15851. 'Anglo-Jewish Notabilities' by A. Hyamson (1949). *Jewish Historical Society of England* and *The Gentleman's Magazine* 2 March 1854, Volume 41 page 445. 'One of the few remaining officers engaged in Battle of Trafalgar'. Gave his Prize Order of £10.14s.2½d. to I. Hammond. ADM238-10. |

*HMS REVENGE (74 guns)*

| | |
|---|---|
| BRANDON, JAMES | Landsman. Born London. Age 20. Joined ship 27 May 1805. Killed in action. ADM36-16546. |
| BRANDON, THOMAS | Landsman. Born London. Age 21. Joined ship 27 May 1805. ADM36-16546. Does not appear to have claimed prize money. |

Dr Cecil Roth in his Presidential Address delivered an admirable paper *'The Jews in the Defence of Britain'* before the Jewish Historical Society of England in the Hall of Magdalen College, Oxford, 27 October 1940. Mention was made of other Jews who, by family legend and tradition, were at the Battle of Trafalgar, namely Isaac Salamon and Barnett Abraham Simmons, subsequently minister in the Penzance Synagogue, who apparently lost a finger. Also a John Jacobs, but some doubt was recorded as to whether he was of the Jewish faith having been born in Arundel. He was aged twenty-five when joining *HMS Victory* as an Ordinary Seaman. ADM36-15900.

At the Battle of Trafalgar there were a number of foreigners who could have been of Jewish birth. Among those noted were Volunteer First Class Philip Mendel aged twenty-seven, wounded aboard *HMS Conqueror*, one of six Russian naval officers. Page 147 *The Trafalgar Roll* by Colonel R H Mackenzie (George Allen 1913). ADM36-16250. And William Abrahams, born Amsterdam, of *HMS Victory* an Able Seaman aged twenty-two. ADM36-15900.

Research is inconclusive because of name changing and lack of definite confirmation. For example, a Benjamin Simmonds, Carpenter's Crew *HMS Thunderer* Ordinary Seaman, born Bristol, aged thirty-eight, joined ship 29 May 1805. ADM37-192 and a Robert Myers *HMS Revenge* Born Leeds, aged twenty-four. ADM36-16545. ('Myers' is a Yorkshire surname and not necessarily Jewish). The earliest note of Jewish communities in Bristol and Leeds was about 1750.

All would have received the Government Grant to those rated Ordinary Seaman and below of £4.12s.6d. and Prize Money of £1.17s.8½d. except Moses Benjamin of *HMS Victory* because he was a supernumerary. However, his son John was permitted to trade freely under an Act of 1816 granting special privileges to the families of men who served in the Navy and Army (*Jewish Chronicle* 20 October 1905) the Certificate reading:-

## MARINERS SOLDIERS AND MARINES

WHEREAS in and by an Act of Parliament made in the fifty-sixth year of the reign of his late Majesty King George the Third instituted an Act to enable such Officers, Mariners and Soldiers as have been in the Land or Sea Service, or in the Marines or in the Militia, or any corps of Fencible Men, since the forty-second year of His Present Majesty's Reign, to exercise Trades, it is enacted, 'that all such Officers, Mariners, Soldiers and Marines as have been at any time employed in the service of His Majesty since the twenty-second day of June One thousand eight hundred and two, and have not since deserted the said service, and also the Wives and Children of such Officers, Mariners, Soldiers and Marines, may set up and exercise such Trades as they are apt and able for in any City Town or Place within the Kingdom without any let, suit or molestation of any person or persons whatsoever or by reason of the using of such Trade' and WHEREAS it appears to be by Certificate under the hand of William Carter, Esq., Principal Clerk in H.M.Admiralty, Somerset House, That Moses Benjamin hath served His late Majesty King George the Third since the twenty-second day of June One thousand eight hundred and two, as a Landsman on board HM Ship *Victory* whereby John, Son of the said Moses Benjamin is only entitled to the benefit of the said Act, THERE AND THEREFORE to will and require all and singular the Serjeants of the Chamber and all other persons whatsoever, not to molest or hinder the said John Benjamin in exercising such his trade within this City or the Liberties thereof according to the said Act.

Given under my hand, and sealed with the Seal of the Officer of Chamberlain of the City of London in the Guildhall of the said City this 13th day of January in the year of our Lord 1846.

## APPENDIX IX

# NOMINAL MUSTER ROLL OF JEWS WHO SERVED IN THE ROYAL NAVY 1750 - 1820.

(See also Appendices V, VI, and VII.)

## COMMISSIONED OFFICERS.

Last known rank is recorded. Reference can be made to the text for careers and sources. The Test Act of 1673 enacted that all persons holding any office or place of Trust under the crown or military were compelled to receive the Sacrament according to the rites of the Church of England, in some public church after divine service on Sunday. This was only repealed in 1829 by the Test and Corporation Acts, when it became legally possible for Jews and Roman Catholics to obtain commissions in the armed forces of the Crown. The following, therefore, would have had to relinquish their Jewish faith:-

Captain Sir Alexander Schomberg
Captain Maximillian Jacobs
Captain Solomon Gideon
Commander Donald Fernandez

## SEAMEN RATINGS AND MARINES

It has been impossible to examine over 10,000 Ships' Musters in the Public Record Office for the period covered. This list is therefore nominal and inconclusive because in addition a seaman's religion goes unrecorded. Accordingly only distinctive Jewish names are here listed, and in particular where Jewish communities were known to exist, as the musters give the seaman's place of birth. Completeness or accuracy cannot be claimed, particularly as name changing occurred. The roll should be usful in connection with other Anglo-Jewish genealogical studies. Names are listed alphabetically, surname first. As much detail as possible is given of the individual's career, together with the sources in the Public Record Office. More details of the ships served in can be obtained from Colledge, J. J., *'Ships of the Royal Navy'*, and background details of the ships' actions with the enemy can be found in James, W., *'The Naval History of Great Britain'* (editions for 1859 and after, when a separately published index of 1895, reprinted in 1971, can be used); also Volumes 4 and 5 of Clowes, W. L., *'The Royal Navy – a History'*, which has a substantial index.

The letters N.G.S.M. represent the Naval General Service Medal. The services of every Officer, Petty Officer, Seaman and Marine during and after the Napoleonic Wars remained unrecognised by the issue of any general decoration until 1847, by which time many who had served were no longer alive. The Naval General Service Medal, 1793–1840, had on the obverse the crowned head of the Queen and on the reverse Britannia seated on a sea horse. The ribbon to the medal was white with dark blue edges, whilst the recipient's name was indented on the edge of the medal. Clasps were issued to the medal bearing the names of the actions, places or ships in which the recipients were engaged. The lists are found at the Public Record Office, ADM171-1 to 5. Recourse has also been made to an authentic roll of recipients compiled by Captain K. Douglas-Morris (Privately printed 1982).

Before admission to Greenwich Hospital pensioners had to go before a board with a certificate covering their time of service in the Royal Navy. Those accepted then had to wait for admission as vacancies arose. By 1814 there were 2710 pensioners at Greenwich Hospital. The Public Record Office holds the papers concerning applications by former ratings and marines for admission into the Hospital as In-Pensioners, under (Reference should also be made to Appendices V, VI and VII) ADM73.

AARON, WILLIAM. Born Essex. Joined *HMS Freija* 20 February 1811 Landsman, age 24. *HMS Elizabeth* 19 March 1811 to 2 July 1815 (ADM37-5061). Awarded N.G.S.M. Boat Service Capture of the French Xebec *Aigle* off Vide, Corfu, 25 May 1814. Went to *HMS Iris* 3 July 1815, discharged one month later. Entered Greenwich Hospital 7 November 1849. (ADM73-1).

BARNARD, CHARLES. Born Bermondsey, London. Joined *HMS Thunderer* Landsman 28 March 1803 to 15 February 1805, then *HMS Hibernia* to 24 July 1810, made Ordinary Seaman *HMS Barbadoes* to 28 September 1812. Able Seaman in last ship *HMS Acasta* to 12 August 1815. Entered Greenwich Hospital 8 January 1841 (number 6935) age 58. Trade of weaver. Height 5' 10½" (ADM73-46 and 60).

BARNETT, RICHARD. Born London. Joined *HMS Vanguard* 28 September 1797, age 22. Landsman. (ADM36-15357) went to *HMS Ceres* 1 November 1801. Ordinary Seaman. Run at Portsmouth 11 March 1802 (ADM36-15305). Shipmate of SAMUEL, ISAAC.

BENJAMIN, JOHN. Born London. Joined *HMS Maidstone* aged 22 on 1 October 1799 (ADM36-15264).

BENJAMIN, JOHN. Born London. Joined *HMS Royal Sovereign* 3 September 1805. Age 34. Ordinary Seaman (ADM36-15754) discharged to *HMS Formidable* 20 December 1805 (ADM36-15755).

BENJAMIN, MOSES. Born London. Joined *HMS Victory* 1 March 1805. Age 21. Landsman. 'Discharged from the service per order of Lord Nelson agreeable to orders from the Lords Commissioners of the Admiralty (being a Jew)'. ADM36-15900 and 15901. Shipmate of MOSS, JOSEPH.

BENSON, LEVEN. Born Stepney. Volunteered *HMS Ceylon* 4 August 1808 age 22. (ADM37-23788). Wounded 17 September 1810.

BRANDON, JAMES. Born London. Volunteered. Joined *HMS Revenge* 27 May 1805. Landsman. Aged 20. Killed in action 21 October 1805. (ADM36-16546). Shipmate of BRANDON, THOMAS, possibly his brother.

BRANDON, THOMAS. Born Shoreditch, London. Volunteered *HMS Revenge* Landsman 27 May 1805 to 10 September 1814. Awarded N.G.S.M with clasp 'Trafalgar'. Shipmate of BRANDON, JAMES who was killed in action, and possibly his brother. Was serving aboard *HMS Revenge* at destruction of French ships in Basque Roads 11 and 12 April 1809, but did not receive an additional clasp to N.G.S.M. *HMS Glasgow* 11 September 1814 to 28 August 1815. Entered Greenwich Hospital 3 December 1845. Age 62, number 8925.

Married. Son and daughter. Last resided Bethnal Green. Trade of horsehair weaver. Height 5'1½". (ADM36-16546; ADM73-4 and 60).

CHAPMAN, BENJAMIN. Born London. Third-class Boy. Killed 10 June 1806 when falling down the hatch-way of *HMS Captain*, Age 18. Letter dated 20 June 1806 from Abraham Goldsmid of Capel Court to William Marsden, Secretary of the Admiralty 'The bearer hereof being the Father of the young man – I shall esteem it much if you will have the goodness to obtain the needful without delay in order that he may be buried according to the Jewish Rites' (ADM37-59; ADM51-1556 and ADMI-4624 piece 137).

COHEN, EDWARD (alias WALSH, GEORGE). Born Greenwich. Entered Greenwich Hospital 5 July 1800 age 69. Saw 26 years' service in the Royal Navy. (ADM73-43).

COHEN, HUGH. Born Belfast. Volunteered *HMS Minotaur* age 35. 1 June 1807. Paid off December 1810. (ADM37-1217 and 2474).

COHEN, JACOB. Born London. Pressed 26 September 1805. *HMS Zealand* Ordinary Seaman. 1 July 1807 joined *HMS Sibylle* aged 41. Discharged 27 April 1809 (ADM37-1441 and ADM36-16921).

COHEN, JOHN. Born London. Joined *HMS Loire* 1 March 1809 age 22. Landsman (ADM37-1959). Awarded N.G.S.M. Clasp 'Guadaloupe' 5 February 1810. Greenwich Pensioner GH 5904.

DA COSTA, BENJAMIN. Born London. Joined *HMS Temeraire* 16 June 1805 age 23. Able Seaman. Made Midshipman 14 July 1805. Discharged 14 January 1806. (ADM36-15851). Awarded N.G.S.M Clasp 'Trafalgar'.

DANIELS, JOHN. Born Canterbury. Joined *HMS Astrea* 1 April 1813. Able Seaman age 26. Still aboard in January 1815 (ADM37-4214). Shipmate of LEVY, DANIEL.

DANIELS, SAMUEL. Born Bristol. Landsman *HMS Sceptre* age 21. Awarded N.G.S.M. Clasp 'Guadaloupe' 5 February 1810. (ADM37-2248).

DE COSTA, ISAAC. Born Whitechapel. Joined *HMS Resolution* from *HMS Princess of Orange* 22 February 1806. Age 20 (ADM37-456). Landsman. Drowned 22 May 1806 when falling from the rigging of *HMS Resolution* (ADM51-1603). Shipmate of EMANUEL, HARRY

EMANUEL, ABRAHAM. Marine. Private sent to *HMS Pompee* 6 January 1800 from H.Q. Portsmouth (ADM36-12486).

EMANUEL, HARRY. Born Bishopsgate. Joined *HMS Resolution* from *HMS Princess of Orange* 22 February 1806. Aged 21. (ADM37-456). Landsman. Sent to *HMS Bucephalas* on 23 March 1809. Ordinary Seaman, then to *HMS Samarang* on 17 January 1811. (ADM37-2501). Shipmate of DE COSTA, ISAAC.

EMANUEL, PHILIP. Born London. Joined *HMS Colossus* 1 November 1804. Age 21, Landsman. (ADM36-15825).

GOLDSMID, DAVID. Born Prussia. Pressed *HMS Balfour* from *HMS Brune* on 24 March 1812 age 36. Run at Portsmouth 18 August 1812. Previously served *HMS Fervent* (ADM37-3309 and ADM6-67-2).

HARRIS, JOSEPH. Born Aldersgate, London. Wounded in the hand aboard his last ship *HMS Tremendous* after 13½ years service in the Royal Navy. Entered Greenwich Hospital 4 September 1840 number 6826 age 64. Married with a daughter. Trade of watchmaker. Height 5'2". (ADM73-46, 60 and 69).

HART, BENJAMIN. See Page 37. *'Seventy Years a Showman'* by G. Sanger 1927. Probably served *HMS Pompee*. Pressed.

HART, HENRY. Born Marylebone, London. Entered Greenwich Hospital 17 September 1837. Age 54. Married, wife's name Sarah, 2 sons, 2 daughters. Last resided in Hackney Road, London. Trade of weaver. Height 5'4". Not wounded. Served 11 years in the Royal Navy, last ship being *HMS Namur* (ADM73-59).

HART, ISRAEL. See page 37, *'Seventy Years a Showman'* by G Sanger 1927. Probably served *HMS Pompee*. Pressed.

HART, JAMES. Born Devonport. Entered Greenwich Hospital number 7778. Age 60. Served aboard *HMS Pelorus*. 15 years' service in the Royal Navy. (ADM73-43).

HART, JOSEPH. Born London. Volunteered *HMS Blake* 16 June 1809 age 21, then *HMS Rippon* 16 May 1813 Ordinary Seaman to *HMS Bellerpoule* until 12 June 1815 discharged to Haslar Hospital. Rejoined 17 June 1824 *HMS Pylades*, then *HMS Winchester* on 1 August 1827 as an Able Seaman until 5 March 1828. *HMS Spartiate* .Paid off 7 July 1831. Admitted to Greenwich Hospital 31 May 1842. (ADM73-12).

HART, LYON. Pressed at Deal 14 December 1812 aboard *HMS Mulgrave*. Discharged 20 February 1813. Per order of Commander-in-Chief from the service, being a Jew. (ADM37-4028).

HART, MICHAEL. Born London. Joined *HMS Blanche* 13 November 1802 age 19. Ordinary Seaman, discharged to *HMS Constance* 3 February 1803. (ADM36-15710).

HART, SAMUEL. Born Bristol. Served 4 years in the Royal Navy. Wounded in left arm and neck. *HMS Unite* (ADM37-46). Last ship *HMS Sparrowhawk*. Entered Greenwich Hospital 18 September 1835. Age 55, unmarried, height 5'7¼". (ADM73-46 and 59).

HART, WILLIAM. Born London. Left Naval Asylum in November 1802 for

*HMS Victory* and then *HMS Ambuscade* on 3 May 1804, age 17. Discharged September 1804 as Boy First Class (ADM37-750).

HENRIQUES, SAMUEL. Born London. Joined *HMS Hecate* 8 September 1809 Boy second class. Age 16. Made Landsman 17 May 1812. (ADM37-3075).

ISAAC, JAMES. Born Portsea. Served 15 years in the Royal Navy, last ship *HMS Active*. Entered Greenwich Hospital 8 February 1833. Married with a daughter. Last resided in London. Height 5'7". (ADM73-59).

ISAACS, EMANUEL. Born London. Joined *HMS Macedonian* 2 August 1810. Landsman. (ADM37-2609). Wounded 28 October 1812 in action with the '*United States*'. (ADM37-3616).

JACOBS, ISAAC. Joined *HMS Prince* from *HMS Frolic* on 31 October 1813, discharged to Haslar Hospital on 1 November 1813. (ADM37-4072).

JACOBS, ROBERT ANGEL. Born Plymouth. Joined *HMS Valiant* 10 June 1794. Age 20. Able Seaman. Discharged to Haslar Hospital 18 August 1794. (ADM36-12139).

KEYSER, JOHN. Born Prague. Joined *HMS Pactolus* 22 September 1815. Second Class Boy, age 17. Discharged to *HMS Severn* 25 February 1816. (ADM37-5790 and 5803). Awarded N.G.S.M with clasp "Algiers" 27 August 1816.

KEYSER, JOSEPH. Joined *HMS Pactolus* 27 October 1815. Master-at-Arms. Discharged to *HMS Severn* 25 February 1816. (ADM37-5790 and ADM37-5803). Awarded N.G.S.M. with clasp 'Algiers' 27 August 1816.

KEYSER, JOSEPH. Born Plymouth Dock. Joined *HMS Pactolus* 14 October 1815. Third class boy, age 14. Discharged to *HMS Severn* 25 February 1816 (ADM37-5790 and 5803).

LEVI, HENRY. Born London. Joined *HMS Britannia* 1 September 1804. Landsman. Age 21 (ADM36-15994). Sent to *HMS Royal George* June 1806 (ADM37-556). *HMS Phoebe* from May 1809 then to *HMS San Joseph* (ADM37-1815). Shipmate of MANUEL, JOSEPH; MANUEL, NATHAN; AND SOLOMON, BENJAMIN.

LEVI, THOMAS. Born Northamptonshire. Joined *HMS Glory* at Plymouth 27 October 1793. Landsman, discharged to *HMS Resolution* 16 April 1794 aged 20. (ADM36-11712).

LEVY, BRYAN. Joined *HMS Prince* 4 August 1813, discharged to *HMS Centaur* 15 November 1813 (ADM37-4072).

LEVY, DANIEL. Born London. Joined *HMS Astrea* age 30 on 1 November 1813. Sent to *HMS Creole* on 24 May until 2 November 1814, paid off. (ADM37-4072 and 4256). Shipmate of DANIELS, JOHN.

LEVY, JOHN (alias COOK, JOHN). Born London. Joined *HMS Merlin* 16 May 1796. Ordinary Seaman. Age 26. Paid off, sent to *HMS Dolphin* 31 July 1801 (ADM36-14464 and 14273: Court Martial ADMI-5360).

LEVY, NATHAN. Born London. Joined *HMS Ceres* 24 May 1805. Landsman. Age 20. (ADM36-15584).

LEVY, THOMAS. Born Chatham. Served for 37 years in the Royal Navy. Last ship *HMS Blanche*. Entered Greenwich Hospital 22 July 1814 age 50. Unmarried. Last resided at Lord Hood Arms. Height 5'5". (ADM73-56).

MANUEL, JOSEPH. Born London. Volunteered *HMS Rippon* 1 August 1776 age 25, Able Seaman, then *HMS Perseverance* until 1783. Rejoined Royal Navy *HMS Dictator* 5 June 1794, then HM Ships *Stability, Van Tromp, Sans Pariel, Grappler* and *Censor*. Bosuns Mate 12 October 1804 age 53. Entered Greenwich Hospital 8 April 1805 after 17 years' interrupted service. Married with a son and three daughters. Height 5'11½" Last resided at 9 St. Catherine Lane, London. (ADM73-16 and 55).

MANUEL, JOSEPH. Born Bethnal Green, London. Volunteered *HMS Britannia* Ordinary Seaman 1 September 1804 to 18 June 1806, awarded N.G.S.M. with clasp 'Trafalgar'. *HMS Royal George* 19 June 1806 to 12 May 1809. *HMS San Josef* 13 May 1809 to 16 August 1814. Entered Greenwich Hospital 15 October 1845. Age 62 number 8883. Married, 3 sons. Trade of weaver. Height 5'4". (ADM73-18 and 60). Shipmate of LEVY, HENRY; MANUEL, NATHAN; and SOLOMON, BENJAMIN.

MANUEL, NATHAN. Born London. Joined *HMS Britannia* 1 September 1804 age 23. Landsman (ADM36-15996). Sent to *HMS Royal George* June 1806 (ADM37-556) *HMS Phoebe* May 1809, then *HMS San Josef* (ADM37-1815) Shipmate of LEVY, HENRY; MANUEL, JOSEPH; and SOLOMON, BENJAMIN.

MEYER, ANTHONY. Born London. Ordinary Seaman. Age 21. *HMS Ethalion* Carpenter's Crew. Awarded N.G.S.M. Clasp 'Martinique' 24 February 1809 (ADM37-1507).

MEYER, GEORGE. Born London. joined *HMS Triumph* 1 March 1798. age 17. Ordinary Seaman. (ADM36-13064).

MOSES, JOHN. Born Birmingham. Joined *HMS Laurel* 18 March 1811. Age 13. Third class Boy.

MOSES, MICHAEL. Born London. Volunteered *HMS Pompee* 20 November 1805 age 28. Landsman (ADM36-17353) sent to *HMS Victory* 1 February 1808 made Ordinary Seaman. Run 16 February 1808. (ADM37-1082).

MOSES, PETER. Born London. Entered Greenwich Hospital 20 August 1825 age 55. Married. Wife's name Sarah. 2 daughters aged 17 and 18. Last resided in

Bermondsey Street, London. Height 5'2". Trade of Barber and Tailor. Served 20 years in the Royal Navy, last ship being *HMS Ajax*. (ADM73-42 and 58).

MOSS, JOSEPH. Born Stoke Newington. Joined *HMS Victory* 1 March 1805. Boy Third Class. Age 14 (ADM36-15900), went to *HMS Resolution* when *HMS Victory* paid-off 6 January 1806 (ADM36-15901). Shipmate of BENJAMIN, MOSES.

MYERS, GEORGE. Born London. Volunteered Landsman *HMS La Chiffonne* 24 June 1803 to 28 August 1811, then to *HMS Egmont* until 19 August 1814. Entered Greenwich Hospital 20 May 1846 at 66 years of age. Married, 2 sons. Last resided St Marylebone, London. Trade of tailor. Height 4'11½". (ADM73-18, 60 and 69).

MYERS, JOSEPH (alias JAMES). Born Portsmouth or Canterbury (records are at variance). Joined *HMS Isis*. Landsman 28 April 1803 to 30 September 1809. Sent to *HMS Hecate* as Ordinary Seaman from 1 October 1809 until 14 February 1814. Awarded N.G.S.M. for capture of Java (July to September 1811). Sent to *HMS Clorinde* until discharged 25 September 1814. Entered Greenwich Hospital age 62 on 16 February 1843 number 7781. Widower with a son and daughter. Blind. (ADM73-18, 60 and 69; ADM37-3075).

MYERS, WILLIAM. Born Whitechapel. Volunteered *HMS Trident* 12 April 1777 age 32, served in HM Ships *Raisonnable, Delaware, Mercury* and *Atlas* until 1783. Able Seaman. Rejoined as a volunteer *HMS Vanguard* 16 July 1790 to 13 September 1791. Left and volunteered again aboard *HMS Albacore* on 24 January 1794, served in HM Ships *Redoubt* and *Sheerness* until 3 August 1803, invalided after 16 years' interrupted service at age of 55. Entered Greenwich Hospital 15 October 1803. Widower with 2 sons and a daughter. Height 5'7". Last resided at 'Sailors Return', Rotherhithe. Trade of Waterman. (ADM73-16 and 55).

NATHAN, SOLOMON. Born Kenningsburgh, Prussia. Private Royal Marines. Served *HMS Andromache* 14 August 1798 to 28 February 1804. *HMS San Josef* 1 March 1804 to 18 March 1806. Discharged wounded. Entered Greenwich Hospital 13 June 1806 age 27, unmarried. Last resided Filgate Street, Whitechapel, London. Trade of tailor. Height 5'7". Blind. One of the many foreigners who served in the Royal Navy during the Napoleonic Wars. By an Act of 1740 (George II Chapter 3) for the better supply of mariners, foreigners were given the privilege to stay in England who had served for 2 years or more upon a British Ship of War or merchant, or other trading ship during time of war, and no other oath or other formality was required as a condition. (ADM36-15963, ADM73-19 and 55).

ROSE, ISRAEL. Captain's Servant *HMS Glory*. Awarded N.G.S.M. Clasp '1 June 1794' (Battle Glorious 1 June). Discharged 12 July 1794 on Admiralty Order (ADM36-11712).

SAMPSON, JOSEPH. Volunteer *HMS Prince* 30 August 1813 from *HMS Asia*. Landsman. Discharged to *HMS Scylla* 29 October 1813. (ADM37-4072).

SAMUEL, BARNETT. Born Hamburg. Private Royal Marines. Served 5 years last ship being *HMS Gladiator*. Wounded. Discharged 21 October 1802 nearly blind. Entered Greenwich Hospital 11 September 1809 age 50. Unmarried. Height 5'3". Dark complexion, grey eyes, dark brown hair. (ADM73-26 and 56).

SAMUEL, ISAAC. Born Chatham. Joined *HMS Vanguard* 4 October 1797. Landsman. Age 22 (ADM36-15357) went to *HMS Royal William* on 8 February 1800 (ADM36-13638). Shipmate of BARNETT, RICHARD.

SCHWEITZER, JOHN. Born London. Pressed *HMS Leander* 14 April 1816. Age 25. Ordinary Seaman. (ADM37-5762).

SMITH, JOHN. Born London. Joined *HMS Hussar* 9 March 1803. Landsman. Age 24 (ADM36-16028). An example of name changing. See Page 169 *'The Adventures of John Wetherell'* by C. S. Forester 1954.

SOLOMON, BENJAMIN. Born London. Joined *HMS Britannia* 1 September 1804 (ADM36-15994). Age 21. Landsman. Then *HMS Royal George* June 1806 (ADM37-556). Shipmate of LEVI, HENRY; MANUEL, JOSEPH; and MANUEL, NATHAN.

SOLOMONS, NATHAN (alias WILLIAMS, NATHAN). Joined *HMS Ceres* February 1814 age 18. Also served *HMS Penelope*. (ADM6-67-3).

VALLENTINE, ISAAC. Born 1793. Founder of *The Jewish Chronicle*. See Obituary *Jewish Chronicle* 18 September 1868.

The possible number of seamen and marines, born of the Jewish faith, who served in the Royal Navy and Marines during the Napoleonic Wars may lie in the region of 300. The average total strength of the Royal Navy and Marines was about 111,000, and a fair proportion could possibly be one-quarter of one per cent. (See comparative proportions in Appendix VI).

# APPENDIX X

## LIST OF STATUTES

31 George II Chapter 10. An Act for the Encouragement of Seamen employed in the Royal Navy; and for establishing a regular Method for the punctual, frequent and certain Payment of their Wages; and for enabling them more easily and readily to remit the same for the Support of their Wives and Families; and for preventing Frauds and Abuses attending such Payments. Under section 30 of this Act of 1758 no more than sixpence in the pound could be deducted for receiving and paying Seamen's Wages or Prize Money.

26 George III Chapter 63. An Act for the further preventing of frauds and abuses attending the Payment of Wages, Prize Money, and other Allowances, due for the service of Petty Officers, Seamen and Marines on board any of his Majesty's Ships. Section 4 of this Act of 1786 established the Inspectors Branch in the Navy Pay Office London.

32 George III Chapter 33. An Act for the Encouragement of Seamen, employed in the Royal Navy, and for establishing a regular method for the punctual, frequent and certain Payment of their Wages, and for enabling them more easily and readily to remit the same for the support of their wives and families. This Act explained and amended an earlier Act of 1758. Section 7 enabled seamen to receive their pay for all past services, whether or not moved from ship to ship, whilst abroad upon the seamens' return to England.

32 George III Chapter 34. An Act for further preventing frauds and abuses attending the Payment of Wages, Prize Money, and other Allowances due for the service of Petty Officers Seamen and Marines on board any of his Majesty's Ships. Under section 7 of this Act of 1792 orders could be made for under £7 to third parties for wages only.

35 George III Chapter 28. An Act to enable Petty Officers in the Navy Seamen and Marines serving in his Majesty's Navy to allot part of their Pay for the maintenance of their Wives and Families.

45 George III Chapter 72. An Act for the Encouragement of Seamen and for the better and more effectual Manning of his Majesty's Navy during the present War. This Act of 1805 consolidated all the previous Prize Acts. Section 5 Prize Bounty; Section 43 Regulations respecting the Condemnation of Prizes; Sections 53 to 59 Prize Agents and Powers of Attorney; Sections 64 to 75 Procedure laid down for Prize Agents to follow in a Prize Cause; Sections 80 to 101 Involvement of Greenwich Hospital with Prize Money; Section 92 prescribed the form of a letter of Attorney for receiving prize money; Section 121 Punishment for impersonating Seamen.

46 George III Chapter 100. An Act to empower the Commissioners and Governors of the Royal Hospital for Seamen at Greenwich to make certain allowances to old infirm wounded or disabled Officers in the Royal Navy, and to provide a fund for the payment of such allowances and for the increase of Pensions to disabled Seamen and Marines. This Act of 1806 was concerned with the amounts of Prize Money Agents had to send for the maintenance of Greenwich Hospital section 2 and Bounty Money section 4. Likewise under

section 1 of the 46 George III Chapter 101 An Act for improving the Funds of the Chest at Greenwich.

49 George III Chapter 123. An Act to explain and amend an Act made in the Forty-fifth Year of his present Majesty for the Encouragement of Seamen; and for the better and more effectual manning of his Majesty's Navy during the present War; and for the further Encouragement of Seamen, and for the better and more effectually providing for the Interest of the Royal Hospital for Seamen at Greenwich, and the Royal Hospital for Soldiers at Chelsea; and to extend the Provisions of the said Act to cases arising in consequence of Hostilities commenced since the passing of the said Act. Sections 35 to 39 deal with the Licensing of Navy Agents for Seamen and Marines.

54 George III Chapter 93. An Act for regulating the Payment of Navy Prize Money, and the Transmission of Accounts and Payment of Balances to Greenwich Hospital.

55 George III Chapter 60. An Act to repeal several Acts relating to the Execution of Letters of Attorney and Wills of Petty Officers, Seamen and Marines, in His Majesty's Navy, and to make new provisions respecting the same.

57 George III Chapter 118. An Act for authorising the Executors or Administrators of deceased licensed Navy Agents to receive Prize Money, Bounty Money and other Allowances of Money upon Orders given to such deceased Agents.

59 George III Chapter 56. An Act to make further Regulations as to the Payment of Navy Prize Orders. Section 4 Licensing Bond increased to £500. Section 10 Prize Orders by seamen to Licensed Navy Agents irrevocable.

## NAVAL GLOSSARY

BOMB VESSEL. OR 'BOMB'. A man-of-war designed to carry one or two heavy mortars mainly for shore bombardment.

BOUNTY. A sum of money paid as an inducement or award.

BUMBOAT. A small Harbour Boat used for carrying bedding, slops, fruit, vegetables and provisions to ships lying at their moorings.

CONDEMNATION. The legal process used in prize law. After hearing all the evidence The High Court of Admiralty (or if abroad the Vice-Admiralty Courts) if satisfied pronounce sentence on the captured vessel in favour of the capturing vessels' crew, who can then proceed to sell the prize with its contents.

CRIMP. One who persuades seamen to desert in order to sell them to another ship to obtain head money. Crimping was an indictable offence of Royal Navy Seamen.

EAST INDIAMEN. Name given to the ships of the various East India Companies. For many years considered the finest ships afloat.

FLAG OFFICER. An Admiral.

LANDSMEN. A form of rank given to British Seamen serving aboard Warships without any naval training, paid less than an ordinary seaman. This form of rating was abolished in 1862.

LOWER DECK. The deck next above the *orlop deck,* the lowest in a ship. An expression to indicate ratings, as distinct from officers belonging to the quarterdeck.

NAVY AGENT. A Trader, more often than not a slopseller, Jeweller or Silversmith who acted for the Warrant Officers, Petty Officers, Seamen and Marines of the Royal Navy in obtaining their wages, allotments, grants and prize money for a small commission. The Navy Agent obtained the Prize Money, on behalf of the seamen, from the Prize Agent.

PIPE TO DINNER. The term used to 'call' the hands to dinner by means of the boatswain's whistle. This was the longest 'call' in the boatswain's repertoire, a low and high whistle with a trill at the end.

PRIZE AGENT. A Person, often a Captain's Secretary or Merchant with legal experience, who acted for the crew of a capturing vessel at the High Court of Admiralty to condemnation, sale and distribution of the proceeds less a commission and expenses. Often the prize agent, being based in London would use SUB-AGENTS in the naval towns and overseas. The prize agent also acted as a petty banker to the Commissioned Officers of the Royal Navy.

PRIVATEER. An armed Merchant Ship, licensed by letter of marque to capture or destroy enemy ships to her owner's profit.

RUN ASHORE. Leave given to Seamen.

SKYLARKING. Playing the fool.

SLOPS. Derived from 'Slip' meaning any garment easily adjusted. Generally sailor's clothing and personal equipment.

SUPERNUMERARY. A person borne on the ship's muster books surplus to her established complement.

WHERRY. A light built boat, pulled by oars and seated for the accommodation of passengers, about 14 feet with a single rower and about 25 feet with four rowers.

# HEBREW GLOSSARY

ARK. An imitation of the Temple with its Holy of Holies wherein the Scroll of the Law is kept and placed at the east end of the Synagogue. Generally covered with a richly decorated curtain.

ASHKENAZIM. Jews of German-speaking and Slavonic Countries. Distinguished from the Sephardim.

BIMAH. The reading desk on a platform from which the people can be addressed. The scrolls of the Law are carried to and placed upon it when the lesson of the day is read.

CHANUCAH. The chief post-Biblical Festival of the Jews, celebrated in memory of the restoration of the Temple Service during the time of the Maccabeans 164 BC, which is held for eight days. It generally occurs about mid-December.

DAYANIM OF THE BETH DIN. An ecclesiastical tribunal which decides cases of Jewish law and is composed of three members known for their knowledge of Talmudic Law. The decision of any two of them is binding. Each member of the Court is called a 'Dayan'.

MENORAH. The eight-branched candelabrum lit on Chanucah, the Festival of Lights.

MINYAN. A Quorum of ten males for the commencement of a service.

MITZVOT. Synagogue Honours, such as taking the scrolls of the Law from the Ark, housing the scrolls, to the reader's desk.

MOHEL. The Official who performs the religious rite of circumcision, eight days after a male's birth.

SEPHARDIM. Spanish and Portugese Jews from the Sepharad mentioned in Obadiah 20. Distinguished from the Ashkenazim in Hebrew pronunciation and in some small ritual differences.

SEPHER TORAH. The Law is read in the Synagogue from scrolls written on sheepskin in long columns containing the five books of the Pentateuch. The ends of the Scroll are attached to handles or rollers of wood upon which they are rolled-up. When not in use they are bound and covered with a mantle, with the two tops of the handles covered overall with a crown or two sets of bells.

TALMUD. The oral law of the Jews together with the commentary, which sums up the whole development of Jewish doctrine and practice after Biblical times up to nearly the fifth century.

TORAH. Commonly applied to the Pentateuch, but in strict theological significance extends to the whole of the Scriptures and refers to the spirit as much as to the letter of the law.

## SELECT BIBLIOGRAPHY


BERMANT C. *The Cousinhood – The Anglo-Jewish Gentry* (Eyre and Spottiswoode 1971).

BLACK D. *Plymouth's Historic Synagogue* (Plymouth Hebrew Community 1961).

BROWNE G. L. *Nelson: The Public and Private Life of Horatio, Viscount Nelson.* (Fisher Unwin 1891).

CHALKLIN C. W. *The Provincial Towns of Georgian England* (E. Arnold 1974).

CLOWES W. L. *The Royal Navy.* 7 volumes (S Low Marston 1897-1903).

EMDEN P. *Jews of Britain.* A series of biographies (Sampson Low 1943).

EMDEN P. *The Brothers Goldsmid and the Financing of the Napoleonic Wars* (Transactions of the Jewish Historical Society of England Vol. 14 1935 to 1939.

ENDELMAN T. M. *The Jews of Georgian England 1714-1830* (The Jewish Publication Society of America) 1979.

FENWICK K. *HMS Victory* (Cassell 1959).

GATES W. G. *The History of Portsmouth* (Charpentier Portsmouth 1900).

GATES W. G. *The Illustrated History of Portsmouth* (Charpentier Portsmouth 1900).

GILL C. *The Naval Mutinies of 1797* (Manchester University Press 1913).

GILL C. *Plymouth. A New History* (David & Charles 1979 Part 2).

HENRIQUES H. S. Q. *The Return of the Jews to England* (MacMillan 1905).

HYAMSON A. M. *A History of the Jews in England* (Chatto and Windus 1908).

HYAMSON A. M. *The Sephardim of England* (Methuen 1951).

JACOB A. M. *The Jews of Falmouth 1740-1860* (Transactions Jewish Historical Society of England. Vol. 17 1951 to 1952).

JAMES W. *The Naval History of Great Britain* 6 volumes (Richard Bentley 1859).

JARRETT D. *British Naval Dress* (J. M. Dent 1960).

KEMP Lt. Cdr. P. *Prize Money* (Gale & Polden 1946).

KEMP P. (Editor) *The Oxford Companion to Ships and the Sea* (Oxford University Press 1976).

LEWIS M. *A Social History of the Navy 1793-1813* (George, Allen & Unwin 1960).

LLOYD C. AND COULTER J. *Medicine and the Navy* 4 volumes. (Livingstone 1961).

LOEWE L. (Editor) *Diaries of Sir Moses and Lady Montefiore* A facsimile of the 1890 edition (The Jewish Historical Society of England and the Jewish Museum 1983).

LONG W. H. *Medals of the British Navy and How they were Won* (Portsmouth 1895).

MacDOUGALL P. *The Chatham Dockyard Story* (Rochester Press 1981).

MASEFIELD J. *Sea Life in Nelson's Time* (Sphere Books 1972).

MEISELS I. S. *The Jewish Congregation of Portsmouth* (Transactions Jewish Historical Society of England vol. 6 1908 to 1910).

NEWMAN E. *Some New Facts about the Portsmouth Jewish Community* (Transactions Jewish Historical Society of England Vol. 17 1951 to 1952).

NICOLAS Sir N. H. *The Dispatches and Letters of Vice-Admiral Nelson.* 7 Volumes (Henry Colburn 1844 to 1846).

PICCIOTTO J. *Sketches of Anglo-Jewish History:* revised and edited, with a prologue notes and an epilogue by J. Finestein (The Soncino Press 1956).

PICTON J. *Memorials of Liverpool, Historical and Topographical* 2 Volumes. Second Revised Edition (Longmans Green 1875)

POLLINS H. *Economic History of the Jews in England* (The Littman Library of Jewish Civilization. Associated University Press 1982).

POPE D. *England Expects* (Weidenfeld & Nicholson 1959).

PRESNAIL J. *Chatham, The Story of a Dockyard Town* (Corporation of Chatham 1952).

ROBINSON C N. Commander *The British Tar in Fact and Fiction* (Harper and Brothers 1909).

RODGER N A M. *Naval Records for Genealogists* (Public Record Office 1984).

ROTH C. *A History of the Jews in England.* 3rd Edition reprinted 1979 (Oxford University Press).

ROTH C. *History of the Great Synagogue* (Edward Goldston & Son 1950).

ROTH C. *The Jews in Defence of Britain* (Transactions Jewish Historical Society of England. Vol. 15 – 1939 to 1945).

ROTH C. *The Portsmouth Community and its Historical Background* (Transactions Jewish Historical Society of England. Volume 13 – 1932 to 1935).

ROTH C. *The Rise of Provincial Jewry* (The Jewish Monthly 1950).

TAYLOR G. *The Sea Chaplains*. A history of the Chaplains of thc Royal Navy. (Oxford Illustrated Press 1978).

TEMPLE-PATTERSON A. *Portsmouth – A History* (Moonraker Press 1976).

WEINBERG A. *Portsmouth Jewry* (The Portsmouth Papers Number 41 1985 The Portsmouth City Council).

WILLIAMS G. *History of the Liverpool Privateers and Letters of Marque with an account of the Liverpool Slave Trade* (Heineman 1879).

WOLF L. *Essays in Jewish History* (Jewish Historical Society of England 1934).

WOOD W. Lt. Colonel (Editor) *The Logs of the Conquest of Canada* (The Champlain Society Toronto 1909).

## INDEX

This index relates only to the text, and does not cover Appendices 1-10. Warship names are in *itallics*, and are British unless otherwise stated. The numeral in brackets after the warship's name indicates the number of guns carried for distinguishing purposes.